Politics and Society in Nottingham 1785-1835

Politics and Society in Nottingham 1785-1835

MALCOLM I. THOMIS

Lecturer in History
University of Stirling

AUGUSTUS M. KELLEY · PUBLISHERS

NEW YORK 1969

Published in the United States by

Augustus M. Kelley · Publishers

New York, New York 10001

SBN 678 06250 1

Library of Congress Catalog Card

No. 78–92499

Printed in Great Britain

CONTENTS

PREFACE

This is an examination of the social, economic, and political life of Nottingham during the so-called 'Age of Revolution' or the years of 'The Making of the English Working Class'. I have set slightly arbitrary limits to the period chosen, beginning just before the impact of the French Revolution and ending with the reform of the Municipal Corporations; but if the neatness of this fifty year span is part of its attraction it will also, I hope, appear a meaningful period of time with some unity and character of its own, especially in the history of Nottingham.

Local history is much more than an aid to understanding national history, and the greatest incentive to the study of Nottingham history is the modern city and the people who live there. I am particularly indebted to Professor Chambers of Nottingham University, who supervised and encouraged this work, to the librarians and archivists of the City of Nottingham, to the staff of the University Library and the County Record Office, to the Editors of the *Transactions of the Thoroton Society* for permission to reproduce material which they have already published, and to my friends in Nottingham who have given me lodgings on visits there.

I am grateful too for help received from the staff of the Bodleian Library, the British Museum, and the Public Record Office.

I

RADICAL NOTTINGHAM

'Travel 20 or 30 miles from home', wrote the *Nottingham Journal* in March, 1835, 'and people have generally in store for you some ejaculation of pity, when they know you are from Nottingham, and the first question asked is "are you all quiet now?", just as if our good old town was continually the scene of some revolutionary tumult or other.'[1]

Nottingham was not, of course, continually the scene of revolutionary tumult, but it did have a reputation for turbulence in the late eighteenth and early nineteenth centuries. Wesley might have commented on the gentleness and sweetness of its people at an earlier time; other people tended to share the view of the M.P. who remarked in 1803 that at Nottingham people were used to riots, riots at every election, riots at the assizes, and riots of every other kind. And this was the reputation that has been handed down of a town renowned above others for its political agitation, led by a combustible and dangerous mob, a provincial public remarkable always for the ferment of political opinion and fiery party spirit, 'turbulent Nottingham, which once had nurtured the Luddites' and twenty years later fired its castle as its contribution to the Reform Bill agitation.[2]

How far contemporaries accepted this view and how they explained it depended very much on who they were. Nottingham

[1]*Nottingham Journal*, 6th March, 1835.

[2]Quoted from *Wesley's Journal* for June, 1777, by J. F. Sutton, *The Date Book of Nottingham 1750–1850* (1852), p. 116; Parl. Debs., Vol. 36, 1238, Mr. Bond, 29th April, 1803; W. H. Wylie, *Old and New Nottingham* (1853), p. 354; C. Brown, *Lives of Nottinghamshire Worthies* (1882), p. 345; A. Briggs ed., *Chartist Studies* (1959), p. 2.

Tories, an excluded opposition permanently at variance with the Whig oligarchy of the Corporation, saw things at their very blackest. As early as 1815 the town appeared doomed to some to be the 'scene of disgraceful outrage of every description', and three years later the Tories wallowed deeper as they contemplated the notoriety achieved by the town through 'its Mob, its Incendiaries, and Assassins', not to mention 'the advocates of Reform' who felt no shame about the town's evil repute. The reformers, not surprisingly, saw the whole subject in quite a different light. To William Cobbett this was 'fair Nottingham' with its public-spirited people, willing to carry on 'the noble struggle', and Cobbett predicted that he would be almost returned to the earth when his blood ceased to stir more quickly than usual at the bare sound of the name. To Lord Holland, elected Recorder of the town in 1809, Nottingham was famed above all for its attachment to the great principles of civil and religious liberty. This, according to the Whigs and the Radicals, was what caused Nottingham to be so grossly libelled; the people of Nottingham thought for themselves and formed their opinions without regard to title or wealth, and in their midst the Established Church and its clergy had but little influence.[3]

It was then largely a question of viewpoint, though both the champions and the detractors agreed that Nottingham had a reputation for activism. They argued about the causes of the reputation and whether or not it was a good thing.

The background to this radical behaviour was a rapidly changing town, growing fast in population and throwing up a host of problems which were to stimulate thought and evoke political responses. The 17,000 people who were estimated to live in Nottingham in 1779 had increased to almost 29,000 by the time of the first official census in 1801, and to more than 50,000 by 1831. In the period 1785—1835 the population of the town roughly trebled itself during the course of half a century. This contemporaries explained in terms of the development of the hosiery and lace trades, which brought substantial immigration into the town, particularly noticeable during the lace-boom of

[3]*Nottingham Gazette*, 21st April, 1815; *1818 Poll Book* (Barnett and Stretton), p. iv; W. Cobbett, *Rural Rides* (1885 edit.), Vol. 2, p. 289; A letter to the Luddites, *Political Register*, 30th November, 1816, in H.O. 40/9; Sutton, op. cit., p. 287; *Nottingham Review*, 16th August, 8th November, 1816.

1824-5 when people were believed to have flocked in from eighty miles around. Natural increase could also be seen as an important factor when birth figures were always well in excess of death figures in all but the worst years of famine and epidemic disease, such as 1801.[4]

It would be dangerous to overemphasise improved medical provision and sanitation as factors in the population rise. It is true that in 1800 Dr. Attenburrow of Beastmarket Hill began to vaccinate children with cowpock free of charge, but not even the proven success of his methods in years of small-pox epidemics was enough to induce the local populace to take advantage of the facilities available to them. The General Hospital opened in 1782 to provide free treatment for the needy, catering for many hundreds annually, and in 1812 a lunatic asylum was completed. All these endeavours indicate an enlightened local attitude to medical provision, but they probably did little more than scratch the surface of the problem.[5]

And undermining such efforts there were always the factors that so alarmed visiting parliamentary commissioners and the more enlightened local residents: defective water supplies before 1830, the absence of public sewerage, a huge number of back-to-back dwellings which housed a population reputedly more densely concentrated than in any other town in the kingdom. Nottingham's unpaved streets were filled with 'pools of filthy water or moist extended dung heaps' in the first half of the nineteenth century; a much quoted comment was the verdict of the town-commissioners of 1844-5 who found no lack of public nuisances in Nottingham since the entire quarters of the labouring classes constituted one great nuisance.[6]

[4] J. P. Briscoe, *Allen's Illustrated Guide to Nottingham and Nottinghamshire Memorabilia* (1890); *The Stranger's Guide through the town of Nottingham*, Sutton and Co. (1827), p. 7; T. Bailey, *Annals of Nottinghamshire* (1852), Vol. 4, p. 187; F. C. Laird, *A Topographical and Historical Description of Nottinghamshire* (1810), p. 142; W. Felkin, *A History of the Machine-Wrought Hosiery and Lace Manufactures* (1867), p. 285.

[5] Bailey, op. cit., p. 183, but see the repeated laments of popular apathy over vaccination in the *Nottingham Journal* and *Nottingham Review* during the next two decades; *Statutes and Directions for the Government of the General Hospital, Nottingham* (1821); M. C. Buer, *Health, Wealth, and Population, 1760-1815* (1926), p. 132.

[6] *The History, Antiquities, and Present state of the Town of Nottingham*, Dunn (1807), p. 4; *Nottingham Review*, 6th August, 1811; H. O. Tarbotton, *Sanitary Operations and Town Improvements*, in *Allen's Illustrated Hand-book and Guide to Nottingham* (1866), p. 85; e.g. J. D. Chambers, *Modern Nottingham in the Making* (1945), p. 7.

Part of Nottingham's trouble was the absence of any major enclosure acts before 1839 and 1845 which allowed common lands, the fields to the North and the meadows to the South, to remain untouched whilst a fast-growing population was crowded into an area which hardly grew in size. The property of the Duke of Newcastle and Lord Middleton, Nottingham Park and Wollaton Park, blocked developments to the west of the town whilst most of the remaining surrounding area was commonable land over which the burgesses of the town, about three thousand in number, exercised partial property rights simultaneously with the freeholders of the land. In spite of the freeholders' wish for enclosure so that they could sell their land for building purposes no act was forthcoming before 1839. It was resisted by the Corporation itself, one of the principal freeholders, whose members wished to retain its patronage rights over the commonable areas, and by the burgesses, who wished to keep their right to inherit, as they became available, small areas called burgess parts which they could rent out for grazing for part of the year. Ironically, the burgesses opposed enclosure in part on health grounds since the town stood to lose its health-promoting open spaces; in fact, non-enclosure had a disastrous effect on the housing and therefore the health of the poorer inhabitants of the town, as well as turning Nottingham into a cramped and unsightly town and restricting in addition its economic development through the non-availability of land for business and industrial purposes. Perhaps the most surprising aspect of the enclosure issue is the fact that the overcrowding and insanitary conditions that it produced did not become an important political issue locally. Instead of stimulating thought and action on how such evils could be eliminated they appear to have been taken for granted, even by the most radical of local leaders, and counted for little politically in comparison with the resolution of the minority group of burgesses to retain their interest in the common lands.[7]

Another part of the problem was the absence of any body or institution with the authority to recognise and deal with such matters. The Corporation of Nottingham felt no wider social responsibility than the preservation of law and order and the administration of the Corporation Estate supposedly on behalf of

[7]For further discussion of the Enclosure issue see J. D. Chambers, op. cit., and M. I. Thomis, 'The Politics of Nottingham Enclosure', *Transactions of the Thoroton Society*, 1967.

the burgesses. It was the duty of individual householders to keep clean the areas in front of their respective houses, not the responsibility of the Corporation, and when some great enterprise for town improvement was undertaken, such as the widening of Chapel Bar in 1827-32, it was financed by public subscription and the Corporation featured only as one subscriber. It was not only in town improvement schemes that the limitations of Nottingham's local government were exposed. In the matter for which the Corporation did accept responsibility, the maintenance of law and order, the efforts of the magistrates to operate through a mere handful of regular constables left the town prey to disorder and it was only at times of particular crisis, such as the Luddite period, that anything approaching an efficient police system was evolved. Much of the burden was in fact carried by privately financed and operated watch committees, which attempted to do the work which the public sector could not cope with, though these bodies always lacked the financial backing to be really effective.[8]

One sphere in which the Corporation appears to have assumed a fairly wide responsibility was that of charity: it was foremost in organising and contributing to funds raised on behalf of the poor or the sick. During the late years of the eighteenth century the corporate body repeatedly bought up large quantities of Irish butter to retail cheaply to the people of Nottingham, which doubtless won them the gratitude of the poor even if it earned them the scorn of the historian Thomas Bailey, who accused them of absurd interference in the laws of trade. As an act of seasonal generosity the mayor gave out 500 12d. loaves to the poor at Christmas, 1787, and this kind of gesture was common. In particular, the Corporation contributed generously to town collections, and the year 1795 illustrated well the strength and weakness of this kind of service. A town meeting assembled in the middle of January to discuss possible relief for those hit by the severity of the winter. It was agreed to raise subscriptions and issue 6d. food tickets to those in need. By 7th February, 6,000 such tickets were being issued weekly. By the middle of the month a new hazard of floods had hit the town, and energies were quickly directed towards the relief of those suffering from the flooding. In June and July the price of corn had become a serious problem

[8]*Corporation Hall Books*, 1786/7, p. 13, 5th January, 1787; *Nottingham Journal*, 15th December, 1792; *Stranger's Guide*, op. cit., p. 16.

and a further public meeting was held to raise funds to provide bread for the poor. Over £1,200 was quickly collected for this latest cause, to which the Corporation contributed £100, and more money was raised by charity performances of a play at the town's theatre. This succession of charitable responses unfortunately had an unsatisfactory ending. When the price of corn fell rapidly at the end of August the committee responsible for buying corn for the poor had such a large stock on its hands to be disposed of that Nottingham was unable for some weeks to enjoy the benefit of national price reductions. After all, it was argued, the committee could not be expected to take a loss; even so the next committee again miscalculated on its finances and purchases the following winter and bequeathed to the town a debt of £350 by the early summer of 1796.[9]

Admirable though these charitable enterprises were, they were by no means adequate to cope with a growing and changing problem. The great growth of population, almost entirely dependent on the hosiery and lace trade, the latter subject to violent fluctuations, the former entering around 1809 a forty-year period of almost permanent depression, meant that charity was an outdated solution to the problems being raised. Machinery to meet the situation did not exist. The Corporation's charitable dispensations were not enough. Nor was existing Poor Law administration a sufficient answer. Neither the indiscriminate application of Speenhamland principles, which forced up the poor rate to astronomical heights before 1820, nor the principles of the 1834 Act, applied in Nottingham under Absolem Barnett from 1819, could meet adequately the increasingly common circumstances of a high rate of unemployment, seasonal and permanent, falling wages and rising prices. And the enforcement of the 1834 Act in Nottingham, as elsewhere, was to be a major factor behind the development of working class politics and the reshaping of the traditional political structure of the area.[10]

[9]*Corporation Hall Books*, 1787/8, pp. 7-8, 18th December, 1787, p. 19, 25th July, 1788, 1788/9, p. 32, 15th July, 1789, 1789/90, p. 53, 1st September, 1790; Bailey, op. cit., p. 125; *Nottingham Journal*, 29th December, 1787, 17th January, 7th, 14th February, 4th, 25th July, 15th, 29th August, 1795, 18th June, 1796; Sutton, op. cit., p. 349.

[10]A. Barnett, *The Poor Laws and their Administration* (1833), discussed both the Speenhamland system and his own 'reforms'.

It could well have been argued, when the Corporation came to be reformed, that the Whig oligarchy had failed to exercise a faithful stewardship on behalf of the town and its interests, though the real political issue that had arisen during the later years was not neglect of the town's welfare. It was more that power had been exercised by an exclusive group than that it had been exercised badly.

It was against this background of growing social problems and an absence of the machinery for their solution that Nottingham acquired its reputation for turbulent conduct and disorder. In the Luddite years of 1811-16 and during the Reform Bill riots of October, 1831, the town hit the national headlines, but even in quieter years Nottingham could maintain a steady output of election riots, recruiting riots, and food riots. The market was a regular scene of disorder in the second half of the eighteenth century with bread, meat, or butter prices creating a succession of popular disturbances during which the mob would often fix their own prices for goods on sale. Industrial disputes produced many ugly scenes before Luddism added a new dimension to the subject, whilst the excesses of the crowds during the French Revolutionary wars were only an extension of conduct which invariably prevailed at election times. The small police resources controlled by the magistrates were ineffective in controlling the ten thousand or more people who would visit Nottingham marketplace on a Saturday, and it is very clear that in these years the people of Nottingham were growing accustomed to taking the law into their own hands when the occasion demanded it. These various outbreaks of disorder reveal a far from deferential attitude towards authority, an attitude from which constructive political radicalism might well arise. There was a growing readiness to disregard authority and please oneself in matters of social behaviour too, for instance, in the willingness to disregard Sabbath observance laws, and this would tend politically to an eventual undermining of both the authoritarianism of the Tories and the control that the Whig leadership of the Corporation was usually able to exercise.[11]

If the apparent willingness of the people of Nottingham to disregard authority and take the law into their own hands con-

[11]For the popular riots of these years see the standard local histories such as Sutton, op. cit., Bailey, op. cit., or J. Blackner, *History of Nottingham* (1815) and M. I. Thomis, *Old Nottingham* (1968), Ch. 5.

stituted a basic ingredient of political radicalism, there were occurring in Nottingham at this time certain developments that would turn this into a more finished product. Human responses were being converted into political behaviour by other social changes that determined Nottingham's history through this period. Sunday schools were advocated as a factor in promoting social cohesion and as part of the answer to crime, but they did incidentally promote education. Regrettably or otherwise a person taught to read the Bible might also lay hands upon the *Age of Reason* or the *Rights of Man*. If Sunday Schools were intended to keep people in their places, they also gave to some the means of changing places. The local radical, John Blackner, said that Sunday Schools had a dual role, to teach 'right notions of the laws of God and of the rights of man', and many Nottingham Dissenters preferred to emphasize the second part. Many local political and trade union leaders of humble background undoubtedly derived their education from Sunday Schools and probably imbibed their first dose of radicalism there if the complaints of certain Anglican parsons are to be believed.[12]

In the period 1785-1835 there was a phenomenal growth of the Sunday School movement in Nottingham, in which the Methodists in particular played a notable role, and also a rapid rise in the number of day schools promoted by religious and charitable organisations and supplementing the older establishments such as the Free Grammar School and the Blue Coat School. As the Anglicans fought to keep pace with the nonconformists who took the lead in establishing both Sunday and day schools, places became more numerous than children to fill them, with only High Pavement and the Free Grammar School having a greater demand than capacity. It has been calculated that in 1834 over 60% of the town's children attended one of the twenty-seven Schools and that 84% were connected with an educational establishment of some sort. This still left the problem of the children of the very poor, whom the Sunday School movement hardly touched, but in 1834 William Roworth and other Evangelicals formed an 'Education of the Poor Committee' and planned to establish new British Schools in the 'most neglected parts of the town'.[13]

[12]Blackner, op. cit., p. 127.
[13]S. D. Chapman, 'The Evangelical Revival and Education in Nottingham', *Transactions of the Thoroton Society* (1962).

It is interesting to note too that the Sunday School movement catered for adults as well as children, and Nottingham has been claimed as the birthplace of the Adult School movement. When the Nottingham Sunday School Union made its fourth Annual Report in 1814, it noted the existence of six schools 'for the instruction of ignorant adults' as well as the provision for almost 11,000 children in the area, and at the end of 1818 Salem Chapel Adult School, established in 1816, had 194 adult scholars in attendance. This trend was encouraged by the setting up of an Artisans' Library which claimed to have more than 700 volumes by July, 1824, which could be joined on payment of a small subscription, with special rates for apprentices. This was an anticipation of the strong Mechanics Institution which was flourishing in Nottingham in the 1840s.[14]

All this is not, however, to suggest the existence of education open to and enjoyed by all. It is clear that all the inhibiting factors associated with the beginnings of popular education, such as religious rivalries and working class indifference, were present in Nottingham, but there was a willingness to make as extensive a provision for education as had at that time been envisaged. And the greater diffusion of education in this period must have had wide social and political repercussions. Gravener Henson, a trade union leader for many years, claimed in 1838 that five times as many people were able to read and write as had been so thirty years earlier when he had been a young man. This was a personal guess but a suggestive one. As early as 1818 the *Nottingham Review* was anxious to claim the local Whig victory of that year as evidence that Sunday Schools and other institutions were spreading knowledge among the poorer classes of society. Fifteen years later the *Journal* from the opposite standpoint appeared to draw a similar inference. It recognised that the rapid diffusion of knowledge was one of the great characteristics of the age and expressed the hope that the knowledge acquired would not be employed in trampling down existing institutions.[15]

The growth of education was parallel in time with the Evangelical Revival and in large part a consequence of it, and the

[14]J. L. Lomax, *A History of Quakers in Nottingham*, 1648-1948 (1948), p. 33; *Nottingham Journal*, 16th April, 1814, 19th December, 1818, 9th July, 1824.

[15]*Report of Select Committee on Postage* (1837/8), XX, 2, p. 209; *Nottingham Review*, 3rd July, 1818; *Nottingham Journal*, 14th June, 1833.

religious life of Nottingham was one of the strongest factors determining the nature of the town and its outlook. The growing irritation with sabbatarian restrictions amongst the people, the conviction of Tories that the French Revolution and its principles had thoroughly undermined all principles of religion, and the conviction of the Methodists and the other Evangelicals that they lived in the midst of sin should not obscure the fact that this was a great period of religious revival. Mrs. Gilbert, the wife of a Nonconformist minister, wrote that on her arrival in Nottingham in 1825 she found a large part of the population, especially the working classes, not only irreligious but broadly deistical. But her pessimistic assessment ignored the tremendous boom that all denominations, Anglican and Nonconformist, were enjoying at the time. Whereas the national average figure for attendance at worship in towns of over 10,000 at this time was 49.7%, in Nottingham the figure was 57.7%. By 1833 there were approximately 12,000 weekly chapel-goers in Nottingham and only 5,000 church-goers, and the Nonconformists were not only numerically the superior force. They also controlled the town's political life through their domination of the Corporation and the town's economic life through their businesses as hosiers, lace-manufacturers, cotton spinners, and substantial tradesmen. It was the Nonconformists who determined the political complexion of Nottingham during this period and controlled the organs of local government.[16]

But if the high politics of the town were decided at the Nonconformist chapels and meeting houses, the low politics increasingly found their centres of organisation in the numerous public houses of the town. There was good precedent for this in the fact that the two main rival groups in the town, the Whigs and the Tories, had always used the higher class establishments, the White Lion Hotel or the Flying Horse, as their election headquarters. During the early 1790s some four or five establishments, such as the Sun Inn, gained reputations for being centres of 'Jacobinism' and later on provided the local branches of the Corresponding Society with meeting places and members. The public houses of Nottingham, wrote John Bowles from London in 1803, were 'nurseries of disloyalty and republicanism', but he was mistaken

[16]Mrs. A. Gilbert, *Biographical Sketch of the Rev. Joseph Gilbert* (1853), p. 68; S. D. Chapman, op. cit.

to make so sweeping a generalisation. During the Luddite period public houses were the places where conspirators met and deals were made, and from the Sir Isaac Newton, Gravener Henson in 1812 conducted his campaign to secure Parliamentary regulation of the hosiery and lace trades. Later the Hampden Clubs moved into the same premises and after the reformers came the revolutionaries. The Golden Fleece housed the conspirators who plotted the downfall of the government in May, 1817, and at The Three Salmons they had a rendezvous with Oliver the Spy.[17]

One further factor that probably contributed to Nottingham's role as a centre of political activism was the degree of social fluidity that existed inside the town. There was no shortage of references to 'the inferior class of people' or 'the lower Order of People', but, in spite of the apparently give-away terms used when charity was being discussed, there were opportunities for members of the lower orders to rise within the town's economic framework. It was the ambition of every stockinger to become a master framework-knitter, taking apprentices, and holding a few frames in a small workshop to be worked by others. Investigation has shown that towards the end of the domestic period, in the middle of the nineteenth century, the great majority of master framework-knitters and undertakers had been drawn from the stockingers themselves or the agricultural population of the surrounding areas. Some even became hosiers. Solly's and Gibson's, two of the town's oldest firms, had been established by the sons of framework-knitters in the eighteenth century; amongst the merchant hosiers listed in 1844 no fewer than eleven were the sons of framework-knitters, and in the early part of the nineteenth century a shoemaker's son, a cabinet-maker's son, and a wheelwright's son all became hosiers. These were exceptional, but it would be surprising if the hereditary leadership of the town's main families had not continued to exercise most control. Lace offered greater opportunities for rising. Absolem Barnett commented in 1833 on the many Nottingham families who had risen to respectability through the bobbin-net boom of 1824-5, and Felkin also

---

[17]Sutton, op. cit. p. 207; J. Bowles, *A Postscript to Thoughts on the Late General Election as demonstrative of the Progress of Jacobinism*, 1803, p. 119; see confessions of prisoners in H.O. 40/3, 40/4, 40/9, 40/10; Nottingham Borough Records, Framework-knitters' Papers, 1812-14; H.O. 42/165, Enfield to H.O. 23rd May, 1817; H.O. 40/9, Oliver's Narrative.

noted that the vast majority of small bobbin-net owners were men of modest origin even if the larger manufacturers tended to be men from a higher social level.[18]

Nottingham was remarkable, wrote Wylie in the middle of the nineteenth century, for the number of self-made men it contained, men who had risen from the humblest positions by their ingenuity and perseverance and attained the highest honours that the town could bestow. He cited William Felkin, the historian of local industries, in his early days an apprentice stockinger but later a successful lace-manufacturer and Mayor of Nottingham, as an example. There were some men of humble origin who, without great social advance, acquired a certain gentility through their poetic or artistic talents which gave them a place in the town's annals; Henry Kirke White, the 'son of a butcher of low habits', went from a solicitor's office to Cambridge University and had acquired a national reputation for his verse by the time of his early death at twenty-one; Robert Millhouse remained at the stocking-frame but wrote poetry in his spare time. But there were more important figures in the political and economic history of the town whose beginnings were modest. John Blackner, who laboured in a stocking-frame and did other manual work, educated himself, became editor of the *Nottingham Review*, a Radical politician, and the author of a very fine history of Nottingham; Gravener Henson, another stockinger, acquired enough education from somewhere to become a trade union leader of national significance, wrote a standard history of the framework-knitters, conversed with cabinet ministers, and gave expert evidence to successive government commissions and enquiries. In fact a whole race of trade union leaders and organisers emerged through the free education that the chapels and churches were providing through this period, and after them the political leaders of the Chartist period.[19]

[18]C. Erickson, *British Industrialists, 1850-1950; Steel and Hosiery* (1959), pp. 81-90; Barnett, op. cit. p. 4; Felkin, op. cit., p. 339.

[19]Wylie, op. cit., pp. 46-7; MSS. relating to the County of Nottingham, in the possession of Mr. James Ward, transcribed and edited by J. T. Godfrey (1890), pp. 64, 102; Bailey, op. cit., pp. 285-6.

2

STANDARDS OF LIVING AND THE
CAUSES OF ECONOMIC MALAISE

The history of the growth of the hosiery trade and its eighteenth-century offshoot, the lace trade, and how they came to be
centred on Nottingham, have been fully described. Local historians such as Gravener Henson and William Felkin knew the
trades intimately and were thoroughly acquainted with their
technological, technical, and statistical sides. Modern historians
have brought the story up to date and provided a more balanced
view of the times through which Henson and Felkin lived,
whilst still relying on these two authorities for much information.[1] In 1785 Nottingham was the centre of the cotton
hosiery trade, though it also manufactured woollen and silk
goods, more closely associated respectively with Leicester and
Derby. It was the centre for point net and warp lace, produced
by experiments on stocking-frames in the second half of the
eighteenth century and eventually to be supplemented by the
superior bobbin-net lace, which was produced in 1808 and soon
became the staple of the trade. In 1812 Blackner calculated that
well over half of the occupied working population of Nottingham

---

[1]G. Henson, *The Civil, Political, and Mechanical History of the Framework-knitters* (1831);
W. Felkin, *A History of the Machine-Wrought Hosiery and Lace Manufactures* (1867), henceforth cited as 'Felkin'. Modern authorities include F. A. Wells, *The British Hosiery Trade*
(1935); N. H. Cuthbert, *The Lace Makers' Society* (1960); D. E. Varley, *A History of the
Midland Counties Lace Manufacturers' Association, 1915-58* (1959); R. A. Church, *Economic
and Social Change in a Midland Town, Victorian Nottingham, 1815-1900* (1966).

were working frames to produce hosiery or lace; in addition great numbers worked on allied occupations, the making and setting-up of machinery and the various finishing processes involved.[2] Cotton-spinning, the one thing which might have given variety to the town's economy, died out during the French Wars, in spite of its promising start. Apart from the retail and service trades connected with any large town, Nottingham was virtually committed to hosiery and lace manufacture and its people to employment inside the two industries, moving between the two but virtually unable to move outside them.

All students of the early nineteenth century standard of living issue now agree on the need to provide local, detailed pictures before the drawing of any firm national conclusions can take place. The hosiery trade, still a domestically-based industry in 1835, has provided one of the rare elements of agreement in that its workers are generally accepted as having experienced a deterioration in standards during the period. It is of some interest that these deteriorating standards coincide with a failure to move over to a factory system of production and a failure to make technological advance.[3]

The movement of wages is clearly a key issue in the problem. As far as Nottingham's working classes were concerned, the majority, the hosiery workers, suffered a severe decline during the period 1785-1835, though this was by no means steady, uniform, or even accurately measurable.

The difficulties encountered in building up a detailed picture are very great. Seasonal variations, such as the expected reductions through winter, always a bad time, must be remembered; so too must the hosiers' practice of spreading out a little work amongst many men for the sake of the frame-rents involved, leaving doubt about the actual time a man was allowed to work as well as the amount he needed to work. Another important factor is that any claim to know exactly what men earned was difficult to substantiate since employers retained a discretionary power to pay appropriately for good or bad work and to make deductions for wastage and error. The complex structure of the

[2]Blackner, op. cit., pp. 245-7.

[3]T. S. Ashton claims that the spread of the factory played a not inconsiderable part in the improvement of conditions of labour, *The Standard of Life of the Workers in England, 1790-1830, Capitalism and the Historians* (1954 ed. F. A. Hayek), p. 128.

trade, the different qualities of manufacture, and the variations required by the individual hosier for individual orders all make generalisation difficult, and when figures are quoted their sources are often suspect. The manufacturer tended to cite the most favourable figures available; the trade union committee picked out the worst cases. The manufacturer believed the stockinger to be a liar; the stockinger believed the manufacturer to be a cheat. Fortunately, these reservations do not prevent the emergence of fairly clear wage trends and the drawing of broad conclusions. There is sufficient general agreement from the various sources to leave no doubt that the framework-knitter of 1835 was much worse paid than his 1785 counterpart.

Before the nineteenth century the framework-knitters were not a particularly depressed body of workmen. If the expression 'poor as a stockinger' was proverbial by 1740, as Henson claimed, against this must be set men's recollections of the 'Golden Age' of the late eighteenth century when the stockinger had his pig or his cow and grew his own vegetables and when wages for the plain cotton worker, one of the poorly paid branches, were 10/- to 12/- and in the most skilled branches up to 30/-.[4] The opinions and evidence of both men and masters suggest that the coming of the French Wars had little effect on wages, which remained, by later standards, at a high level. Supplying the demands of the armed forces kept trade brisk and recruitment helped to check the growth of numbers in the industry. The *Review* estimated that the average weekly wage of a stockinger in 1792 was 17/- but this figure is too high. It was already possible for certain branches to endure severe temporary slumps, as when the two-needle cotton workers were able to clear only 7/3d. in September, 1792, although this was exceptional. This branch was calculated to have averaged a net wage of 10/6d. in the period 1794-1803, whilst silk workers were earning nearly £1, clear of deductions, in the years immediately afterwards. This suggests that an average wage was in the 13/- to 15/- range until the war began to make its impact felt. It was in this period, before and during the first stages of the war, lamented the Rev. J. T. Becher, a county magistrate, that workmen took to 'the discussion of politics' and substituted 'the dissipation of the ale-

[4]Henson, op. cit., p. 98; *Nottingham Review*, 12th June, 1818; Felkin, op. cit., p. 117.

house' for devotion to duty, when they found they could survive on a four day week.[5]

The situation changed around 1809. Interference in trade by enemy and government action produced a slump and wages fell in the next two to three years by an estimated one-third. This accords with the plain silk worker's statement that he was averaging 12/- per week in 1812 as a fairly highly paid stockinger and the statement of the Arnold framework-knitter that 7/3d. was about the general average in 1811 before frame-breaking began. It is significant that hosiers who claimed to be paying as much in 1812 as they had for some years were now heavily involved in 'cut-up' production, which was recognised as one of the best-paying branches of hosiery. Frame-breaking temporarily secured a rise of about 2/- per dozen all round. This was quickly lost. In 1814 the men's union claimed to have achieved a small rise in all branches, and 1814 was remembered as the last time the stockingers appeared to be returning towards their former relative comfort. From 1815 decline again set in and there occurred the great turn-outs of 1817 and 1819. In 1817 the men claimed to be averaging 8/- to 9/-, struck against reductions, and accepted a settlement well below pre-war rates. Two years later they were forced, after a further prolonged strike, to accept a settlement appreciably below the 1817 agreement for all kinds of stockings, giving one of the poorest, and certainly the most numerous of branches, the two-needle workers, alleged earnings of 4/- to 7/- per week. In 1820 they claimed to be averaging 5/- per week and to be having great difficulty in getting paid by the 1819 list. In fact, apart from the years 1824-5, the 1819 settlement, so bitterly resented at the time, was the unattainable standard to which men tried vainly to have the hosiers adhere. During the temporary buoyancy of 1824-5 some wages rose even beyond the 1817 level. This lasted in some branches for only a few weeks. By October, 1825, the 1819 price list had been reached in cotton hose, and the decline continued. Even the best hands, according to the Journal, could earn no more than 9/- to 10/- per week towards the end of the boom.

[5]*Nottingham Review*, 12th June, 1829; *Nottingham Journal*, 15th September, 1792; *Nottingham Review*, 29th November, 1811; *First Report from the Select Committee on Framework-knitters' Petitions*, 1812, 11, p. 24; Newcastle MSS, Ne.C. 4919b, J. T. Becher to H.O. and to Newcastle, 12th February, 1812.

By February, 1827, the men were claiming that they were worked so far below the 1819 statement that they could not live and that an 80 hour week was giving them a mere 6/- to 7/-, which was 2/- to 3/- less than had an unemployed man with three children who was breaking stones and being maintained out of the rates. And apart from small seasonal rises, which were quickly lost, this position hardly altered for a quarter of a century.[6]

The precise earnings of men in the different branches of hosiery are impossible to determine. William Felkin, in citing their earnings in 1833, allowed for tremendous variations. He believed that those knitting worsted received 3/- to 6/- per week, those in cotton 4/- to 7/-, the silk-workers 6/- to 12/-, and those making cut-ups 10/- to 21/-. Sample earnings from men in the 1833 turn-out varied from 3/2d. per week to 8/8d.; and in 1832 the men had calculated their average earnings at 6/6d. Over thirty years, down to 1833, Felkin believed that all wages in hosiery had fallen by about 30%. This would undoubtedly have been greater but for the introduction of cut-up manufacture, which provided a new and better paid employment. Alfred Power, one of the 1833 factory commissioners, believed, on the basis of a number of interviews with employers, that Felkin's estimates were on the low side, though they were in accord with another local estimate of 1832 by J. Clayton, who found that wages in cotton had fallen by about one-third since 1792 and in silk by a half. The *Review* calculated the average decline from 1792 to 1829 to be by about half, but its figure of 17/- for the former year was too high. Later, Felkin generalised that in the forty years after Luddism the average earnings of stockingers were no more than 6/- per week. He was undoubtedly the best qualified as a statistician and the most experienced man in matters of the trade to come to a conclusion. He was also respected for his integrity

[6]*First Report of the Select Committee on Framework-knitters' Petitions*, 1812, II, p. 30; *Report of Select Committee on Laws affecting Export of Machinery*, 1841, VII, Appendix 3, p. 233; *Second Report of the Select Committee on Framework-knitters' Petitions*, 1812, II, pp. 65-100; Felkin, op. cit., p. 439; H.O. 42/140, G. Coldham to H.O., 11th August, 1814; *Nottingham Review*, 12th September, 1817, 20th August, 1819, 2nd March, 1820, 31st October, 1825; *Nottingham Journal*, 7th January, 1826; *Nottingham Review*, 16th February, 1827, 27th October, 1826.

by both masters and men and not concerned to present figures favourable to one side.[7]

Another factor which gives the wage figures of the 1820s and 1830s an even bleaker appearance is the fact that after 1819 stockingers living in the parish of St. Mary's, which contained four-fifths of the town's population, were not allowed to supplement their wages from parish relief on behalf of themselves or their children. Absolem Barnet became overseer in that year and, anticipating the 1834 Act, steadfastly refused to make up wages. In this way he reduced the annual pauper bill for the parish by £5,000 over 14 years, in spite of a rapidly growing population.[8]

Along with his figures on incomes, Felkin supplied reminiscences from relatives and acquaintances on the length of hours that men had needed to work for their weekly wages. These tended to confirm the men's suggestions that a ten-hour day had sufficed in 1760, by 1821 fourteen hours had to be worked and by 1835 it was sometimes necessary to put in sixteen or eighteen hours of labour in the day.

Again, Power felt that Henson had exaggerated a little and suggested seventy-five hours as an average working week.[9] Whatever the precise position these trends of falling wages and rising hours lay a firm basis to the argument that the framework-knitter in the hosiery trade experienced a marked decline in his standard of living in the period 1785-1835. The latter is an entirely arbitrary date in this context, for there was to be no improvement for a further twenty years.

His lace-working contemporary was better off. The aristocracy of the framework-knitters, the lace-workers, though subject to more violent fluctuations in demand and therefore wages, managed to earn several shillings more than the hosiery workers

[7]W. Felkin's Statement on Present State of the Hosiery Trade, *Nottingham Review*, 31st May, 1833; *Report of Select Committee on Laws affecting Export of Machinery*, 1841, VII, Appendix 3, pp. 234-6; *First Report of the Commissioners on the Employment of Children in Factories*, 1833, XX, 1, p. 556; *Nottingham Review*, 27th April, 1832, 12th June, 1829; Felkin, op. cit., p. 239.

[8]*Reports of Commission on Operation and Administration of Poor Laws*, 1834, XXVIII, Appendix A, Part 1, pp. 600-3.

[9]*Report of Select Committee on Laws affecting Export of Machinery*, 1841, VII, Appendix 3, pp. 232-3; *First Report of the Commissioners on the Employment of Children in Factories*, 1833, XX, 1, p. 556.

in the worst of times. In the best, in 1824, when the expiry of Heathcoat's bobbin-net patent helped to produce a tremendous boom period, their wages rose to astronomical heights and some of the most highly skilled men were said to have earned as much as £5. Then followed a slump and partial recovery which produced an estimated wage of 24/- by 1829, reduced by further depression to 18/- in 1833 and 16/- in 1836, though the *Review* talked of wages in the 30/- to 40/- range in the intervening year, 1834. In 1838 Gravener Henson stated that the great mass of lace-workers earned less than 12/- per week, though men employed on fancy production could earn good wages. But the lace-workers felt other pressures upon them. The hand-operators were by 1829 finding the competition of the power-driven, factory-based frame increasingly difficult to combat and could expect to be reduced by one-quarter to one-third in wages against the power operatives. Also, by 1833 wider or speedier machines were compelling non-users to produce a quarter more lace net to maintain their earlier rates. As with the hosiery workers, wages were falling, and attendant pressures of longer hours and harder work were developing.[10]

If Nottingham failed to follow national trends in its experience of calamitous wage reductions it did at least share the nation's rising prices. Here again a comprehensive picture is unattainable, but information is sufficient to indicate general trends. And there is no lack of comment on what people thought was happening even if their impressions were not always accurate. When Clayton in 1832 estimated wage-reductions of one-third since 1792 he also concluded that the cost of food and 'other necessaries of life' had risen by a quarter in the period. This is the most conservative estimate given by a local commentator. It contrasts with the list compiled in September, 1811, which estimated that food prices had trebled in twenty years, and a further list of December, 1812, which suggested that they were two or three times as high then as they had been in 1782. It is not without significance that these claims were made in 1811-12, when food prices locally reached their peak for the 1785-1835 period. The great rises occurred before 1812 and there was then a levelling

[10]Felkin, op. cit., p. 332; *Report of Select Committee on Laws affecting Export of Machinery*, 1841, VII, Appendix 4, p. 243, Appendix 5, p. 246, Appendix 6, p. 256; *Nottingham Review*, 27th March, 1835; *Report of Select Committee on Postage*, 1837-8, XX, 2, p. 218.

off, with little change in the second half of the period. In 1829 the *Review*, producing a very detailed chart of many food prices, estimated that beef, mutton, veal, pork, bacon, cheese, and ale had on average risen by 60% since 1792. Coal too had risen from 5d. per cwt. in 1792 to 8d. or 9d. in 1829. Many of these items barely featured in the diet of the poor and the figure of 60% seems high. The *Review's* concern to present an over-pessimistic picture, for it had opposed all governments throughout the period, together with proffered national figures for the period, suggest that Clayton's 25% rise on food and 'other necessaries of life' is a more helpful guide, though any rise at all would be disastrous for people suffering a 30% reduction in wages over the same period.[11]

Again, a really detailed picture would involve the tracing of every fluctuation and the noting of every price fall as well as the general rise. Corn in particular was susceptible to wide fluctuations. In December, 1813, after a long lean period, there was a rapid fall in corn prices, and it was reported that the poor could again afford to buy bread. 1821-2 was also noted as an easier period; with prospects of a good harvest in 1821 the poor were again able to obtain 'a sufficiency of the necessaries of life'. The better times were clearly indicated, it was thought, by the calling of thirty-three lots of banns at St. Mary's one Sunday in December, and the Spring of 1822 brought further evidence of falling prices. But such brief moments of relief were few. The more familiar story was of rising prices and great distress locally. In December, 1816, for instance, the labouring poor were said to be experiencing worse conditions than for forty years. A poor harvest had doubled the price of bread over a few months and put potatoes beyond the reach of the poor, a situation that continued throughout the Spring of 1817. At such times public outcry against those supposed responsible for the high prices was great. During the poor harvest of 1800 large bands, reputedly 1,000 strong, left Nottingham and visited the villages, intimidating the farmers, millers, and corn-dealers, and committing acts of depredation. In the town itself the butchers and bakers were frequently pillaged in some market skirmish; bakers were commonly accused,

[11]*Nottingham Review*, 27th April, 1832, 27th September, 1811, 18th December, 1812, 12th June, 1829; Silberling's Price Index in J. H. Clapham, *An Economic History of Modern Britain* (1926), Vol. 1, p. 602.

sometimes found guilty, of giving short weight. Coal prices, it was believed, were kept high through a combination of owners in the area, and almost everything that came into Nottingham from the country was prey to 'forestalling, engrossing, and re-grating', against which the magistrates had to maintain perpetual vigilance.[12]

Trends in wages and food prices together ensured that the diet of the Nottingham stockinger after 1811 was, for much of the time, little above starvation level. Occasionally he spoke out and gave details, as when a stockinger wrote, in April, 1812, of his family and their diet of barley-bread, old milk, and pota-toes. Sometimes the poor could not buy bread: sometimes potatoes were beyond their means. A man on subsistence level in November, 1826, 'must never taste a drop of ale . . . not a single pipe of tobacco, nor a pinch of snuff. His wife and his children, even in sickness, must not taste a drop of tea, nor morsel of butter to their bread . . .', and such accounts were innumerable. The situation was summarised by the 1844-5 Commissioners on Towns: the diet of the Nottingham working classes was described as 'low and precarious', 'universally stated to be poor'; it con-sisted principally of bread, potatoes, milk and herrings, 'while all other and better articles are strangers to the tables of the poor', a description supported by Felkin. This was not the selective presentation of material by commissioners with an axe to grind but a description that could not have been otherwise with the wage-rates and food prices that are known to have existed.[13]

The supposed contrast between the delights experienced by the domestic worker and the grim conditions of the early factory worker is no longer acceptable, and whatever the joys of the independent stocking-knitter of the mid-eighteenth century it is clear that his still home-based successor of the early nineteenth century was working harder than ever before for lower wages and that his children were working at an earlier age than ever be-

[12]*Nottingham Review*, 10th December, 1813, 7th September, 1821, 14th December, 1821, 19th April, 1822, 6th December, 1816, 3rd January, 2nd May, 1817; H.O. 42/51, Correspondence between Nottingham and H.O., September, 1800; Bailey, op. cit., p. 184; Sutton, op. cit., p. 247; *Nottingham Review*, 16th March, 30th March, 1810.

[13]*Nottingham Review*, 1st May, 1812, 3rd November, 1926; Appendix to *Second Report of Royal Commission on the State of Large Towns and Populous Districts*, 1845, XVIII, p. 255; Felkin, op. cit., p. 458.

fore. The independence associated with working at home or in a neighbour's small workshop meant nothing if a fifteen-hour day had to be worked, and the relief of spending a day in the delivery of goods or the collection of materials was merely a further grievance, adding more hours to the working week. The sight of the whole of a stockinger's family at work by candlelight until 10 or 11 o'clock at night would be familiar enough. Children would be employed in some subsidiary task from a very tender age and could expect to move into a frame themselves as soon as they were big enough to manipulate it, an exercise they soon mastered. The mill-owner was hardly an impartial commentator, but there is little reason to suppose that Henry Hollins of Mansfield was wrong in claiming in 1816 that the lot of a child in a well-run cotton-mill was better than that of a twelve-year-old operating a stocking-frame.[14]

The garrets and small workshops of the hosiery trade were untouched by the 1833 Factory Act, as were the workshops and factories of the lace trade. Felkin supported the latter's exclusion in 1833 because he feared that if lace factories came under the Act manufacturers would be deterred from transferring to power-operated, factory-housed machinery, which he believed to be necessary for the salvation of the trade. In any case, if the Factory Act's main benefit was the introduction of shorter hours, this in itself would be of no help to either the hosiery or the lace-worker, who needed to put in even longer hours to combat falling wage-rates. Conditions inside the lace trade varied much. Felkin praised the new factories housing power-driven bobbin-net machines. They were healthy establishments, he maintained, not hot or confined like the smaller workshops and required no legislative interference. The Commisioners of 1844-5 emphasised the other side of the picture, the small workshops and attics, the low, ill-ventilated apartments, unregulated, overcrowded with children, wretched places compared with which 'Factories are Elysiums'. They spoke of the moral and physical conditions prevailing, which tended to the deterioration of the health of all those who worked in the lace and hosiery workshops, and lamented that legislation had passed them by. Their conditions had not passed entirely unnoticed. The *Review* had questioned

[14]*Report of Select Committee on State of Children employed in Manufactories*, 1816, III, p. 189.

the propriety of excluding lace from the workings of the 1833 Factory Act and campaigned against the evils of night work in lace factories which put children and young men on the streets late at night or early morning. In 1839 Richard Oastler, married to a Nottingham woman, Mary Tatham, not sharing Felkin's satisfaction, campaigned against children's conditions inside Nottingham lace factories, and in 1843 the Children's Employment Commissioners presented a grim report on the condition of children generally who were employed in both hosiery and lace, stressing the detrimental effects particularly on their health and education.[15]

The health of the working population, determined by such factors as their ability to buy food and their working conditions, inevitably suffered during this period. The bobbin-net machine might pay more than the stocking-frame and its worker might therefore be better fed, but he was also more prone to chest disease in operating it. Work in a stocking-frame caused rapid physical deterioration from an early age. The stockinger could expect diseases of the respiratory and digestive organs from his early association with the cramping frame. His working hours and the nature of the labour made him prone to various diseases of the eyes. Dr. Williams reported in 1845 a great growth of disease amongst framework knitters, a growing inability to shake it off, and a rapid deterioration in their general condition. The stockinger was a man apart, whose occupation could always be identified from his physical appearance.[16]

A further factor in determining the health of the working man was the standard of working-class housing available and sanitation arrangements provided. In 1844 Thomas Hawksley, the engineer with the Water Works, a talented and an enlightened

[15]*First Report of the Commissioners on the Employment of Children in Factories*, 1833, XX, 1, p. 520; *Report of Select Committee on Laws affecting the Export of Machinery*, 1841, VII, Appendix 4, p. 241; Appendix to *Second Report of Royal Commission on the State of Large Towns and Populous Districts*, 1845, XVIII, p. 251; *Nottingham Review*, 7th November, 1834; J. C. Weller, *The Revival of Religion in Nottingham*, p. 243, B.D. Thesis, University of Nottingham, 1957; *Second Report of the Commissioners on the Employment of Children*, 1843, XIII, pp. 35, 38.

[16]*Report of Select Committee on Laws affecting the Export of Machinery*, 1841, VII, Appendix 3, p. 238, Appendix 5, p. 247; *Report of Royal Commission on the Condition of Framework-knitters*, 1845, XV, p. 107; Appendix to *Second Report of Royal Commission on the State of Large Towns and Populous Districts*, 1845, XVIII, p. 256.

man, explained to the Town Commissioners what a number of people had long realised, that Nottingham was paying a high price for its failure to enclose its common lands and expand outwards. The town contained, it was suggested, three times as many people as it could safely accommodate; slum property owners, including Corporation members, were erecting the maximum number of houses in the minimum amount of space and opposing enclosure in order to keep their houses occupied. These notorious back-to-back dwellings were erected on four sides of a court, which could be entered by means of a low tunnel in one corner. Their construction was bad and their sanitation crude, with a characteristic open sewer running down the centre of the court. Only Bombay, it was asserted, in the entire British Empire, had worse slums than Nottingham. In the worst housing areas a life expectancy of fourteen or fifteen years was lower than that recorded in any other part of the Empire, and the naturally well-sited town had an overall figure of 22.3, which was seven below the national average. Hawksley believed that through public administration alone it would be possible to reduce the mortality rate prevalent among the labouring classes and thereby promote their 'comforts, happiness, intelligence and pecuniary interests'.[17]

It has recently been pointed out that Hawksley's bleak picture must be seen in conjunction with two major improvements in working-class housing that occurred in the half century before Hawksley gave his evidence. In the first part of the period many working class families moved from primitive cottages and cramped apartments to the greater comfort of three-roomed brick and slate terraced houses; in the second part the better-off workers, those in lace rather than hosiery, migrated from the town centre into the new suburbs springing up beyond the 'green belt', such as New Radford and Hyson Green, where they lived in five-roomed houses in villages which were regarded as model communities.[18] But this still left a serious problem.

In 1812 Blackner had identified more than 300 enclosed courts with open sewers; in 1832 at the time of the great cholera epidemic a Board of Health was established which calculated that between seven and eight thousand of Nottingham's eleven

[17]Ibid, pp. 130-47.
[18]S. D. Chapman, 'Working Class Housing in Nottingham during the Industrial Revolution', *Transactions of the Thoroton Society*, 1963.

thousand houses were 'back-to-back' with shared conveniences. Here 'this terrible scourge, the cholera, fixed itself . . . in streets, and courts, filthy, ill-ventilated, and crowded with inhabitants, too poor, dirty, or dissipated to procure necessary food, or use the most common measure to secure health'. The better housed part of the population virtually escaped.[19]

When all these factors have been considered, it is probably necessary to agree with Dr. Williams, in 1845, when he identified poverty as the main cause of the wretched condition of the people of Nottingham. The *Review* concluded in 1829 that the relation of wages to food prices was then such that in order to maintain his standard of 1790 a man needed to work three times as long. The day did not permit this and so it concluded that the man's comforts must be diminished. Even allowing for the *Review*'s overestimate of both the rate of wage decline and the rate of price-rise, its conclusion was an understatement. Survival had replaced comfort as the aim of the working man. In March, 1816, Lord Rancliffe had vainly challenged Castlereagh to visit Nottingham and say whether prosperity or misery prevailed. A year later things were worse. The poor were experiencing a 'deplorable state of wretchedness, were obliged to sell their belongings, and many homes were destitute of clothes, furniture and bedding'. There was still, however, the illusory year of 1824 which caused the town temporarily to flourish and the framework-knitters to appear better-dressed than for years. But the decline set in and each successive year added to the history of growing distress.

'To give a true picture of our real situation', wrote two framework-knitters in February, 1827, 'would stagger belief, and were it possible to obtain a general knowledge how many get on from day to day, without money, credit, furniture, cloathing [sic] etc., would be equally astonishing and out rival the greatest romance. Look upon our battered garments, our pale countenances, the deep melancholy that sits upon our brow, the feebleness of our steps. . . .'[20]

[19]Blackner, op. cit., pp. 72-4; Chapman, op. cit.; *Report upon the Past and Present Sanitary State of Nottingham* (1849), p. 4.

[20]Appendix to *Second Report of Royal Commission on the State of Large Towns and Populous Districts*, XVIII, p. 256; *Nottingham Review*, 12th June, 1829, 15th March, 1816, 3rd January, 1817, 23rd July, 1824, 16th February, 1827.

C

At the height of summer, 1829, the *Review* lamented that not even in the disastrous year of 1819 had the poor been as poor as they were then. Each year brought new superlatives, the depression 'beyond all parallel' of 1831, a situation 'never worse' than in 1832. Yet worse was to come. In 1845 it was reported that 'altogether, the condition of the working inhabitants of Nottingham, as respects their habits of life, occupations, dwellings, diet, clothing, bedding, and fuel, not to speak of the immorality, improvidence, and want resulting therefrom, offers a spectacle of the most lamentable description'. Earlier Felkin had described the same people as 'ill-fed, ill-lodged, ill-clothed, with careworn and anxious countenances, they are a class by themselves...; hopeless poverty', he added, 'is producing fearful demoralisation'. Some years later he found them even worse and ruefully commented on the disappearance of furniture from their homes, the deterioration in their dwellings, their few, poor quality clothes.[21]

The story of working-class living standards in Nottingham through the period 1785-1835 is one of deteriorating conditions in those aspects of life which have often been taken as criteria of judgement. The decline belonged particularly to the second half of the period and was particularly felt by the hosiery worker. It was not a uniform decline, either in its impact or its timing, but it is clear that during the final decade of the period Nottingham was in almost perpetual depression, alleviated by only very transitory periods of buoyancy, and that distress was extremely severe and very widespread. In such a context it seems meaningless to undertake any assessment of the 'quality of life' as opposed to the standard of living.

The reasons for this low standard of living for so many of Nottingham's people are many and complex. Critics were never lacking to blame the working classes themselves for their plight and to offer them advice. The *Review*, for instance, during the Luddite trouble in 1812, suggested that the poor could improve their position by greater industry and frugality. This line was particularly characteristic of the Evangelicals, who believed that

---

[21]*Nottingham Review*, 31st July, 1827, 23rd December, 1831, 12th October, 1832; Appendix to *Second Report of Royal Commission on the State of Large Towns and Populous Districts*, XVIII, p. 255; *Report of Select Committee on Laws affecting Export of Machinery*, 1841, VII, Appendix 3, p. 238; *Report of Royal Commission on the Condition of Framework-knitters*, 1845, XV, p. 111.

salvation, spiritual and material, was very much within the individual's own control. Felkin, who knew more than most about working-class conditions and who cared more than most, could never escape from the influence and example of his grandfather, a humble framework-knitter, who by hard toil, abstemious conduct, and frugal living, had built himself a comfortable house, provided adequately for his family and won universal esteem. The grandson was from the same mould, and he measured others by the same standards. When Felkin enquired in 1837 into the affairs of the Nottingham Savings Bank, set up in 1818 for the benefit of the working classes, he found no working class depositors and condemned workmen for their lack of diligence and thrift. At the same time his own investigation of wages was showing that the stockingers had not the means to meet their family budget, let alone for investment in a Savings Bank. He blamed them too for their failure to provide for their children and their lack of foresight. Absolem Barnett portrayed the working classes as basically idle, in spite of the sixteen-hour day of the framework-knitter, and pleasure-loving, ready to waste their time and substance in public houses and incapable of making provision for the morrow; whilst John Rogers, a hosier and a further Evangelical, was to condemn stockingers, as a body, as liars and idle people.[22]

It is difficult, with knowledge of working class conditions in this period, to accept this censure as fully justified, though on one point, inability or refusal to plan and look to the future, the complaints of the Evangelicals were supported by leaders of the men themselves. Trade union leaders repeatedly complained that the men were interested in organisation only during times of depression and would not organise for the future when times were good and machinery needed to be built up. Gravener Henson, during his frustrating campaign to secure Parliamentary regulation of hosiery and lace, in 1812, complained that the men were dilatory and seemed bent on their own destruction. He reprimanded

[22]*Nottingham Review*, 1st May, 1812; W. Felkin, *The Stout-Hearted Weaver, The Story of William Felkin I, 1745-1838*, Felkin MSS. (1872); *Remarks upon the Importance of an Enquiry into the Amount and Appropriation of Wages by the Working Classes*, 1837, pp. 5-9; *Report of Select Committee on Laws affecting Export of Machinery*, 1841, VII, Appendix 4, p. 243; A. Barnett, *The Poor Laws and their Administration*, (1833), p. 4; *Report of Royal Commission on the Condition of Framework-knitters*, 1845, XV, Appendix to Report, Part ii, pp. 90-2.

them again for their indifference and inertia over the threatened restoration of the Combination Laws in 1825. In 1838 he told of his inability to elicit a modest contribution of 1d. per week from workmen for the Artisans' Chamber of Commerce. A similar response was met a decade later by Feargus O'Connor, the Chartist leader, who found that the working classes of Nottingham were interested in what he had to say only as long as they had not a few shillings in their pocket. When they had, their interest ceased. This short-sightedness, even perversity, was summarised by Thomas Hawksley in 1844 over the issue of enclosure, when he stated that the working classes almost always acted in direct opposition to their own interest. But however true these comments about working-class mentality, they will not serve as an explanation of the economic malaise that afflicted Nottingham during this period. A 'live for today' philosophy was understandable in a situation of almost perpetual depression, but it does not explain how that depression came about.[23]

The reasons for the plight of Nottingham's local trades have been examined in great detail elsewhere and it is convenient here simply to summarise some of the main arguments involved.[24]

Many people, both workmen and employers, saw their problem in personal terms, with the avaricious hosier or the lazy workman as the villain, according to one's viewpoint. But Felkin's impartial verdict that neither the masters nor the men were better or worse than their counterparts in other industries is as conclusive a verdict as can be reached in the dispute.[25]

The grievances most immediately felt by the men were the weekly deductions and abatement of about one-sixth of their gross wage which were levied according to the customs of the trade. Of these the heaviest was the weekly frame-rent which the workman paid, probably to the hosier, for the hire of his machine. This could be anything from ninepence to two shillings according to the size of the frame and would be charged whether

[23]Nottingham Borough Records, Vol. 8, p. 147; Place MSS., B.M. Add. MSS. 27803, 374, G. Henson to F. Place, 24th April, 1825; *Report of Select Committee on Postage*, 1837-8, XX, 2, p. 221; *Nottingham Review*, 6th September, 1850, quoted by R. A. Church, op. cit., p. 151; *First Report of Royal Commission on State of Large Towns and Populous Districts*, 1844, XVII, p. 329.

[24]See the authorities on the trades cited previously.

[25]*Report of Royal Commission on the Condition of Framework-knitters*, 1845, XV, Appendix to Report, Part ii, p. 3.

the machine was in employment or not. Frame-renting was a source of immense profit to the owner, who could safeguard his rent by stinting, or spreading out the work, when employment was scarce. It is surprising that the workmen did not press for complete abolition of frame-rents in their parliamentary campaigns, for this easy profit caused the industry to be flooded with excessive machinery by speculators, but their attitude remained ambivalent. It was the ambition of many journeymen that they might one day become frame-owners themselves and enjoy the profits of frame-rents, and so they chose to regard them as inviolable property rights.[26]

Another form taken by deductions was the truck payments of some employers and as late as 1845 there were complaints that Nottingham was itself still suffering from this, in spite of earlier assurances that the practice was confined to outlying country districts.[27] But more irksome, because more arbitrary, were the petty deductions and swindles said to be practised by the employers over allegedly dirty goods, loss of materials, or mistakes in manufacture. In order to avoid these reductions the men repeatedly demanded the introduction of schedules to specify the price to be paid for particular work and tickets which specified the amount of raw material given out, for what purpose, and at what price.[28]

But all these grievances arose out of a belief that the condition of the workmen derived from the evil practices of men, which could be eliminated by goodwill or appropriate legislation. Regulation might have removed many of the irritants but it would have left many fundamental causes of depression untouched. The workmen had only one major contribution to make to the bigger issue of what was wrong with the trade as a whole rather than what caused their immediate sufferings; this was the belief that inferior manufacturers were responsible for the de-

[26]Ibid, pp. 41, 56; J. D. Chambers, 'The Worshipful Company of Framework-knitters, 1657-1778', *Economica*, 1929.

[27]A. Barnett, *The Poor Laws and their Administration* (1834), p. 7; *Report of Royal Commission on Condition of Framework-knitters*, 1845, XV, Appendix to Report, Part ii, p. 70; Frequent successful prosecutions of employers in Nottingham both by magistrates and the enterprising trade union leader, Gravener Henson, reveal the continuation of the practice of truck-payments through this period.

[28]*First Report of Select Committee on Framework-knitters' Petitions*, 1812, 11, pp. 20-1; *Report of Royal Commission on Condition of Framework-knitters*, 1845, XV, p. 69.

cline of both point-net lace and hosiery in the period 1800-45. The argument has tended to centre on 'cut-up' stockings, which first appeared in 1795, stockings made by stitching together sections cut from a large piece of knitwear rather than articles fashioned as they were knitted in one piece. The view that inferior goods ruined the market for better class products was shared by a number of employers and has been widely accepted by historians. In fact, the innovators were probably responding to an existing depression rather than creating it; by modifying their techniques they were helping to create new markets and secure their own survival, and cut-ups constituted the hosiery trade's one growing point through decades of depression. Against this must be balanced the argument that the persistent failure of the trade to revive during the first half of the nineteenth century suggests that the innovators would have been better advised to turn their attention to methods of manufacturing orthodox articles more cheaply rather than to production of ingenious imitations which continued to offend the craftsmen and many of the manufacturers, to technological advance rather than to technical ingenuity. As far as the decline of point-net lace was concerned, this is now explained entirely outside the context of inferior production and in terms of the superior bobbin-net lace, which was soon to monopolise the trade, and the failure of the British to keep pace with the French in techniques of dressing.[29]

A more penetrating analysis of the problems of the trade came from the manufacturers than from the men, though even here was to be found a mixture of reasons and excuses. A popular belief and a correct one was that hosiery, and lace to a lesser extent, were the victims of perpetually changing fashion. Trousers and boots, for instance, dealt successive blows to hosiery. William Felkin's view was that the trade should have been capable of responding to the challenges that fashion-changes presented; instead men indulged themselves in self-pity and accepted the situation apathetically.[30] Another factor, believed by some to be another

[29]F. A. Wells, op. cit., and R. A. Church, op. cit., are the two historians who have really examined critically the popularly accepted case against 'cut-ups', whilst D. E. Varley, op. cit., p. 4, has similarly looked at lace goods in a wider economic and historical context.

[30]Felkin, op. cit., p. 434; *Nottingham Journal*, 7th April, 1821; *Report of Royal Commission on Condition of Framework-knitters*, 1845, XV, p. 93, Appendix to Report, Part ii, p. 82.

face-saver, was the French War. Though it might be argued that the closing of European markets and other interferences in normal trade only brought to a head evils from which trade had long been suffering, it is clear that the wars did substantial damage which even the leaders of the men had to acknowledge.[31]

One problem of which the manufactures were conscious and of which they claimed to know at least part of the explanation was the failure of the hosiery and lace export trades to expand significantly in contrast with other English manufactures. After the French Wars, with their temporarily closed markets, were over, exports did not revive, and in 1824 the *Journal* commented: 'our exportations to the Continent are very trifling'. Stagnation in trade, when the productive capacity of both hosiery and lace continued to increase throughout this period, was a disaster. One suggested reason for this was the export of men and machines to Britain's rivals, such as France, which the government did little to check and the free-traders much to encourage. Rivals were being presented with machinery that had an almost unlimited life, it was agreed, together with a great deal of technical know-how, and were thus given the means to establish their own industry. Another problem was said to be the ability of Britain's competitors to undersell her; Saxony, for instance, was allegedly able, in spite of a 30% tariff, to put hosiery on the British market more cheaply than native manufacturers. This was supposed, at the time, to be the consequence of sweated Saxon labour, but modern opinion is rather that Saxon industry was technologically ahead of Britain.[32]

Perhaps the most commonly agreed cause of the almost permanent depression in hosiery, and the periodic one in lace, was the fact that the industries were over-populated and produced

[31]*Nottingham Journal*, 11th November, 1809; *First Report of Select Committee on Framework-knitters' Petitions*, 1812, II, pp. 10-11, 24, 48; *Nottingham Review*, 12th January, 1816; *Nottingham Journal*, 7th April, 1821, 12th January, 1822; F. A. Wells, op. cit., p. 99.

[32]*Nottingham Journal*, 27th November, 1824; Felkin's Statement on State of the Hosiery Trade, 1833, op. cit., *Nottingham Review*, 21st February, 1834; *Nottingham Journal*, 12th January, 1822; *Report of Select Committee on Artizans and Machinery*, 1824, V, pp. 274-8; Place MSS., B.M. Add. MSS. 27803, Place's pencilled comments on *Report of Select Committee on Artizans and Machinery*, 1824, V; *Report of Select Committee on Laws affecting Export of Machinery*, 1841, VII, p. 144; *Nottingham Journal*, 27th November, 1824; R. A. Church, op. cit., p. 28; *Nottingham Review*, 21st February, 1834; L. Brown, *The Board of Trade and the Free Trade Movement, 1830-42* (1958), pp. 162, 204.

more than they could sell. The concern of the workmen for the maintenance of apprentice regulations and the non-employment of 'colts' was not just a concern for the preservation of high standards of craftsmanship but arose from a need to control the number of people entering already overcrowded trades. But it was impossible to halt the influx of labour into hosiery when Nottingham offered no sufficiently large alternative to absorb the population, and the stockinger's art was one which people readily picked up. The seriousness of the over-abundant labour supply was, of course, increased by the fact that, with falling wages after 1809, men needed to produce ever more goods to earn the same level of wages, one more pressure contributing to the situation of a glutted market. And if the labour force expanded beyond the needs of the trade so too did the machinery that it was to operate. In the period 1812-44, years of static export trade and only modestly increasing home demand, the number of stocking frames in the hosiery industry rose from nearly 30,000 to almost 50,000 and, after the tremendous lace-boom of 1824-5, when anyone pretending to mechanical skill attempted to throw a bobbin-net machine together, overstocking of the lace trade with machines was a greater complaint than it had been before. All attempts to reduce or abolish frame-rents with a view to discouraging investment in frames met with the same outraged complaints that property rights were being attacked. Nor were the workmen blameless in this; they accepted the argument that the industrious and careful journeyman should himself have the opportunity of becoming a frame-proprietor, a clear symptom of obsolescence in both the organisation of the hosiery industry and the techniques it employed. And arguments based on property rights, together with the aspirations and suspicions of the workmen themselves, were sufficient to defeat the case for reducing or abolishing frame-rents, with disastrous consequences both for the trade and the workmen.[33]

The most remarkable thing about the hosiery industry during

[33]*Nottingham Journal*, 7th April, 1821; *Report of Royal Commission on Condition of Framework-knitters*, 1845, XV, pp. 106, 129-30, Appendix to Report, Part ii, p. 45; *First Report of Select Committee on Framework-knitters' Petitions*, 1812, 11, pp. 16, 18, 35; Felkin, op. cit., pp. 332, 437, 464; *Nottingham Journal*, 22nd July, 29th July, 28th August, 30th September, 11th November, 25th November, 9th December, 1809; *Nottingham Review*, 13th October, 1809, 10th September, 1813.

this, the so-called age of 'Industrial Revolution', was its static nature. Its basic machine, the stocking-frame, was very largely as invented by Parson Lee in the reign of Elizabeth; its motive power was supplied by its operator, and it was housed in the workman's home or in a small workshop capable of holding several frames. The industry achieved in the first half of the nineteenth century its 'peculiar characteristic of having escaped the propelling and invincible power of steam, to which even the winds and the waves may be said to have been constrained to submit'. The trade did not consider its outlook to be conservative; no man in Nottingham opposes improvements, wrote the *Review* in August, 1829; since they were going on all the time this would be insane. There was, however, a longing for the past, a characteristic of most societies. The argument was advanced in January, 1818, that workmen spent too much time on production and so over-produced. They should be spending some of their time growing food; if all men with families had a good garden they could grow their own food and at the same time help to solve the problem of over-production. Henson, the trade union leader, shared this dream of an idealised world where the workman allocated a large part of his time to subsistence gardening. It is possible that the 'bag-hosier', the middleman who carried raw materials and finished goods between manufacturer and workman, was disliked in part because he formalised the worker-status of the framework-knitter, keeping him at his frame the whole time without the need, or excuse, to occupy two days a week otherwise. It is impossible to generalise about worker attitudes to the idea of a factory-based hosiery industry. A magistrate offered the conventional argument in 1845 that the men would not tolerate factories; restraint would be too great and factories would arouse their great hostility; and there was later, in 1855, the ironical offering from an employer that the beauty of the stocking-trade lay in its domestic character. Whatever the response in later years, the problem scarcely arose before 1835 since no one apparently entertained the idea of a factory industry at this time.[34]

[34]*Report of Royal Commission on Condition of Framework-knitters*, 1845, XV, p. 25, Appendix to Report, Part ii, p. 55; *Nottingham Review*, 28th August, 1829, 12th June, 1818, 12th August, 1833; C. R. Fay, *Life and Labour in the 19th Century* (1947), p. 225, quotes a Nottingham hosier.

The reason for this was in part the experience of lace. A newer industry with shorter traditions, it had never been based upon workmen's homes because of the difficulties of housing the heavy machines there. The workshop or factory unit had grown in size through the 1820s and the application of steam-power been introduced. But the latest innovation became just the latest in the developments blamed for the unhealthy state of trade. Steam power came under heavy attack in the late 1820s, and in April,1834, it was said that the steam-engine was ruining the poor workmen. Trade was falling into the hands of 'capitalists', who were congregating their machines in factories and applying steam-power to them. The interests of the men, it was said, were not the same as those of the employers. Felkin agreed that the inevitable effect of steam-driven machines was to cause orthodox operators to have to increase their output or to drop their prices accordingly.[35]

These lessons were, if crudely understood, hardly conducive to an enthusiastic approach to steam-power on behalf of hosiery workers, and the hosiers themselves had no wish or need to step up production. The excessive labour supply, the low wages paid, and the excessive production of hosiery were all deterrents to the application of power. So too was the frame-renting system, which gave the frame-owners, usually the hosiers themselves, a vested interest in the retention of the domestic system and a reluctance to employ men in their own factories where there would be no justification for requiring a frame-rent. What Felkin described as 'illegitimate profit', frame-rents, went far, he believed, in accounting for 'torpor in the trade'. Industry was left stationary. Sometimes it was argued that the function of the eye in co-ordinating the movements of the body meant that human motive-power could not be replaced. This was not so. The general principles for the application of power to hosiery manufacture had been long known. The problem of working a rotary frame had been solved early in the century and in 1829 Warners, a firm of Loughborough framesmiths, had set up a power-machine but abandoned experiments to improve it. Felkin believed that power could and should be applied, though

---

[35]*Nottingham Review*, 28th November, 1828, 4th April, 1834; *Report of Select Committee on Laws affecting Export of Machinery*, 1841, VII, Appendix 4, p. 243.

he had reservations about its ability to reproduce all the hosiery processes and greater doubts about its ability greatly to improve working class conditions. It would, however, be a boon to the worker in saving his physical energy, and this relief would in itself have been a substantial gain. Felkin realised what circumstances held back the application of power in Nottingham, but showed in 1845 that it had already been applied successfully in Philadelphia in opposite circumstances to counteract high wages and high production costs. It would also, as Absolem Barnett pointed out in 1845, make possible, besides the abolition of frame-rents, the ending of the plaguing deductions men experienced and give them at last a genuine, meaningful wage.[36]

Factory production and the application of power could not in themselves solve all the problems of the industry and might in themselves produce more. But they could make the life of a stocking-maker easier by taking the infinite toil from his work and reducing his working hours, and by producing faster they could produce more cheaply and hope to make British hosiery again competitive. Until their introduction Nottingham's principal industry would remain technologically obsolete and commercially stagnant, for where technology stopped stagnation occurred.[37] The pioneer innovators were to be Hine and Mundella in the 1850s, who introduced steam-power and factory-production for hosiery and combined this with providing an immense quantity of out-work for domestic finishers in their own homes. In so doing they trebled wages, gave the factory its most glowing testimonial to date, and saved the industry. To supplement this enormous contribution it was, however, necessary that Nottingham's overwhelming dependence on hosiery, and to a lesser extent lace, should be broken. Only by a diversification of her economy in the second half of the nineteenth century, with the emergence of engineering, chemical, and tobacco firms of national significance, did Nottingham provide for people who could not hope to continue to be eternally absorbed into the new, factory-based, power-operated industry

[36]*Report of Royal Commission on Condition of Framework-knitters*, 1845, XV, pp. 91, 92, Appendix to Report, Part ii, pp. 29, 63-4; C. Erickson, *British Industrialists; Steel and Hosiery* (1959), p. 178.

[37]J. D. Chambers, 'Victorian Nottingham', *Transactions of the Thoroton Society*, 1959; 'Vale of Trent, 1670-1800', *Economic History Review*, Supplement 3, 1957.

as they had been, with such disastrous consequences, into the old. In any debate on the merits and demerits of the 'factory-system' it must be conceded that it was the only possible salvation left to hosiery and that its belated arrival was a tragedy to a whole generation of framework-knitters.

3

THE HOSIERS AND LACE
MANUFACTURERS

The health of Nottingham's economy was the particular responsibility of the manufacturers who controlled the hosiery and lace trades; their response to trade problems would help determine the welfare of most people in the town.

Any general view of these men must, of course, take into account the committed position of those who sought to judge them. The Rev. J. T. Becher, a Southwell magistrate, for instance, disliked the hosiers as a body, emphasising their beginnings 'without fortune or education'. He believed that only a minority had a firm attachment to the established government and found in them much that was frightening to him. Recent inquiries have shown that almost all Nottingham hosiers in the middle of the nineteenth century were in fact from the local establishment of families, even if they failed to measure up to Becher's county standards in pedigree and politics.[1]

The most easily detected partisanship is that of the workmen in their moments of great anger. The hosiers, wrote one in February, 1811, when reductions were threatened, 'pull the poor man's teeth out of his head one by one, and the flesh off his bones, and put it in their pockets; they care not at all for the lives of their poor workmen, by whose labour they have made themselves rich'. The Luddism of 1811-12 was widely attributed to the 'wanton cruelty' of the employers, among whom Richard

[1]Ne.C. 4919b, J. T. Becher to H.O. and to Duke of Newcastle, 12th February, 1812; C. Erickson, op. cit., p. 121.

Eaton, soon to be Editor of the *Nottingham Gazette*, was known for his 'hostility to suffering mechanics'. There were undoubtedly selfish masters to exploit the workmen and reduce their wages, as Henson claimed, and occasionally men would be victims of capricious conduct such as that of a hosier, Hardstaff, who was alleged in 1812 to have set on great numbers of men in a fit of insanity and turned them off again at a moment's notice. But even the spokesmen of the workmen were ready, even eager, to admit that the hosiers as a whole were not ill-disposed towards them. It was good tactics, as well as the truth, to reiterate the belief that the vast majority of hosiers sympathised with them; they were allegedly frustrated in their good intentions only by the 'evil practices' of a small minority. It was 'not through desire to injure the workman, but to undersell each other' that prices were not maintained in 1817, the men believed. The great majority, argued Henson, were averse to reductions but lowered rates to remain competitive; once the few began to undercut 'the want of good faith in a few—destroyed the confidence of the rest'. The men always distinguished between the 'unscrupulous' and the 'respectable' and maintained that the majority were in the second category. Henson's mature verdict in 1838, when, admittedly, he was no longer a trade union militant, was that, in spite of the many disputes that had occurred, he believed there to be no better set of masters in the world, taken as a body, than the hosiers and lace manufacturers of Nottingham.[2]

William Felkin, knowing and sympathising with both sides, lamented in 1832 the depreciating value of labour, an attitude he believed to be shared by most employers. He pointed out that in the first thirty years of the century hosiers' profits had proportionately declined even more than wages and that the number of large manufacturers was much diminished. This supports what appears at first to be the standard self-pity of the business man, the hosier's lament of August, 1819, that manufacturing had for some years past been attended with more loss than profit. It is clear that the hosiers had a most precarious existence.

[2]*Nottingham Review*, 1st February, 15th February, 1811, 4th November, 1814; G. Henson and G. White, *A few remarks on the state of the Laws at present in Existence for Regulating Masters and Work People* (1823), pp. 87-8, Place MSS., B.M. Add. MSS. 27804, 3; *Framework-knitters' Papers*, 1812-14, F.17; *Nottingham Review*, 25th July, 1817, 2nd October, 1829; *Report of Select Committee on Postage*, 1837-8, XX, 2, p. 212.

Bailey was wrong to claim the almost total disappearance of the eighteenth-century firms in the early decades of the nineteenth century. But mortality figures, as revealed by local directories, were very high. The 127 hosiery firms of 1815 had by 1844 fallen to 56. There seems no reason to dispute Felkin's judgement in 1845 that the hosiers were no less just and honourable as a body than other men. Many, he said, had for a long time deeply lamented the depression of wages but knew of no remedy. Any investigation of hosier attitudes must accept that the hosiers, like the workmen, were seeking, equally unsuccessfully, an answer to the problems of their trade. The same could also have been said about the lace-manufacturers. The ending of Heathcoat's bobbin-net patent in 1824 produced a great proliferation of independent machine-owners and small manufacturers. When the boom ended they faced problems of overproduction and falling prices, and almost 500 small owners disappeared in the years 1833-6 as a result of these pressures and the competition of power-driven machinery.[3]

This sharing of common problems is clearly shown in the attitude of the hosiers to wage agreements. Wages were, in general, paid according to list prices, negotiated, with as much goodwill as the situation permitted, between masters and men. The 1787 statement, followed by two decades of economic stability and relative prosperity, worked well, but from about 1809, when slumps were separated by periods of only slightly less depression, settlements lasted for only a few years each and were almost impossible to enforce. From the workers' viewpoint the problem was the underpaying master. From the hosiers' viewpoint the trouble was the workmen who agreed to work at rates below list-prices, and the hosiers were quite ready to shift the onus of responsibility for the maintenance of prices onto the workmen themselves. Both Felkin and Henson agreed that the preliminaries to Luddism involved agreement between a group of hosiers and representatives of the men that the latter would attempt to force up the rates of underpaying manufacturers, even restrict

[3]Felkin's Statement on the State of the Hosiery Trade, 1833, op. cit.; *Nottingham Journal*, 28th August, 1819; Bailey, op. cit., p. 123; see local directories for 1815, 1834, 1844; *Report of Royal Commission on Condition of Framework-knitters*, 1845, XV, Appendix to Report, Part ii, p. 3; *Report of Select Committee on Laws affecting Export of Machinery*, 1841, VII, Appendix 6, p. 251.

manufacturers in the quality of articles they were making. During the strike of 1820 the larger manufacturers contributed to the funds of the men as the strike was against those employers who were paying below the 1819 statement, the undercutting masters, the enemy of men and manufacturers alike. When a further strike was organised in 1821 labour was withdrawn, according to Benjamin Taylor, the leader, 'in compliance with the wish of many gentlemen hosiers'. And again in 1823 the hosiers were still working to secure from the men guarantees that they would not take work below statement prices. When the hosiers disagreed amongst themselves, as they often did, on the question of wages, the workmen were often invoked to apply the necessary pressure on defaulters. The men did not relish this shifting of responsibility knowing that the alternative to working at low rates was often not working at all, and the condition of the trade after 1809 was usually such as to offer protection neither to the workman who might be reduced nor the manufacturer who might be undercut. What made permanent co-operation between masters and men even more difficult was the vexed question of 'cut-up' production, for the big manufacturers who were always the last to reduce prices and the most ready to co-operate with the men to maintain list-prices were also the people who were giving offence to the men by their production innovations such as cut-up stockings. Conversely, the hosiers who felt sympathy with the men over cut-ups were those likely to be guilty of undercutting.[4]

On the subject of workmen's combinations as well as on wages the approach was empirical rather than doctrinal. Henson believed that very few masters favoured the Combination Laws. After their repeal, Francis Place waxed eloquent on the approbation of the Nottingham masters for the satisfactory state of affairs that now existed. This mutual satisfaction of Place and the Nottingham party is not surprising, for Place took credit for both the carrying of repeal and the defeat of Henson's more radical proposals of the previous year which would have imposed severe restrictions on the Nottingham employers. Occasional hostile outbursts were reported against trade unions.

---

[4]Felkin, op. cit., p. 230; *Report of Select Committee on Artizans and Machinery*, 1824, V, pp. 270, 280; *Nottingham Review*, 2nd March, 1821, 14th November, 1823.

Henson himself related the case of a man almost prosecuted under the Combination Laws for merely asking a person to attend a meeting, whilst lace manufacturers were, in February, 1834, reputed to be compelling children to sign a declaration against the existing union. For most of the time, however, neither hosiers nor lace-manufacturers were particularly sensitive on the matter. There was, for instance, no refusal to employ union labour, such as a tailoring concern declared in 1825. The Combination Laws were certainly invoked from time to time but so infrequently and under such circumstances as to suggest that the employers took it for granted that the men would organise. The men were often encouraged in their activities. They received backing from sympathetic employers on their appeals to Parliament, they received contributions from employers when they organised a sick and unemployment fund in February, 1820, and sometimes when they were on strike; their committees were received by the employers as a matter of course over wage negotiations, and a joint committee of employers and workmen on wages was set up in March, 1834.[5]

And as the workmen combined with little interference from their employers, so did the latter act together from time to time with no restraint. The enterprising Henson, who had the temerity to invoke the Combination Laws against the hosiers in 1811, without success, knew that a successful prosecution would have meant only a non-deterring fine and that social opportunities were such as to make effective combination possible on a purely informal basis.[6] He seems to have raised the only local challenge. Inevitably the masters met to discuss wages; trade restrictions and the whole practice of list prices demanded this. The workmen repeatedly demanded that these meetings should occur for the discussion of wage-increases; it would have been strange had they not occurred to discuss 'wage freezes' and reductions.

An early combination of the manufacturers was the hosiers' counter-union of 1777-9 which fought the men in their attempts to secure legislation for the trade; on this occasion hosiers

[5]*Report of Select Committee on Artizans and Machinery*, 1824, V, p. 281; Place MSS., B.M. Add. MSS. 27, 798, Place to Hume, 20th June, 1825; *Nottingham Review*, 28th February, 21st March, 1834, 18th February, 1820; *Nottingham Journal*, 31st December, 1825.

[6]*Report of Select Committee on Artizans and Machinery*, 1824, V, pp. 280-1.

D

made a secret agreement that £500 should be forfeited by anyone who should employ Caleb Herring, one of the men's leaders, at any time in the future. The hosiers also acted together
repeatedly for the recovery of runaway apprentices and the
prosecution of anyone who assisted them. They combined to
fight Luddism in 1811 and again to prosecute machine-breakers
in 1814; they combined, if not unanimously, again to oppose
Parliamentary regulation in 1812; they combined to fight the
Union Society in 1814; and in 1825 a Hosiers' Association was
formed to resist current demands for higher wages. In fact, any
trade matter involved some degree of combination amongst the
employers. What invariably antagonised the workmen was not
a tendency to combine, which seems to have been taken for
granted, but the failure, from time to time, of the hosiers to
act together. Effective combination amongst the hosiers, the men
continued to believe, would have eliminated most of their own
problems, for the majority, they thought, shared their views on
what was wrong with the trade. The failure of the hosiers to
act as a united body on maintaining wage-rates and production
standards, or in 1811-12 to present a united front to the Luddites,
was believed by people outside the trade to be its great weakness.
There were numerous Hosiers' Associations throughout the period
1785-1835 but they had no continuous existence and inevitably
collapsed when they had completed the job that brought them
into being. Even more necessary for the success of campaigns
in the lace trade in the 20s and 30s was co-operation between
lace-manufacturers. Committees of bobbin-net machine owners
tried throughout this period to persuade the whole trade to act
together on matters of common interest, in particular restriction
of output, but effective employers' combinations were almost
as difficult to realise as unions of the men.[7]

   A central argument in the debate between masters and men
concerned the need for Parliamentary regulation of the hosiery
and lace trades, the imposition of certain modes of conduct and
production that could not legally be infringed. When the men's
leaders petitioned for this in 1812 they were convinced to the
the last moment that they were acting on behalf of the whole
trade and that they would not be opposed. In fact, after a be-

[7]Henson, op. cit., pp. 386, 415; Felkin, op. cit., p. 446.

lated start, many prominent houses organised an opposition, met the workmen's delegates in acrimonious exchanges in London, and swept aside the case which the men had so convincingly put to the Parliamentary Committee. It was one thing to condemn fraudulent goods; it was another to invite Parliamentary 'interference' in the basic rights and customs of businessmen. In accordance with an economic orthodoxy approved by Place and Hume, they refused to accept schedules which fixed precise rates for particular jobs and to be bound by any contractual relationship with their workmen. Furthermore, they denounced any attempt to dictate to them what they should make and how they should make it. They would make what they could sell, and that was the end of it. The split inside hosier ranks was now evident. Previously the masters had generally conveyed the impression that they disapproved of the cheap products that some firms had begun to make. Now they went to London not only to defend successfully their right to non-interference but to demolish the widely-accepted argument that cut-up production was a bad thing. The split remained, and many continued to believe, as Felkin's frequent restatements of the case show, that cheap, inferior goods, alleged to be fraudulent, were destroying the market for the better articles. A few sympathetic employers, especially lace-manufacturers, agreed to apply part of the men's programme unofficially, and in 1823 a further bid was made, but the battle was lost. Cut-ups were never outlawed, and parliamentary regulation was not introduced, but the view that unfettered production and trade were best, though widely held at Westminster, remained a more doubtful issue as far as Nottingham was concerned.[8]

'The gentlemen from Nottingham,' reported the 1841 Commissioners on the export of machinery, 'also state themselves to be advocates of free trade in the abstract, but claim an exemption in regard to machinery used in their own manufactures'. This love of free trade when profitable and protection when necessary well summarises the mixture of theoretical commitment and practical opposition that characterised Nottingham attitudes. On the Corn Laws the manufacturers were free-traders. Long before 1815

[8] *Framework-knitters' Papers*, 1812-14, Fs. 149, 150, 166, 173; *Second Report of Select Committee on Framework-knitters' Petitions*, 1812, II, pp. 65-100.

these had been repeatedly condemned; in June, 1813, the *Review* described farmers as 'direct tax-gatherers upon the commercial and manufacturing interests to fill the pockets of land-proprietors'. The classic case against the Corn Laws had been formulated and developed in Nottingham at the time of the 1815 Act and in 1821 nearly 8,000 signatures were gathered in Nottingham in support of 'open ports and free trade'. Reduce taxes and abolish duties (though not on imported hosiery and lace) it was argued in January, 1817, until labour is cheap, 'not with a starving but with a thriving and healthy poor'. This mixture of humanitarian and economic motives was behind Nottingham's protest through four decades. Like the Anti-Corn Law League later the Nottingham free traders preferred not to emphasise the argument, indiscreetly let out in November, 1824, that foreign corn must be allowed into Britain so that wages and costs could be lowered.[9]

Free trade was good for corn, for imported raw materials, and for exported manufactures. It was important too to break continuing monopolies such as that of the East India Company. Nottingham lace, it was believed, was almost unknown East of the Cape, and it was imperative that India and China should be thrown open to the trade. But free trade was not always a good thing and opposition to protection for agriculture did not mean opposition to all protection. Support the agriculturists over the Corn Laws, John Wright urged the hosiers with no little irony in March, 1834, and they will help you to prevent the importation of Saxon stockings; this seemed reasonable enough to him but his deal was spurned, for it brought out the great inconsistency of the Nottingham manufacturers as free traders and highlighted their special pleading. Free trade becomes really desirable only when an industry is in so strong a position that it can out-sell its rivals abroad. This was not the case with either lace or hosiery and so these trades demanded not free trade but enough intervention to ensure fair trade.[10]

In 1785 Pitt's commercial proposals for Ireland had been strongly opposed by the entire body of Nottingham's hosiers

[9] *Second Report of Select Committee on Laws affecting Export of Machinery*, 1841, VII, p. xiv; *Nottingham Review*, 25th June, 1813, 2nd February, 1821, 17th January, 1817; *Nottingham Journal*, 27th November, 1824.

[10] *Nottingham Review*, 16th March, 1832, 28th March, 1834.

on the grounds that cheap food and low wages made the Irish unfair competitors against the Nottingham trades. As Britain's economy moved towards free-trade in the nineteenth century it came up against the protected economies of Europe; and where there were rival industries, French lace and Saxon hosiery, Britain, in particular Nottingham, felt itself to be suffering. And so the 30% tariff on Saxon stockings was supported, though not believed to afford adequate protection. A bigger grievance was the 50% duty which the French placed on British lace. In June, 1834, a memorial was presented to the government protesting against the introduction of English bobbin-net yarn into France without any corresponding admission of bobbin-net lace. To send the means of production without ensuring the British right to compete with French production seemed unreasonable, and the almost entire exclusion of English bobbin-net from France, in contrast with France's ability to export to Britain on easier terms, long remained a grievance.[11]

The issue that really aroused the protectionist side of the Nottingham manufacturer was, however, the export of machinery. There was strong dislike of the right of men, 'the very flower of our trade', to cross the channel, taking their secrets with them, but this could hardly be stopped. Bulky machinery was another matter, and on this the manufacturers of Nottingham tried several times to act. When Hume's enquiry into Artizans and Machinery was announced the owners of bobbin-net machines called a meeting to oppose any provision for the free export of machinery and formed a committee to look to this question 'of great importance to the prosperity of this large manufacturing town'. Rather curiously, the case of the machine-owners was most fully presented by Gravener Henson, who was at the same time arguing the case against the Combination Laws on behalf of the men, but who always liked to feel he was able to speak for the entire trade. He explained the dangers of supplying Britain's rival with the machinery that could put France on equal terms with Britain. The argument that a trade in machines was valuable to the framesmiths was rejected by William Shoults on the grounds that the long life and high state of perfection of

<hr>

[11]Parl. Debs., Vol. 25, 702, D. P. Coke, 24th May, 1785; *Nottingham Review*, 13th June, 1834.

the lace-frame would soon render future production unnecessary. In the opinion of the *Journal* the free exportation of machinery was a bad thing, if carried out for the benefit of foreigners.[12]

Lace machinery had illegally left the country before 1824 with the authorities making little effort to check its departure. It continued to do so after 1824 in spite of being an excepted category. The authorities, apparently unwilling to take firm steps to prevent this, even when supplied with full information, continued to show a marked indifference to the clamourings of the Nottingham interest. In August, 1833, the bobbin-net owners again appointed a committee to work for the prevention of machine export. They offered rewards for information regarding illegal exports and offered to finance the return passage of Nottingham workmen in France who could come back to provide evidence. Evidence was collected but the committee broke up without completing its test case. For a time it had, in 1834-5, held in check the export of machinery, but with its collapse the process was renewed. Trade in machinery, said Felkin in 1841, was no compensation for a major decline in the lace trade. On this issue the sectional interest of the lace-manufacturers, and to a lesser extent the hosiers, had driven them to assert a fierce nationalistic outlook and break completely with the thorough-going free-traders.[13]

One of the chief problems of both hosiery and lace was the failure of the market for products to expand at the same rate as the industries' productive capacity. The problem might have been solved by greater diversification of articles and a greater effort at winning new markets. Up to a point this was tried. Lace manufacturers also attempted to correct the situation by manufacturing less, a difficult policy to enforce but at least an attempt to introduce an element of planning into production, which hosiery as a whole seems to have lacked, though it suffered just as acutely as lace from glutted markets. The general willingness to introduce artificial restrictions of output again indicates an outlook far removed from those who accepted the natural laws of supply and demand as sufficient in themselves to take care of trade. Lace could be hit very badly by such an event

---

[12]*Report of Select Committee on Artizans and Machinery*, 1824, V, pp. 274-8, 374; *Nottingham Review*, 26th March, 1824; *Nottingham Journal*, 27th March, 1824.

[13]*Report of Select Committee on Laws affecting Export of Machinery*, 1841, VII, pp. 144, 151, 175; *Nottingham Review*, 27th September, 1833, 21st March, 1834.

as the King's death in 1820, which prompted a complete stop-
page of bobbin-net production for almost six weeks. For periods
each year machine-owners agreed to complete stoppages of a few
weeks or a restriction of hours to twelve or eight per day. There was
uncontrolled output in 1824 and most of 1825, the great boom
period, but by September the owners were agreeing to work
no more than an eight hour day. The idea behind restriction was
that by a lowering of output prices could be kept steady; the
danger was that unless the restriction were rigidly observed those
who abstained were only creating an easier market for the unscrupulous who continued to work. There was always danger
that Nottingham's rivals would thrive whilst she herself rested
and great efforts were always made, sometimes successfully, to
ensure the co-operation of substantial manufacturers, as Heathcoat of Tiverton, in the restriction. Some thought that the steam
factory owners would use restriction by the independent owner
to crush the latter, though in the Winter of 1828-9 there was
complete unanimity amongst independent and factory operators for a period of over two months in which a prescribed
limit was rigidly observed. It was widely believed that such restrictions did have a beneficial effect upon the industry and
preserved stability. Even if they did not restore high prices,
they did at least, Felkin believed, slow the rate of falling, though
some owners advanced the case of completely unrestricted production to flood the market and force prices so low that the many
inferior machines built in 1824-5 would be driven out of existence
and the whole factory movement halted by the unprofitable
state of trade. There might have been some value to the trade in
the former but the latter could have been only a disaster. Differences on the efficacy of restriction and defaulters who broke the
agreements caused the organising committee of machine owners
to resign in 1829, but a new committee was chosen, and periodic stands and reduction of hours remained the pattern. Tension
remained between the small owners and the factory-operators,
for it was the former who experienced the greater distress in
absorbing the losses created by falling prices. And the feeling was
prevalent throughout the trade in 1835 that any further machine-
building and any further speeding up of processes could only
cause supply to exceed demand and threaten the precarious stability which had been achieved. And so it can be seen that even

in this section of Nottingham industry, which, in contrast with hosiery, moved increasingly over to a factory system, and has been described as a 'progressive' industry, restricting output in both machinery and manufactured goods was seen as the best answer to trade problems.[14]

A supplement to restriction, or perhaps an alternative which could have rendered it eventually unnecessary, was invention and innovation. In mechanical ingenuity the Nottingham workman had long possessed a high reputation. If the stocking-frame had remained in principle the creation of Parson Lee in the sixteenth century, ingenious adjustments had permitted a great variety of articles and designs to be produced on it, and its application to lace had opened a whole new field in which native skill could develop. Unhappily, the lace trade was bitterly, and permanently, divided by feuds arising out of patent-claims, infringements, and alleged plagiarising. The local press was full of injunctions from inventors against those who were thought to be illegally using their work. Henson felt that the operation of the patent laws was so inefficient and corrupt that it discouraged genius and denied men their just rewards. The most important patent-holder of them all, Heathcoat, whose bobbin-net patent allowed him to confine production to licence-holders until 1823, was believed by some to have reached his invention by stealing the ideas of others. Litigation featured regularly in the history of the lace-trade; but the trade could at least respond to the need to perfect its articles through what Felkin called a 'cultivation of the fine arts on correct and scientific principles'. And if there was tension between the independent owners and the factory owners there was at least a development of new units of production and the application of power to the mechanical processes. Hosiery, by contrast, could modify its patterns and framesmiths could expend their ingenuity in vain. What was required here was not the skill to produce fancy articles, for these were a thing of the past, but a thorough reorganisation of the entire industry so that the simple articles required of it could be produced quickly and cheaply without the endless tedium and infinite manpower that

[14]*Nottingham Review*, 4th February, 1820, 30th September, 1825, 3rd March, 1826, 9th January, 1829, 3rd February, 1826, 9th October, 1829, 22nd May, 1835; *First Report of the Commissioners on the Employment of Children in Factories*, 1833, 1, p. 371; R. A. Church, op. cit., Ch. IV.

stocking-knitting involved in 1835. For reasons already considered, the hosiers did not respond to this challenge, the greatest of all facing the industry, before the second half of the century.[15]

[15]H. H. Swinnerton, *Nottinghamshire* (1910), p. 131, states, 'The little smith of Nottingham was far famed. It is probable that he derived his skill in metal-work from the Danes'; Place MSS., B.M. Add. MSS. 27807, Henson to Place, 31st May, 1825; *Nottingham Review*, 18th July, 1817; *Report of Select Committee on Laws affecting Export of Machinery*, 1841, VII, Appendix 6, p. 255.

4

THE TRADE UNIONS

The economic situation which developed in Nottingham during the period 1785-1835 was hardly a promising setting for trade union activity, which thrives in buoyant rather than depressed conditions. The early history of trade union activity in Nottingham, as elsewhere, presents a tantalising, incomplete story but one with sufficient details to provide a general idea of how widespread activity was in the late eighteenth and early nineteenth century, what forms it took, and how far it was regarded as permissible conduct by the authorities of the day. It would certainly be a mistake to believe that all early trade union activity was of a secretive, disapproved kind, and equally mistaken to view the legislation of 1799/1800 as marking a distinct break in official attitudes to the question.

The patterns of trade unionism seem clearly established in the decade before the Acts of 1799/1800. In these years there was no regular or permanent union inside the main trades of the town. The most common form of activity was, as might be expected, the practice of workmen in a particular industry or in a particular branch of an industry coming together for the purpose of requesting an increase of wages. They would sometimes hold a general meeting for formulating this request. At other times they would devise some temporary machinery, a committee with Chairman and Secretary, empowered to negotiate on their behalf. A more complex organisation for this purpose that arose in this period was devised by the framework-knitters in the two-needle branch in 1794, when their committee was the outcome of a delegate conference representing twenty-eight villages in the Nottingham area. Sometimes these requests for a rise were successful. Often the outcome is not known. A common result would be for a number of the masters in a trade to agree to requests and others to reject them. In November, 1787, the cordwainers, having achieved this partial success after a request for an increase, attempted to publicise the names of the best-paying masters so that workmen could choose to go to them in preference to the others, and this sort of practice must have occurred unofficially much of the time. Sometimes, as in August, 1796, when the journeymen cabinet makers applied for a rise, the request would be turned down, and the men would then attempt to set up some organisation for a longer struggle. Often the negotiations would be no more than a single meeting or a letter in the local paper. What is quite clear is that the requests for rises were standard practice and that the workmen felt no inhibitions about making them. The request would be accompanied by an attempted justification, usually rising prices, and the case would be given what publicity it could get through the press or public meetings or both. The magistrates normally played no part in these negotiations, though it was alleged by workers in the twilled branch of hosiery in January, 1796, that the magistrates, like the men, favoured an open conference between the hosiers and representatives of the men so that the dispute might be settled. Indeed, it is the avoidance of dispute which seems to have been the chief concern of the magistrates, and it is significant that when men combined for peaceful negotiations which were harmoniously completed, one way or the other, the word 'combination' was not heard or not considered applicable. The two-needle branch of framework-knitters who applied for an increase in May, 1799, specifically disavowed 'all combinations of any sort to raise our wages'.[1]

What did or did not constitute a combination was a matter dealt with empirically and neither the authorities nor the public, before or after 1799, were concerned with the letter of the law when what were regarded as the customary processes of negotiation were followed. It was when these processes threatened

[1] *Report of Select Committee on Laws affecting Export of Machinery*, 1841, VII, Appendix 3, p. 233; *Nottingham Journal*, 14th, 28th June, 5th July, 1794, 10th November, 1787, 20th August, 9th January, 1796, 1st June, 1799.

to lead to breaches of the peace that 'combinations' came to be discussed. In September, 1792, a Nottingham hosier, William Hayne, received a threatening letter and at the same time someone wrote to the Mayor, informing him of the existence of 'diverse combinations' amongst the framework-knitters. He and his fellow magistrates therefore issued a public warning against such activities, described as having 'a manifest tendency to end in tumult and disorder'. They expressed their determination to put into execution the laws against combinations and to take every step to protect individuals and preserve the peace and good order of the town. Their prime concern was the maintenance of law and order in the town, and not the safeguarding of local industrialists against trade union action. Later in the year several journeymen cordwainers were indicted for combination and conspiracy against the masters in that they had endeavoured to entice other journeymen from their masters, the standard description of efforts sometimes made to leave an under-paying employer without a labour force. Another example of unacceptable conduct occurred in March, 1794, when a disturbance developed after a framework-knitter had been dragged from his home and made to promise not to work for less than a prescribed sum. In October, 1794, after framework-knitters in the two-needle branch had been organised and negotiating for increases throughout the Summer, they were warned at a meeting by their leaders to guard against conduct offensive to the magistrates. The actions of meeting, organising, and negotiating were clearly not offensive, and it was breaches of the peace which the men's leaders feared as likely to bring down the wrath of the magistrates upon them.[2]

The year 1794 was clearly a time when the authorities were rather more sensitive on the issue of combinations. At the county assizes in August the hosiers brought a prosecution against a number of stockingers for riot, conspiracy respecting their wages, and agreeing not to work below certain prices. Unfortunately for the prosecution, several key witnesses absented themselves and the trial could not proceed. Chief Baron Macdonald, with an injudicial belief that the defendants were guilty, delivered an address on 'the henious nature of the offence of conspiracy and

[2]*Nottingham Journal*, 8th September, 13th October, 1792, 15th March, 18th October, 1794.

its ruinous tendency to manufactures'. It is perhaps of some significance that this reference to the harmful effects of combination
on industry itself was made by an outsider. Local opinion had
so far concentrated on the question of the threat to law and order.[3]

In 1796 the Master Cabinet Makers of Nottingham were faced
with what they described as 'a most impudent, unreasonable,
and unlawful combination' of journeymen, undertaken for the
purpose of raising wages. They resisted the demands and found
new workmen. Later the old ones began to threaten the lives
of the new men and attack their property. The Master Cabinet
Makers now formed themselves into an association for self-
protection, for, they claimed, they themselves were now being
threatened. The journeymen denied the allegations and demanded
that they should be proved before a magistrate. They were not,
either because they were unfounded or because the Masters did
not wish to call in the authorities. The dispute had been given
little public ventilation whilst it remained at the stage of wage-
demands, dismissals, and replacement of workmen. It was only
when threats to life and property were involved that the employers saw fit to publicise their side of the case and complain
about combinations.[4]

In the decade before Pitt's Combination Acts various trends
can be seen emerging. A readiness to make wage-demands,
backed up if necessary with organisation, is evident amongst
many sorts of workmen. Hosiery and lace-workers enjoyed a
tradition of free association 'to enjoy matters relative to the
trade'; in addition, shoemakers, masons, builders, tailors, and cabinet
makers all advanced wage claims in the period with what publicity they could get and did not fear being labelled 'combinations'
at this stage of negotiations. The distinction between peaceful
negotiation and behaviour threatening disturbance seems to
have been accepted as vital on all sides, and combinations never
seem to have been condemned for consequences that were purely
industrial. In December, 1792, a loyalist meeting was held in Nottingham which condemned amongst other things combinations
'which must inevitably tend to interrupt the public tranquility'.
A developing back-ground of war and anti-Jacobin feeling in
Nottingham, which reached a peak in the Summer of 1794 and

[3]*Nottingham Journal*, 16th August, 1794.
[4]*Nottingham Journal*, 7th January, 1797.

prevailed until the war lost its popularity, helped to magnify feeling against trade union activity when it appeared to threaten order. Also, the succession of food-riots in Nottingham with which the magistrates had to cope would increase their sensitivity to movements which might end in disorder. The middle years of the decade posed a number of problems to the local authorities and it is perhaps surprising that declarations and actions against combinations were not more numerous and severe than they were, for there is little to indicate a hostile climate of opinion which cannot be explained in non-industrial terms.[5]

In the period of the Pitt Combination Acts trade union activity became more widespread and more ambitious in its scope, especially from about 1809 when economic conditions began to deteriorate. The most common form of initiative undertaken by the workmen still remained the petition to the manufacturers, the traditional way of ventilating a grievance, of which low wages was the most common kind. In February, 1805, a joint committee of the plain silk and two-needle cotton workers 'waited on the hosiers' to press a wage claim. As often happened, some hosiers agreed and others temporised. Sometimes a petition would meet with quick success; in September, 1811, for instance, makers of plain black silk stockings received an immediate rise on advancing their claims. Sometimes the petition was the first note sounded in a planned struggle, when the workmen had organisation ready to operate a strike. Such were the petitions in the winter and spring of 1814, when the men were sounding out the opposition and preparing for a trial of strength. On other occasions the 'humble petition' reads like a very forlorn hope and registered disapproval of a trend which the framework-knitters knew they were powerless to reverse, as in March and May, 1816, when the makers of plain silk stockings complained of the abandonment of regulations by certain hosiers. Usually the petition concerned wage increases or threatened abatements, more often the latter, though occasionally the manufacturers would be approached on another theme. In November, 1809, the journeymen silk hose makers asked the manufacturers to mark the quality of their hose with figures and regulate the number of 'jacks' for each quality; whilst the framework-knitters in the neighbourhood of Calverton

[5]S. and B. Webb, *History of Trade Unionism* (1920), p. 75; *Nottingham Journal*, 22nd December, 1792; Bailey, op. it., pp. 142-3, 158, 167.

appealed to their employers in May, 1816, to eliminate their peculiar grievance of truck-payments.[6]

But the petition was increasingly being replaced, or at least supplemented, by more ambitious and positive action, relying less on the goodwill of the employer to respond and more on the ability of the organisation of the men to enforce their demands. The most menacing action of this type, because it occurred during the Luddite period and at a time, 1814, when economic conditions allowed trade unions some prospect of making headway, was the Society for Parliamentary Relief, established by Henson and his colleagues in Nottingham to succeed the unsuccessful organisation of their 1812 campaign for Parliamentary regulation. Experts such as Sir Samuel Romilly were consulted and the Society's statutes carefully worded to respect laws against combinations and Corresponding Societies, though Home Office legal advisers were later inclined to think that the Society was nonetheless offensive. It was said to be modelled on the Methodist class system and had groups throughout the hosiery districts. It was believed to have a weekly income of £100-£150 from the town of Nottingham alone, which could well have been so at the time of its greatest strength, for after a year's existence it had in November, 1813, a membership of 1455 in Nottingham, 935 more in the country areas, and total funds of £200. Like its 1812 predecessor it exercised a watching brief over the general welfare of the trade, identifying and publicising the complaints of workmen; but unlike its predecessor it had the strength and prevailing economic conditions to permit the pressing of wage claims; it also showed enterprise by itself entering into the manufacturing business to give work to members and to raise funds. Through the winter and spring of 1814 other manufacturers experienced growing apprehension of intimidation from the Union and one contemporary view was that the men had the strength to dictate their own terms. This is certainly an exaggeration and the men themselves claimed only the achievement of small rises in most branches. Where these were not gained, the Union furthered its claims with limited strike action against particular employers, and it was one such effort against Ray Brothers and

[6]*Nottingham Journal*, 16th February, 1805; *Nottingham Review*, 27th September, 1811; 22nd March, 31st May, 1816; *Nottingham Journal*, 18th November, 1809; *Nottingham Review*, 3rd May, 1816.

Beardmore and Parkers in July, 1814, which, together with the belief that the Union was promoting frame-breaking, prompted the using of the Combination Acts against it.[7]

The period 1817-24 experienced strikes on a greater scale, involving bigger areas and larger numbers, but at no time in this period did the men's organisations appear so potent as in 1814. In July, 1817, William Raworth appealed to the men to form committees in every area in order to safeguard prices. It was a preliminary to negotiations for securing the adherence of hosiers to a statement of prices, below the 1811 level but of a kind the men were ready to accept. Following their failure to secure unanimous acceptance of the plan, framework-knitters throughout the Midland Counties left work in their thousands, refusing to work for the abated prices which the employers offered. In Nottingham the strike was perfectly orderly and conducted with great decorum. The authorities admitted this but feared that the calm would not last. Towards the end of September the men started drifting back. By early October they were mostly at work, having secured no better terms than previously offered.[8]

Two years later, in what some always regarded as one of the most critical years in the town's history, their position was even more forlorn. The framework-knitters of Nottinghamshire resolved to co-operate with the workmen of Leicestershire and cease working below the prices they had received in 1817. On August 9th, 1819, the two-needle branch, the plain cotton operatives, stopped work, left their frames, and assembled in the town. On the 19th over 6,000 gathered in the town to parade with placards urging 'Give us bread', and the frames of hosiers who abated the men were brought back to Nottingham to the hosiers' shops. Again the men behaved 'quietly and without any disturbance' and apart from the 'outrageous combination' reported

[7]Framework-knitters' Papers, 1812-14, F. 171; H.O. 42/138, Coldham to H.O., 10th May, 1814; H.O. 42/137, Correspondence between H.O. and Coldham, February, 1814; H.O. 42/138, Allsopp to H.O., 22nd April, 1814; H.O. 42/135, William Woodcock of Mansfield to H.O., 16th November, 1813; H.O. 42/138, Sculthorpe, Clerk to County Justices, to H.O., 12th April, 1814; H.O. 42/139, Coldham to H.O., 24th May, 1814; 42/139, J. T. Becher to H.O., 10th, 14th May, 1814; H.O. 42/140, Enfield to H.O., 11th August, 1814.

[8]*Nottingham Review*, 25th July, 12th September, 10th October, 1817; H.O. 42/170, Enfield to H.O., 10th, 25th, September, 1817.

Enfield, the town clerk, 'conduct is peaceable'. The Duke of Newcastle, asked to intercede on behalf of the men, was equally impressed by their 'reasonable' behaviour, but unable to ignore that they had entered into a conspiracy. Towards the end of September the men began to drift back at the rate offered by the hosiers, with no gain to show for their prolonged strike. Enfield, not unsympathetic towards the men and an opponent of the ministry, took the opportunity to point out to the central government that they must expect trouble unless something were done to procure 'some immediate supplies for the necessary wants of the workpeople'.[9]

In March, 1821, the cotton hose workers made a further abortive bid to keep the hosiers to settled price-lists by striking, an attempt repeated through the three hosiery counties in the Spring of 1822. And yet again in July, 1823, the Nottinghamshire cotton workers met to consider further proposed abatements. Again it was resolved to form committees in every district, raise subscriptions from those in full employment, and use the money to support those in 'temporary unemployment' whilst the underpaying employers were 'brought up'. The inevitable 'stand' was decided upon in Nottinghamshire, Leicestershire, and Derbyshire and took place through October, but again without success. Strikes, however long, seemed inevitably to result in a return to work on whatever terms the hosiers would give. And if the hosier expressed a willingness to be accommodating, he could probably be so only because the lay-off had enabled him to build up business to be completed. The men had no means of keeping their employers to their agreements once the back-log of work had been cleared.[10]

One of the most interesting strikes of the period was that of bleaching hands at Basford, on the outskirts of Nottingham, in February, 1822. Apart from the unexceptional demands for wage-increases, the men also attempted to fix the prices that their employers should receive from the hosiers for the work which they did. In addition, they made detailed proposals about additional

[9]*Nottingham Review*, 13th, 20th, August, 3rd, 24th September, 1819; Sutton, op. cit., p. 353; H.O. 42/194, Enfield to H.O., 1st, 2nd September, 1819; H.O. 42/193, Newcastle to H.O., 31st August, 1819.
[10]*Nottingham Review*, 2nd, 16th March, 1821, 12th April, 1822, 18th July, 15th August, 10th October, 1823.

E

overtime pay, hours to be worked in Winter and Summer, apprenticeship terms to be enforced by their employers, unemployment pay to be received if the men were inconvenienced through the scarcity of work, and holidays to be enjoyed by the workmen. This represents easily the most ambitious programme advanced by any local group during this period for it advanced the right to regulate the employer in ways of which the vast majority had not so far dreamed. The outcome of these demands can be readily imagined.[11]

A more passive response to the perpetual threat of wage reductions was the formation of societies or committees for the purpose of scrutinising price-lists and enforcing adherence to them. It was a variation in the normal technique as it hoped to anticipate and avoid the need ever to hold strikes. Protective action was taken by the committee of the point net lace hands in July, 1810; when threatened with abatements their committee secretary, George Waterfall, issued an order that the committee 'expected to see every man there (at a meeting) who worked at a point net frame'. A common front shown to employers would, it was hoped, deter them from taking hostile action. Another suggestion was made by the 'Freeholders, Farmers and Traders' of Arnold, in July, 1817, who proposed a permanent union of masters and men to keep constant vigilance on prices, in the belief that the goodwill of honest men was all the problem required for its solution. More popular was the frequently tried bluff of collecting all available information about underpaying employers in the hope thereby of exercising a deterrent: in November, 1819, for instance, the two-needle branch appointed a committee to sit and note any infringements of the recently agreed 1819 statement. The following month a workman was paraded round the town on an ass and a hosier carted through the town in effigy, the one accepting work below statement prices, the other offering it. But such attempts as these never succeeded for long when work was short and workmen were glad enough to take it on any terms.[12]

The other type of organisation used by the workmen in hosiery and lace was that modelled on the Sick Club or Friendly Society, a collecting society which attempted to make provision

[11]*Nottingham Journal*, 9th February, 1822.

[12]*Nottingham Journal*, 7th July, 1810; *Nottingham Review*, 18th July, 5th November, 1817, 17th, 24th December, 1819.

during good times for worse times ahead. This was the solution
that Felkin always favoured, arising perhaps from his grandfather's belief that 'each man, by his economy, sobriety, and
industry (should) so provide, as that it should never be worth his
while to accept of unreasonably reduced wages'. But the virtues
of William Felkin I were not given to all men, and the deteriorating conditions of trade in the nineteenth century made
such prudent management impossible. The planning of such
funds by a union was often recommended, and in the period
1819-21 attempted. The stockingers' committee which had conducted the 1819 strike in the two-needle branch began, at the end
of September, to establish a Union Friendly Society as a safeguard against unemployment and to provide temporary relief
for those unable to find work at list prices. It received the distinguished patronage of the Corporation, which donated £30,
and a number of 'Gentlemen and Tradesmen' of the town also
formed a committee to act with that of the men. The silk stocking workers quickly joined the scheme. In February, 1820, the
hosiers themselves blessed the idea and planned to make their
contribution, and, with the support of all the local press, the
Nottinghamshire and Derbyshire Framework-knitters' Friendly
Society appeared to be making good progress. It relied jointly
on the contributions of the employed members and public subscriptions, but appeals for more had repeatedly to be made. As
late as March, 1821, the Society was still functioning normally,
and money was still being collected from those in work, but in
that month a further long strike was begun, and money in hand
became converted into a strike fund, which the men's advisers
had always warned against. In November, 1823, the two-needle
branch was again reported to be uniting in societies like sick
clubs to prevent men from having to take cheap work, but this
attempt also faded out. It is significant that the major enterprise,
the 1819 Society, had survived only during the inter-strike period
when relatively favourable conditions prevailed. This apparently
more sophisticated method of combating unemployment and
reductions could only succeed when the unemployment and
reductions were small. When they became extensive and insup-
portable, the men felt the need to make a further 'all or nothing'
challenge.[13]

[13] W. Felkin, *The Stout-hearted Weaver*, op. cit.; *Nottingham Review*, 1st, 15th, 22nd
October, 1819, 18th February, 28th April, 1820, 2nd, 16th March, 1821, 28th November,
1823.

What emerges clearly from the period 1800-24 is the great variety of organisations of a trade union type which were to be found in Nottingham and district during this period, inside both principal trades of the town and in other occupations, which sought to impose conditions upon employers in the management of their businesses. On at least fifteen different occasions strikes occurred as a result of these associations and combinations, but on five occasions only were the Combination Laws used against the striking men. Gravener Henson was to maintain in 1823 that the Combination Laws were not so burdensome as the law which made men liable to prosecution for leaving work unfinished, and it is true that female lace-runners, bobbin-net workmen, framesmiths, and cobblers were all imprisoned under the law, but there is no means of knowing when these cases arose from trade union activity and when simply from criminal intent or pure inertia. What is clear is that the Combination Laws were ignored on many occasions when they could have been invoked, which gives to the cases of their enforcement a particular interest.[14]

The first was a simple case, in June, 1804, arising out of a strike of boot and shoe makers for increases of 1/- per pair on boots and 6d. on shoes. The Masters produced a counter-organisation, rewards were offered for information, and one man was convicted on the charge of entering a combination to obtain an advance in wages and was given three months' imprisonment; four others, convicted of having left work in an unfinished state, were similarly sentenced. The incident is a good illustration of the purely passive role of the magistrates; the initiative came entirely from the employers, who were themselves much better organised than the men for the purpose of fixing wage levels, an offence under the Acts.[15]

A more interesting case occurred in March, 1807, when three journeyman tailors were convicted of combining and sent to prison for two months. In April a fourth was also convicted, but the strike went on, and this in spite of a warning from the Recorder of Nottingham that combination was a dangerous tendency and that official leniency would give way to severity if the men did not return to work. The pressure on the employers was

[14]G. White and G. Henson, op. cit., p. 51.
[15]Nottingham Journal, 1st, 15th, 22nd June, 13th July, 1805.

such that they divided. Some agreed to the men's terms: others refused. By the end of May, with the dispute unsettled, some masters were offering constant employment at a guinea a week, a good wage and practically what had been sought, to anyone who would take it, for many tailors were leaving the town rather than accept defeat. Demoralised by the defections of some of their number, the employers began to attack each other in the local press, and one firm was accused of surrender to the men's demands and the re-employment of one of the leading organisers of the combination. It seems that given a favourable economic situation the men could successfully divide their employers and that not even the enforcement of the Combination Laws, let alone their existence, was a strong deterrent.[16]

In October, 1810, the Laws were invoked over a dispute in lace. On Henson's testimony, a wage reduction of one-twelfth had occurred in the trade following the introduction of a machine for measuring lace, known as the 'rack'. The men welcomed the regulation but not the reduction. A strike occurred in 1810 and four journeymen lace-workers, including John Blackner, local historian and later editor of the *Nottingham Review*, were sentenced to a month's imprisonment for combining to advance wages and attempting to control William Nunn, their employer, in the management of his work, for he refused to introduce the rack. When the men were released they were conducted from gaol with a 'band of music and the cheerful greetings of a great concourse of spectators' and then proceeded to the Sir Isaac Newton, the usual place of their committee meetings, to enjoy dinner for eighty at the expense of the landlord and friends. They were accepted as heroes rather than criminals, and William Nunn bought himself some unfavourable publicity by his resort to the law.[17]

By July, 1814, when the next prison sentences were awarded, a lot had happened. In particular the Luddites had been at work and all attempts to track down their leaders had failed. In the early summer of 1814 there was a growing feeling amongst employers and magistrates that the Union Society was promoting the breakings and they organised a joint committee, with the town clerk as Secretary, to prosecute frame-breakers. This close

[16]*Nottingham Journal*, 28th March, 11th April, 23rd, 30th May, 1807.
[17]*Nottingham Review*, 26th October, 23rd November, 1810.

and formal association of municipal authorities and hosiers was a novel development brought about by the crisis; in fact, no evidence was produced against Luddites but the committee was able, by the use of spies, to catch two men in the act of collecting funds for the support of the current strike of silk stocking workers. The men were convicted and given a month's hard labour in the House of Correction, and the Union appears to have collapsed in consequence. It is clear that the very existence of the Union is not enough to explain the prosecution, for the magistrates had known of this for two and a half years and been approached by the men on many occasions. Their action in July, 1814, seems to have arisen in part from the authorities' determination to make a gesture, albeit a fruitless one, against Luddism when they believed that they had at last found the responsible party, partly from the grave concern at the widespread successes of this the most successful trade union attempt to date, and partly from the rather cheeky resolve of the Union to make an example of two particular firms, a gesture which could hardly be overlooked. The frustrations and fears of magistrates and hosiers alike combined to produce the prosecution of 1814.[18]

The final prosecution, in April, 1821, was not produced by fear of Union power. At the end of February the two-needle branch of cotton hosiery, who claimed to be working a fourteen to eighteen hour day for 5/- per week, went on strike for the 1819 agreement, which was being undermined by some hosiers. They were widely supported in their cause and public subscriptions were taken out to support them. The strike dragged on, public charity was forthcoming, churches and chapels collecting for the men, and the hosiers, with no incentive to have work resumed, were in no hurry to terminate the dispute. The town magistrates warned the men against acts of violence against property, but the strike was conducted peaceably and there was no official interference from the town authorities. On April 7th, however, the county magistrates, invariably at odds with the borough officials, arrested and charged two committee members with offences under the Combination Acts and issued warrants against fourteen more. The men were, however, acquitted on insufficient evidence, though not before defending counsel, Mr.

[18]H.O. 42/139, Coldham to H.O., 22nd May, 1814; *Nottingham Journal*, 9th July, 1814; H.O. 42/140, Coldham to H.O., 7th July, 1814.

Hopkinson, had pointed out the equal liability of the hosiers under the Acts and the impracticability of sending 4,000 or 5,000 men to prison. At the end of the month the magistrates struck again, and this time four leaders were convicted and given a three months' sentence, though this conviction was quashed on appeal over a technicality. And so this last attempt at enforcing the Combination Laws in the town, made by the county authorities, was frustrated. In many ways it was a surprising prosecution, a 'monstrous one' in the eyes of a modern authority. The men's combination had been formed to resist abatements, not to advance new claims, and this sort of association had not been challenged before. The Acts, said the men's counsel, had never been intended for such a case as this; and the intrusion of the county magistrates, on the instigation of an unnamed manufacturer, emphasised the unusual nature of the case. At all events the men escaped, and it is clear that the Acts had taken only a light toll of Nottingham strikers before their repeal in 1824.[19]

They had taken no toll of combining masters, but this was general. The *Review* argued in July, 1814, that workmen should have the same facility for prosecuting their employers for combining to reduce wages as the latter had for prosecuting workmen who combined to advance them. In theory this equal right did exist for anyone with the skill to make use of it. One such man was Gravener Henson, who attempted to bring a prosecution against combining employers in 1811. The magistrates, according to Henson, refused to receive his information even though the combination was publicly advertised in the press, a notice signed by four parties which declared that they had agreed to reduce the wages of their workmen. The grounds for refusal were that Henson could not show in which parish the men had met to make their agreement; Henson regarded this explanation as inadequate.[20]

What appears then from an examination of the period of Pitt's Combination Laws in Nottingham is a magisterial policy essentially of non-interference, and it is necessary to ask why the

[19]*Nottingham Review*, 9th, 16th, 30th March, 13th April, 4th May, 1821; *Report of Select Committee on Artizans and Machinery*, 1824, V, p. 281; M. D. George, 'The Combination Laws Reconsidered', *Economic History*, 1927.
[20]*Nottingham Review*, 15th July, 1814; G. White and G. Henson, op. cit., p. 81; *Report of Select Committee on Artizans and Machinery*, 1824, V, p. 280.

magistrates did not take greater trouble to enforce the law of
the land. The answer lies partly in their own view of their function in society, clearly evident in the pre-1799 period, which
was to maintain good order in the area of their jurisdiction. When
that was threatened, as in Luddite years, they were willing to
act, but on the whole strikes were surprisingly peaceful and there
was usually little real cause for concern about breaches of peace.
If the employers demanded interference and law-enforcement
the magistrates' hands were forced, but they preferred not to act.
Reporting on the strike of 1817, Henry Enfield, the town clerk,
wrote that the magistrates had no power or right to interfere
in the dispute; their duty was to watch the public peace and to
act only if complaints were made or violence broke out. This
was the opposite view to that of John Parker, a hosier, who felt
that the magistrates ought to interfere to break the combination,
but the town authorities stuck to it in 1817 and also during the
1819 strike. Enfield again rejoiced that there was no disturbance
and that conduct was peaceable except for the existence of an
'outrageous combination', which in itself did not seem to worry
him. And in March, 1821, the Nottingham magistrates warned
the striking framework-knitters not against breaking the Combination Laws but of the need to avoid acts of violence against
property. On the same occasion the High Sheriff of the County
explained that any interference from him on his own initiative
would be 'improper and useless'.[21]

In view of this record, it was hardly reasonable for Henson to
maintain, as he did in 1823, that the magistrates had regarded all
the men's attempts at improvement as sedition and resistance to
government and every active man as a dangerous instigator to
be watched. He had a personal grievance in that magistrates had
refused his evidence for a prosecution of the masters in 1811,
but he must certainly have known that the men too had experienced the lenience of their policy of non-enforcement. Non-
interference was in fact quickly being erected into a principle of

[21]H.O. 42/170, Enfield to H.O., 10th September, 1817; H.O. 42/194, Enfield to H.O.,
1st September, 1819; *Nottingham Review*, 30th, 23rd March, 1821; J. L. and B. Hammond,
The Skilled Labourer (1919), state that the Nottingham authorities were not so friendly
to the men as those at Leicester. This they infer from a remark by the Duke of Newcastle
that men on strike in 1819 had entered a conspiracy and were not therefore entitled to
legal assistance. As lord-lieutenant Newcastle spoke for the county, but never for the town.

national life, and *laissez-faire* in industrial matters meant allowing
the parties concerned in disputes to work out a solution for themselves. The town's principal industries were already working
according to fairly well-established, if unsatisfactory, patterns.
Wage negotiations were a normal part of relationships and magistrates felt little need to interfere in these questions.[22]
   An important factor in the explanation of official attitudes
is the general atmosphere in which industrial disputes occurred.
Conditions in hosiery were such as to ensure the framework-
knitters a large measure of popular sympathy throughout the
period, as is shown by the readiness with which public subscriptions were opened and supported when the men were on strike.
This sympathy was in part shared by the magistracy and gave rise
to the claims made by the men that the magistrates themselves
did not approve of the Combination Laws. A writer in September, 1819, spoke of combinations 'which the laws condemn,
but which the magistrates connive at, and the public applaud'.
'It is notorious in this neighbourhood', wrote the *Review* in
1824, 'that when the workmen in the Nottingham manufacture
are run down in their prices they frequently combine and a
general stand takes place'. The Acts clearly held no terrors for
the men. The whole period of their operation was one of open
combinations, of different kinds of organisations of workmen,
public meetings, appeals through the press, approaches to local
dignitaries, and even to Parliament itself. On occasions the magistrates themselves were approached for help in disputes, and their
approval was often sought. When the mechanics and workmen
of all the trades in Nottingham petitioned for the repeal of the
Laws in 1824, the Mayor granted them the use of the town hall
for the purpose of collecting signatures, which was hardly the act
of an oppressive magistrate. In fact the magistrates as a whole had
been known, it was alleged in March, 1824, to express great
reluctance to invoke the Acts from the strong belief that they
were 'opposed to every principle of sound policy, even to the
common dictates of humanity'.[23]
   And the feelings of society's guardians were believed to be
shared by society as a whole. When the workmen claimed that

[22]G. White and G. Henson, op. cit., pp. 88-9.
[23]*Nottingham Review*, 3rd September, 1819, 20th February, 2nd April, 26th March,
1824.

their committees of 1814 were 'sanctioned by public opinion' they probably spoke correctly. The Combination Laws were considered very partial on the side of the masters, said Benjamin Taylor, a Union leader, when he gave evidence in 1824; every man from the highest to the lowest had been sympathetic towards them in the great strike of 1821. Gravener Henson went so far as to express the belief that very few masters even favoured the laws. John Blackner, the local historian, himself one of the few people to be imprisoned locally under the Acts, believed the law to be 'marked with such direct partiality as to make it odious in the eyes of those who seek to further their own views by taking advantage of its provisions—the facilities it affords for punishing the employed over what it affords for punishing the employers is the cause of its being held in general abhorrence'. He then went on to observe that the workmen, by conducting their opposition in peace, had successfully linked public sympathy to their cause. The *Review* printed and shared Blackner's views on the partiality of the Acts.[24]

The workmen themselves claimed that the Combination Acts were oppressive. Benjamin Taylor spoke in 1824 of men who acted in fear of the law and demanded the right and freedom for men to strike their own bargains, though this would have been of very doubtful value to them in the existing state of the hosiery trade. Henson expressed the belief that the Acts kept wages down, whilst the silk hose and glove workers referred to the 'most degrading restrictions arising out of the Combination Laws, which are now almost universally decried as equally unjust and oppressive'. Yet Taylor himself admitted that the 1821 prosecution had stimulated rather than diminished the men's enthusiasm; and it is difficult to understand Henson's claim that wages were kept down as a result of the Acts; the absence of the Combination Laws would not have meant strong unions and not even strong unions would have meant higher wages. It was a theoretical rather than any practical restraint that the Acts had exercised on the workmen of Nottingham. When the newly-won right to combine was threatened in 1825 and Francis Place was organising workmen's evidence to forestall the government, he received a dispirited letter from Gravener

[24]*Nottingham Review*, 8th April, 1814; *Report of Select Committee on Artizans and Machinery*, 1824, V, pp. 271, 281; Blackner, op. cit., p. 235.

Henson in which the latter lamented his inability to rouse the workmen of Nottingham to the perils of their position and complained of their complete apathy on the issue. It seems that the Acts were by no means the actual bogey that a few believed them to be, and there had certainly been no history of strict enforcement to make them an object of terror to the men of Nottingham.[25]

The year immediately following the repeal of the Combination Acts was a period of almost general wage demands and numerous 'turn-outs' in different branches of hosiery and also amongst the journeyman tailors and stone-masons. This arose less from the new liberty that repeal allowed than from the greater prosperity of 1824-5 which all groups were anxious to share and suggests that for once trade unions were not seen entirely as defence mechanisms but organisations that could be used to exploit favourable situations, which many of them now did. The two-needle branch, among the poorer paid workers, appealed for their right to participate in the general prosperity and struck in November, 1824, but their appeals went unanswered. The long strike carried on into January, 1825; it was not 'for mastership or honour', said the men, but for a fair wage, but the labour of these men was less in demand than that of other branches. The poor framework-knitters and their families, wrote the *Review*, were literally starving in the midst of plenty, and they were forced back to work on terms which showed scarcely any improvement.[26]

From this time on general turn-outs such as this and the great efforts of 1817-23 no longer occurred. A stockinger later claimed in 1833 that the poverty and distress attending the mass turn-outs were the main reason why the big strikes had stopped and why he did not expect them to be repeated. The futility of the strike when their position was so weak was evidently accepted, and the men resorted to the traditional appeals to the hosiers,

[25]*Report of Select Committee on Artizans and Machinery*, 1824, V, pp. 272, 281; *Nottingham Review*, 26th March, 1824; F. A. Wells, op. cit., p. 122, surprisingly supports the Henson view. He says that fear of the Combination Laws prevented the men from forming any permanent organisation and so masters could not be held to agreements; Place MSS., B.M. Add. MSS. 27803, 374, Henson to Place, 24th April, 1825.

[26]See *Nottingham Review* for 1824-5; *Nottingham Journal*, 24th November, 1824; *Nottingham Review*, 7th January, 1825, 17th December, 1824.

being glad to accept whatever was forthcoming. Threats of strikes were usually unfulfilled, and when a request concerning prices in December, 1827, met with only limited response it was followed by only limited strike action against four principal offenders. This was not a sign of strength, as when the Union attempted to teach a lesson to Ray Brothers and Beardmore's in 1814, but an indication of weakness to do no more than make a gesture. In the Winter of 1832 and Spring of 1833 the two-needle branch again appeared ready to repeat a challenge on the scale of 1819. Meetings were held of delegates from the three hosiery counties and preparations were made 'to secure good understanding and prevent confusion when the grand crisis shall come'. It did not come and the only consequence of the preparations was what one of the men later described as an 'ineffectual very partial turn-out' in March, 1835.[27]

Other better paid groups still persisted in the attempt to raise or retain their wages by strike action. Workers in plain silk hose were the most tenacious and long-suffering in their efforts, organising large and ineffectual strikes in most years in the period 1824-35. Another group which could still threaten to cease work altogether rather than submit to reductions and still carry out its threat was the drawer and pantaloon branch, which struck in 1825 and 1827, whilst the cut-up workers, amongst the best-paid of all hosiery workers, were still willing to strike in 1833. But even these branches could do no more than defer reductions by temporarily abstaining from work and temporarily re-creating a demand.[28]

The new emphasis in this post-repeal period was away from the conventional actions of individual branches of the trade, carried out over as big an area as could be organised, occasionally supplemented by co-operative enterprises on behalf of all branches of hosiery, and towards the principle of general union. This idea involved the participation of trades outside hosiery and lace; its purposes were less clearly defined but its promise, perhaps because of this, seemed great. Through the principle of general union,

[27]Felkin's Statement of 1833, op. cit.; *Nottingham Review*, 7th December, 1827, 1st, 22nd February, 1828, 4th January, 1833; *Report of Select Committee on Laws affecting Export of Machinery*, 1841, VII, Appendix 3, p. 234.

[28]*Nottingham Journal*, 10th December, 1825; *Nottingham Review*, 27th April, 1827, 13th September, 1833.

the working men of all Nottingham trades were given a first suggestion that they were a class with grievances in common and that their combined action could be a source of power.

There is a little evidence to suggest that as early as 1818 Gravener Henson had conceived the idea of a general union on a national scale of men engaged in the manufacturing trades. Manchester magistrates reported that the men in their area were supporting such a scheme which was believed to have originated in Nottingham. Henson was at this time doing a lot of travelling and making contacts, but if this was his scheme it failed to make any headway in Nottingham itself and its life was short. It was Henson who outlined the first scheme for a general union on a purely local basis in May, 1829. It was time, he said, that the working classes, like everyone else, had their committees, and he proceeded to advocate a union of all Nottingham trades. A committee was chosen of two representatives from each trade present at the original meeting, and many trades outside hosiery and lace, cabinet-making, joinering, and painting, for instance, were represented. A subscription of 1d. per week was to be collected from all members, and the aim of the union was to keep up journeymen's wages.[29]

This scheme never got off the ground, but it was quickly followed in August, 1830, by Doherty's ambitious National Association for the Protection of Labour, organised in Nottingham along similar lines to those previously suggested by Henson and with a similar purpose. By October eighteen trades had joined, and on October 20th, a Nottingham 'mechanic' expressed the sanguine belief that the National Association was increasing a hundred-fold in comparison with the Political unions or Co-operative Trading Societies and could not now be suppressed. Different trades continued to join by branch or by district through the Winter of 1831. Weekly committee meetings were held in Nottingham and in March a national conference was held there. This was appropriate, for Nottingham was at this stage the only organised area outside Lancashire. In the period July 31, 1830, to September 10, 1831, Nottingham contributed over £228 to the Association's funds, an amount exceeded only by Rochdale and Manchester, and was by far the largest contributor outside

[29]H.O. 42/181, James Norris, Manchester, to H.O., 11th October, 1818; *Nottingham Review*, 15th May, 1929.

the cotton area. But the early enthusiasm was not maintained. In January, 1831, the bobbin-net lace hands formed themselves into the Lace Makers' Union, a sure sign that the 1824-5 boom was now thoroughly played out, and joined the National Association, but the failure of Lancashire to support their strike of 1831, after Nottingham had generously contributed to the funds of the cotton spinners earlier, led to Nottingham defections. When a delegate from the National Association headquarters came to Nottingham in the August few attended his meeting. The continued decline was later blamed on people's preoccupation with Parliamentary reform and the attendant excitements, and a meeting to revive the Association, held in March, 1832, was adjourned with no progress made. Ever the optimist, Henson was within a week proposing a union of the mechanics of Nottinghamshire, Derbyshire, and Leicestershire. The time was favourable, he said, and they should aim to increase the value of labour and support any effort to do this. Though 'many influential supporters' were said to be emerging, this plan also failed to develop.[30]

When the idea re-emerged in October, 1833, it produced much more alarming reactions than ever before. This time it was the bobbin-net lace hands who gave the lead by announcing their enrolment in a secret order of Operatives' Trades Union for Clothiers and the establishment of a local lodge in connection with the Bradford Union of Operative Classes. Great numbers were apparently initiated into the secret order, and the taste for 'Union' quickly grew. A Nottingham Trades' Union sprang up, incorporating all the principal trades of the town and it affiliated to the Grand National Consolidated Trades' Union. By January, 1834, the Union was publicly demonstrating its size and organising impressive displays to accompany the funeral of a member or any similar function that could be exploited. When an employee of Joseph Banks of Basford, a manufacturer of silk stockings, was ordered to make a wide piece, he informed his employer that the men had a union and would resist such practices; all twenty-eight of the firm's workmen came out on strike.

[30]*Nottingham Review*, 13th August, 8th October, 5th November, 1830; S. and B. Webb, op. cit., pp. 122-3; G. D. H. Cole, *Attempts at General Union* (1953), pp. 26, 30-1, 177; N. M. Cuthbert, *The Lace Makers' Society* (1960), pp. 19-20; *Nottingham Review*, 26th August, 1831, 24th February, 9th, 16th, 23rd March, 1832.

It was claimed that out of 470 silk glove hands in Nottingham and district over two-thirds were in the Union, and some alarm began to be felt. At the end of March a mass demonstration took place on the Forest at which the sentences on the Dorchester Labourers were deplored and the whole policy of the Whig government was attacked. There was even talk of a 'Universal strike' if the sentences were not revoked. Towards the end of the meeting the Nottingham 'Female Union' appeared, and both Unions went in procession back to the Market Place, accompanied by a band which played 'God save the King' and 'Praise God from whom all blessings flow', thus establishing loyalty to Church and State, though the texts of their anthems seem hardly appropriate to the men's conditions. More meetings were held, still anti-government in tone, but by the middle of May the enthusiasm had waned. A further mass demonstration attracted no more than 100 unionists and broke up in disorder, and a fortnight later the *Journal* was able to bring its readers much comfort; the trade union at Bulwell had dissolved, its regalia had been sold, and there was additional evidence coming in that 'the working classes are coming to a right understanding of these clubs'.[31]

In 1835 wages in hosiery were an estimated one-third below those of 1790 and in lace they had been generally falling for ten years; nor had the workmen succeeded in persuading or compelling their employers to accept the many regulations of trade outlined in the abortive bills of 1812 and 1823. It is then hardly possible to speak of trade union success in the period of 1785-1835. Any example of effective trade union action in this period is to be found almost entirely outside the main industries, amongst tailors or joiners, or other unrelated groups. The boom year of 1824 sent lace wages soaring and even helped some hosiery hands to secure their requests, but more typical was the case of the cotton drawer branch a year later who struck for eleven weeks, and then went back at the same price they had received previously, or the silk hose workers who struck in 1830 and returned without an advance, finding their trade badly

[31] G. D. H. Cole, op. cit., p. 68; *Nottingham Review*, 25th October, 8th November, 13th December, 1833, 17th January, 21st February, 7th March, 1834; *Report of the Proceedings of the Public Meeting held on Nottingham Forest, 31st March, 1834, on the Six Members of the Trade Union at Dorchester* (1834); *Nottingham Journal*, 16th, 30th May, 1834.

affected by the declining health of the King. The lesson of all such cases was clear; if the men combined and struck when trade was not in a good state their action simply recoiled on them.[32]

The inevitability of the failure of strike action in unfavourable circumstances was gradually felt by the men themselves. An Arnold framework-knitter with decades of trade union activity behind him stated in 1833 that he believed no turn-out had been productive of real good and that he himself had favoured only representations to the masters. This was the view of Felkin's grandfather, that combination had never had a beneficial effect, and others were willing to develop the argument that the men, far from gaining, had always done themselves great injury by striking. As early as 1819, the *Journal* claimed to have witnessed too many combinations not to know that they could not end in a single practical good, a view which the not unsympathetic *Review* was also to share. The workmen would meet nothing but disappointment through the trade unions, wrote Thomas Warsop, in April, 1834, and it was true that the unions had brought them little else to that point. Let the framework-knitters disavow combinations, wrote another in January, 1831; if they would wait patiently they would by their exemplary conduct gain many friends. The advice was not very encouraging, but aggression brought no more reward than stoicism.[33]

If the futility of combination was the main argument employed against it, other disadvantages were also seen. The *Journal*, in December, 1824, attacked the 'baneful system of turning-out'; youths on strike were learning the habits of vice and indolence which were replacing industry and morality. Absolem Barnett, with his concern for public economy and the welfare of the poor, believed that trade unions aggravated the evils they sought to cure and increased pauperism. Strikes, it was also argued, were a threat to capital, which ought to be protected. If threatened, it would be withdrawn, and manufacturers would transfer their business from Nottingham to areas where trade unions did not

[32]*Nottingham Review*, 3rd June, 1825, 14th May, 1830.

[33]Felkin's Statement of 1833, op. cit.; W. Felkin, *The Stout-hearted Weaver*, op. cit.; *Report of the Royal Commission on Conditions of Framework-knitters*, 1845, XV, Appendix to Report, Part II, p. 147; *Nottingham Journal*, 12th June, 1819, 25th April, 1834, 1st January, 1831.

exist. In order to prevent this, it was urged, manufacturers should refuse to employ men who joined trade unions. On a few occasions 'non-union' shops were maintained, but the cases concerned tailors or builders and not workmen in hosiery or lace.[34]

Yet hostility to trade unions was never very pronounced until 1833-4, when the general union of that period aroused opposition in many quarters. The *Review* had declared ten years earlier that it was no friend to striking 'which ought to be rarely if ever done'. Now it firmly instructed trade unions to confine themselves to their 'just and legitimate object', that of preventing wage-reductions and providing assistance to members in distress. The *Mercury* also joined the condemnatory chorus; trade unions were acting under delusions, claiming to exercise power they did not possess, and attempting wrongfully to dictate to their employers. The *Journal* was even more outspoken on the 'rashness and folly' of involvement in trade union activity. In March, 1834, it attacked the intimidatory methods allegedly used to coerce men into joining and the individuals who served as delegates or committee men, 'leeches which suck the very heart's blood of the operatives'.[35]

But the greatest and most poignant disillusionment was still to come and was that of Gravener Henson himself, who had been in active association, usually as leader, with virtually every trade combination in the area for a quarter of a century and who was still in the early 1830s advocating general union. By 1838 his ideas had changed:—

'When I was young', he told the Select Committee on Postage, 'I was engaged in many extensive turn-outs, but since that period I have always acted upon the policy of endeavouring to bring both parties together . . . I have acted both for the masters and men . . . I consider that if the masters and men can be brought together there will be very little combination; it is only when they have been kept asunder that they have disagreed.'

And Henson worked henceforth to promote workmen's interests not through trade unionism, which he found oppressive, but

[34]*Nottingham Journal*, 11th December, 1824, 15th November, 1833, 31st December, 1825; A. Barnett, op. cit., p. 5; *Nottingham Review*, 6th December, 1833.

[35]*Nottingham Review*, 12th November, 1824, 2nd May, 1834; *Nottingham Mercury*, 23rd November, 1833, 5th April, 1834; *Nottingham Journal*, 14th March, 1834.

F

through schemes to encourage invention and in other ways to stimulate trade, that all might benefit from its revival.[36]

It was not, however, the defection of its leaders, the resistance of employers, the opposition of newspapers, or the prejudices of society which caused trade unions to record such a list of failures. Henson, earlier, or Benjamin Taylor might blame the Combination Laws for their oppressive nature and tendency to keep down wages or the secret combinations of masters over their glasses of wine, unchallenged by the local authorities, but this was to caricature the situation. Nor were problems of trade union organisation to blame. It was, as historians have pointed out, difficult to organise trade unions inside industries scattered over three counties in small units of production. Men were so far apart, organised in so many small districts, and separated into so many different branches of the trade that effective organisation was impossible.[37] But these technical points were not of great importance. It would be mistaken to suggest that trade union organisation of a sufficient calibre would have produced greatly different results.

It would be equally mistaken to suppose that the emergence of trade union organisation in Nottingham, whatever this indicated elsewhere, was evidence of improving working class standards and the existence of a large class well above subsistence level. Trade unions in hosiery and lace were for defence and not for attack. The M.P. who informed the House of Commons that combinations occurred not when wages were low but when they were high had no experience of Nottingham. When someone informed the Duke of Portland that the stockingers were attempting to secure a rise in 1820 William Rutherford wrote to inform him otherwise:—

'Permit me my Lord kindly to assure you this is not the case with us at this time, it is to maintain that rate of wages only which was agreed to by the manufacturers themselves . . . which rate of wages is very moderate.'

And it was almost always so, for wages were almost always falling. In desperation the men turned to organisation and strikes. In better times they allowed their organisation to decay, as their leaders so frequently and so bitterly complained. 'Reviving

[36]*Report of Select Committee on Postage* (1837-8), XX, 2, p. 221.
[37]e.g. J. D. Chambers, *Nottinghamshire in the 18th Century* (1932), p. 119.

trade', wrote the town clerk, George Coldham, to the Home Secretary in February, 1814, 'should take away all occasion for combining' and he looked forward, mistakenly, as it transpired, to the ending of his immediate problems. The men's unions indicated their weakness, not their strength.[38]

Whether economic laws are amenable to Parliamentary amendment or not, Nottingham's principal trades in this period neither suffered nor enjoyed Parliamentary interference and in their unregulated state demonstrated several lessons. The clearest, as far as trade unions were concerned, was bluntly stated in the 1845 Report on the condition of the framework-knitters, which pronounced that 'Nothing can be more untenable than the professed object for which the union is formed—the maintenance of an established list of prices for labour, nor anything more certain than its ultimate down-fall'.

This sounded harsh and doctrinaire. It was in fact demonstrably true as far as Nottingham experience went. Trade union successes were either confined to good years, such as 1814, or 1824, when trade was good enough to allow the unions success, or else occurred in industries other than the area's basic ones. In the basic ones the men really did appear to be the prisoners of economic laws, almost powerless to determine their own position. If the men struck in depression periods when demand was low, as in 1819, the hosiers could do little to help; the strike would prove a complete loss to the poor workmen, they were told, and they were urged to put their trust in divine providence. When the trade was overstocked and work was scarce, there occurred the inevitable struggle to get it. Men were 'competitors with each other for employment' and inevitably offered to take work below list prices in order to get it at all. And so the list collapsed, not because of black-leg treachery, but from inescapable pressures. When a strike went on long enough to give the manufacturer a chance to clear his stocks or even build up further orders it was possible that a rise would be given; when normal work was resumed and the demand satisfied prices would fall and the men would be powerless to hang on to what they

[38]T. S. Ashton, *An Economic History of England: the 18th Century* (1955), p. 234, and elsewhere, draws an optimistic inference from trade union growth; Parl. Debs., Vol. 88, 410, 14th April, 1824; Portland MSS., Pw H, 1010, William Rutherford to Portland, 8th October, 1820; H.O. 42/137, Coldham to H.O., 20th February, 1814.

had temporarily acquired. If, under coercion, a master were forced to pay high wages he would suffer great losses and would eventually go out of business. These were the arguments that gained increasing currency, not only with the manufacturers but also with men not involved in the trade and sympathetic to the plight of the workmen. There is no evidence to suggest that the manufacturers were somehow thriving when trade stagnated and declined, and the failures of the trade unions, like the bankruptcies of the hosiers, were the consequences of industrial stagnation rather than the human malevolence of any one group.[39]

[39]*Report of Royal Commission on Condition of Framework-knitters*, 1845, XV, pp. 81, 122; *Nottingham Review*, 27th August, 1819, 3rd October, 1823, 23rd April, 1824, 6th December, 1833.

5

THE LUDDITES

The most dramatic of all techniques employed by the working classes in this period to further industrial ends was that of machine-breaking, or Luddism, as it became known in 1811. Frame-breaking had a long history in the hosiery industry, where trade union organisation was difficult and direct sabotage could often be applied more effectively. Henson cited a case of frame-breaking in 1710 against a London employer who had grossly infringed Charles II's Charter to the Worshipful Company of Framework-knitters by taking no fewer than forty-nine apprentices at one time. In 1779 the framework-knitters of Nottingham broke their employers' frames 'in characteristic fashion' on the failure of their attempted Bill to regulate the trade, and in 1787 the *Journal* reported the smashing of a wide frame by men with blackened faces.[1]

Luddism in Nottingham and district was bound by its nature to give rise to a host of myths and misconceptions, some of these contemporary, others appearing later. It was variously suggested at the time that the Luddites were French agents, working at Bonaparte's instigation, paid to sabotage the war effort on the industrial front, embarrassing the government and absorbing its military forces; that the Luddites were receiving their instructions from Cobbett and other national leaders of the reform movement in London; that they were local Tories whose aim was, presumably, to discredit all reform movements, and, even more

[1]Henson, op. cit., pp. 95-6, 401-4; J. L. and B. Hammond, op. cit., p. 226; *Nottingham Journal*, 3rd November, 1787.

ludicrous, that Luddism was a scheme put up by the Ministry of the day to enable it to place areas under the heel of military despotism. Uninformed commentators in the House of Lords made their contribution to the general misunderstanding by wrongly attributing the outbreaks of violence to newly invented machinery or improved machinery which was creating widespread redundancy. And recently, attempts to apply a clear formula have produced misleading descriptions of Luddism as 'simply a technique of trade unionism' and 'simply the product of extreme economic distress'.

Luddism was not 'simply' anything. It was an infinitely complex phenomenon, the strands of which are barely separable, a movement which has successfully defended many of its secrets against the investigations of both contemporaries and historians.[2]

There is a fairly large basis of agreement about Nottinghamshire Luddism. The main outline of the story is beyond dispute. The breaking of stocking-frames started in March, 1811, was resumed with great intensity through the autumn and winter of 1811-12, began again in the spring of 1814, and continued sporadically until the notorious Loughborough 'job' of June, 1816, when Heathcoat's lace factory was attacked. After that it gradually died out, though occasionally breakages occurred in the 1820s. It is generally accepted that this was not simply random destruction by criminals but an enterprise of great organisation and discrimination, a 'premeditated plan of systematic aggression', choosing particular victims for particular reasons.[3] It has been observed that frame-breaking went on with the apparent cooperation of those working in the frames against a background of popular support, though how far people were terrorised into giving their blessing and how far they gave it spontaneously is still open to question. The authorities, local and central, found it impossible to secure the necessary information to uncover the Luddite organisation in spite of their willingness to expend great

[2]Nottingham Borough Records, M.429, Fol. 26; H.O. 42/117, Newcastle to H.O., 16th December, 1811; H.O. 42/121, N.T. Haines to H.O., 22nd March, 1812; *Nottingham Review*, 30th October, 1818; Place MSS., B.M. Add. MSS. 27809, Place's account of the years 1815 onwards, p. 18; Parl. Debs., Vol. 57, 967-9, 26th February, 1812; E. J. Hobsbawm, *The Machine Breakers, Past and Present*, 1, 1952; A. C. Wood, *History of Nottinghamshire* (1947), p. 284.

[3]Parl. Debs., Vol. 57, 865, Mr. Sinclair, 20th February, 1812.

sums of money, and throughout this time domestic troubles tied down so many troops as to make the Luddites almost as great a military problem as the French.[4] On all these points there is agreement, but the points at dispute are still sufficiently fundamental to indicate doubt about what exactly happened as well as what interpretation to put upon events.

It seems beyond doubt that Luddism was produced by a combination of factors arising inside the hosiery and lace trades and factors arising from the general condition of the country and people at the time. The Whig critics of the government, and of the war in particular, had little difficulty in explaining Luddism without any reference to circumstances in the specific industry. It was provoked by unparalleled distress, the result of the government's having reduced the commerce of the country 'to a gambling speculation'. The war, the decrees of Napoleon, and the Orders in Council were all blamed, and Nottingham's trade, being much dependent on exports, must have been hit very hard. If explanations of the trouble were all variations on the same theme, their recommended cures ranged from the highly ironical proposal that doctors should get together to find out how to eliminate appetite, to the more widely urged view of Major Cartwright that only Parliamentary reform could rid the country of government corruption, which had been responsible for the economically disastrous war.[5]

The years 1811-12, with depression conditions following hard upon the relative boom year of 1810, undoubtedly brought a very distressing situation to Nottingham. John Smith, M.P., told the House of Commons in February, 1812, that he had never witnessed so much misery as on his previous visit to Nottingham. This impression is supported by the numerous letters to the press from distressed stockingers who were unable to feed their families even in full employment; unemployment figures are incalculable because of the degrees of unemployment that the organisation of the industry allowed, but Felkin believed that in January,

---

[4]Full accounts of the events are to be found in J. L. and B. Hammond, *The Skilled Labourer* (1919) and F. Darvall, *Popular Disturbances and Public Order in Regency England* (1934).

[5]Parl. Debs., Vol. 57, 603, Earl of Lauderdale, 4th February, 1813, John Smith, 14th February, 1812; *Nottingham Review*, 1st March, 27th September, 1811, 8th May, 27th December, 1812.

1812, almost half of the town's population was being relieved
from poor rates. A system of relief tickets was later devised and
large subscriptions opened on behalf of the poor. The committee
quickly distributed 10,000 of the 6d. tickets which could be ex-
changed at food shops. One case was quoted of a man so wasted
and emaciated that he was unable to cope with the food he
received and died when he tried to eat. The many pitiful accounts
are impressionistic rather than scientific evidence of distress,
but there is good reason to see 1811-12 as a particularly severe
period. Food prices locally were never higher in the period
1792-1829, with the exception of flour, which was exceeded
only in the famine years of 1800 and 1801. Then it had risen to
7/- a stone. Now it rose to 6/-, and the estimated average net
weekly wage of the framework-knitter was little higher than
this at this time. Not surprisingly Felkin believed hunger and
misery to be the basic causes of Luddism, and he later recalled
that through the winter of 1811-12 the almost universal cry was
'give us work at any price—half a loaf is better than no bread'.[6]
    If the troubles of 1811 are to be seen against a background of
general distress arising from the war, the Continental System,
and the interruption of normal trading relations with Europe
and America, they must also be specifically related to their own
industrial background. It was the way that the industry responded
to the national problems and its capacity for producing its own
that were directly to produce Luddism in Nottinghamshire. The
war closed markets, creating what Mr. Secretary Ryder called
an 'unfavourable situation of trade', and the depressed trade
brought down wages. But the prohibition of British goods from
foreign markets only accelerated a crisis which, some realised,
had been building up for a long time. Hosiery had long been
acquiring its characteristic weaknesses of an over-large and ever-
increasing labour force producing for a market expanding at
an insufficient rate and repeatedly losing old trade as changes in
fashion rendered the ornate unacceptable and made the plain
and simple standard requirement. Stocking-frames had mul-
tiplied way beyond the demand they had to satisfy, and their

[6]Parl. Debs., Vol. 57, 814, 14th February, 1812; e.g. *Nottingham Review*, 29th November,
1811; Felkin, op. cit., pp. 231, 239; *Nottingham Review*, 22nd, 15th May, 1812, 12th June,
1829; *Report of Select Committee on Laws affecting Export of Machinery*, 1841, VII, Appendix
3, p. 233; W. Felkin, *Story of William Felkin III*, 1795-1874.

owners, in many cases pure speculators, drew an improper
return from the industry through the frame-renting system
which ensured the over-population of the trade. When the war
began to make its severest impact, from about 1809, the industry
was in no position to meet the crisis. It is of importance to note
that Luddism first broke out within a context of obsolete
technology and organisation, where industry was both over-
manned and by-passed by technological innovation, and not in
a classic Industrial Revolution context of factories and powered
machinery.[7]

There were two ways chosen by manufacturers to combat
the trade depression. One was to reduce wages in order to try
to stimulate trade and open new markets by cheaper production.
This was attempted by Thomas Brocksopp and Company,
along with four other large hosiery firms, and Brocksopps were
the first to have frames broken. This group declared their reluctance to reduce rates but explained the cut on the grounds
that many of their workmen, using their own or privately owned
frames, as opposed to frames owned by the hosier, were accepting other work at lower rates, thus compelling Brocksopps
and their associates to reduce theirs in order to remain competitive. If the men would cease to accept low rates elsewhere,
they would gladly restore theirs. Unfortunately for these firms,
their action was repudiated by a majority of the hosiers who
signed in March a declaration to abide by list prices. There was
a widespread belief that five firms were exploiting the war
situation to reduce their workmen, and it was over the question
of wage reductions that Luddism began in March, 1811.[8]

The case of the framework-knitters against these hosiers was
clear and widely accepted. They were suffering from what one
of their leaders called 'the unprincipled oppressions of an avaricious few', and even the Duke of Newcastle thought that they
had unquestionably been treated badly by their employers. But
for the conduct of the hosiers, said Lord Middleton, there would

[7]Parl. Debs., Vol. 57, 810, 14th February, 1812. Recent developments in the trade are
well summarised in Ne.C. 4919b., J. T. Becher to Newcastle and H.O., 12th February,
1812. The standard accounts leave no justification for retaining the occasionally voiced
idea that the Nottinghamshire Luddites were 'anti-machinery'.
[8]Felkin, op. cit., p. 230; Report of Select Committee on Artizans and Machinery, 1824, V,
p. 280.

have been no Luddism, whilst County Magistrate Becher of Southwell contrasted the 'honour and humanity' of some hosiers with the undercutting of others whose profits were 'oppressively extorted from the starving necessities of the poor'. Luddism was blamed on meanness, on wanton cruelty, and generally deplorable conduct from those who had made the reductions. It was an easy case to make, and its validity has very recently been endorsed. But it must be remembered that Becher who blamed the hosiers also blamed the general developments in the industry for the conditions of 1811 and was clearly torn between a condemnation of the hosiers and an understanding of the situation which produced their reaction, showing a concern for impartiality which not all have been concerned to observe.[9]

The alternative way of stimulating trade was to try to produce different, cheaper goods which might create new demands when the old ones were flagging. This was the response of the hosiers who began to manufacture 'cut-ups' and the lace manufacturers who started to produce single-press lace. It was the frame producing the cut-up that was particularly sought out by the Luddites for destruction, and belief in the harmful effects of this type of production was a prime article in the creed of the framework-knitters. Although the validity of this argument has been accepted by almost all historians, it is probable that the men's views were in part rationalisation. Luddism began over wages and not over production techniques, and the first man to have his frames broken, Thomas Brocksopp, had actually declared against cut-up production. He had offended over wages. George Coldham, the town clerk, informed the Home Office in December, 1811, that Luddism had arisen out of an attempt to force the market by lowering wages, which corresponded to the account later written by Felkin of the events preceding the outbreaks. The London magistrates who arrived in January, 1812, also reported that Luddism was initially a question of wages, whilst some local historians continued to suggest that the only real object of the Luddites had been to preserve wages.

[9]Ne.C. 4920, Thomas Large to Newcastle, 26th March, 1812; H.O. 42/117, Newcastle to H.O., 29th December, 1811; H.O. 42/119, Middleton to H.O., 11th January, 1812; Ne.C. 4919b, J. T. Becher to Newcastle and H.O., 12th Februry, 1812; *Nottingham Review*, 4th November, 1814; E. P. Thompson, *The Making of the English Working Class*, 1963, pp. 530-2.

The men began to act against the cut-up frames only after Luddism had been fully launched. The depression was evident enough; its precise causes were not. Many manufacturers argued against cut-ups; and these articles, requiring a minimum of skill to produce, were a convenient thing for the workmen to blame. And so the wide frame producing cut-ups was singled out for destruction even though its pernicious influence must be considered doubtful.[10]

A recent account of Luddism has portrayed the conflict as part of the class-war between the hosiers and the framework-knitters, occurring at a crisis point in economic thought and development when paternalism was fighting a losing battle against the doctrines of *laissez-faire*. It has concluded, not surprisingly that the Luddites were justified in their struggle, both morally and in terms of expediency.[11]

Seeing Luddism as part of a class conflict has involved the acceptance of ideas that during the French wars the stockingers were beaten down to poverty by the deliberate policy of the hosiers. The latter were intent, it is alleged, on lowering wages; in fact they were intent on lowering production costs, which is not necessarily the same thing. The 'least scrupulous', who did in fact lower wages, have been implicitly condemned as evil men. And equally evil was the willingness of manufacturers to introduce cut-ups when trade was already stagnant. This is, however, to miss the point that it was this stagnation which made necessary cut-up production; and far from being the work of cheap labour these new articles actually gave some of the best weekly earnings to be had in stocking-manufacture in the area. As was seen earlier, there was always a wide sympathy amongst the manufacturers for the plight of their employees, and the men themselves frequently recognised this. The problems of 1811 faced the whole of the trade and not just the workers. It is a very partial view which sees only the hardships of the workmen, and the latter themselves went beyond this and spoke not of their

---

[10]See Framework-knitters' Papers, 1812-14, and *First Report of Select Committee on Frame-work-knitters' Petitions*, 1812, 11; Felkin, op. cit., p. 230; H.O. 42/117, Coldham to H.O. (December) 1811; Nottingham Borough Records, M.429, Fol. 16; J. Orange, *History and Antiquities of Nottingham*, 1840, Vol. 2, p. 878.

[11]The following is a discussion of the account and interpretation of E. P. Thompson, op. cit., pp. 530-602.

own sectional interests but of the general 'good of the trade'. The problems of the Luddites were common to masters and men alike. The masters did not utilise the war and the circumstances it produced to beat down the workers. They had themselves opposed the war, had agitated against it, and were, as Major Cartwright informed the Luddites, not their enemies but fellow-sufferers from its economic consequences.[12]

It is also to over-dramatise to suggest that Luddism occurred at the crisis point in the abrogation of paternalist legislation and was a gesture of defiance against the imposition of *laissez-faire* principles upon the industry. *Laissez-faire* and capitalism had already won. The cost of both machines and materials ensured that hosiery should be established on a capitalist basis from the start. When the industry moved away from London to the Midlands it escaped from the authority of the Framework-Knitters' Company, and the abortive attempt of the latter to reassert control in the early years of the nineteenth century illustrated the demise of such ideas as the traditional apprenticeship period. Nor was the frame-owning hosier and capitalistic frame-owning speculator a novelty, for the knitter who owned his own frame had joined the minority by 1775. What arose in 1811 was not the issue of whether the capitalist should be free to destroy the customs of the trade, for many had already fallen, but whether the industry could survive by paying traditional rates and producing its usual range of articles or whether it should attempt to give itself a boost by introducing novelties and dropping certain accepted standards. Some manufacturers took the latter view; the Luddites took the former. It has been suggested that the Luddites were both morally right and practically wise. Yet the discussion on morality and principles is hardly relevant. The manufacturers of cut-ups were not exponents of 'unrestrained industrial capitalism' who sought 'to destroy the customs of the trade'. This was no exposition of principle to be resisted by adherents to a contrary principle, not license for the manufacturer versus the will and conscience of the workers. It was a question of expediency, which is almost admitted when it is suggested that the framework-knitters made

[12]*Report of Select Committee on Laws affecting Export of Machinery*, 1841, VII, Appendix 3, p. 238. In Framework-knitters' Papers, 1812-14, there is repeated use of the term 'good of the trade'. *Nottingham Journal*, 3rd January, 1812.

the most realistic assessment of the short-term effects of their activity. The Luddites should more properly be judged for their realism than for any standard of right which they allegedly supported; and their realistic assessment of the situation will be examined later.[13]

The most lasting and suggestive impression left by the events and discussions which preceded and accompanied Luddism is not, in fact, of a class war building up between employer and employed, but of a common crisis point being reached by both sides, suffering from the same grievances and both having doubts and difficulties over the solution to be offered to their problems. And when the crisis did come the clearest division was not between masters and men but between some masters on one side and the men and the rest of the masters on the other. When unpleasant solutions were attempted to revive the industry they, like the war, created havoc amongst the hosiers as well as amongst the men. Every commentator noticed the absence of agreement amongst the hosiers and the acrimonious divisions in their ranks. Felkin mentioned their disagreements over wages, under-cutting, and standards of production. John Smith, M.P., commented like many others on their differing attitudes to truck-payments. Becher reported on their divisions which led up to the crisis and on their failure to act together once it was on. Another remarked that the hosiers spent all their time attacking each other in public prints instead of coming to common agreement about trade problems. But they attacked each other on the very points that the Luddites attacked—undercutting, cut-ups, and standards in general. The grievances of the men were grievances of many of the masters. They were truly the common victims of one great problem, how to promote the revival of an industry, and the readiness of many masters to back the men who petitioned Parliament for a regulation of trade in 1812 indicated that frame-breaking, in its first phase, had failed to drive any strong wedge between masters and men and create a situation of class war. It is perhaps too crude and too simple to speak of Luddism as 'less . . . an agitation of workmen, than . . . an aspect of com-

[13]A. Redford, *The Economic History of England, 1760-1860* (1931), p. 10; P. Mantoux, *The Industrial Revolution in the Eighteenth Century* (1961), p. 223; F. A. Wells, op. cit., p. 69; J. D. Chambers, *The Worshipful Company of Framework-knitters*, op. cit., and *The Vale of Trent, 1670-1800*, op. cit.

petition between the backward and the progressive . . . manufacturer' and of the 'latent or passive Luddism of the employer',
but it would be folly to ignore that the interests of men and
masters were often identical and that, as a strong decrier of the
hosiers admits, many hosiers would applaud the aims if not the
methods of the Luddites. Luddism must have seemed an answer
to some of the masters who were struggling for survival as well
as some of the men, and neither the causes nor the course of
Luddism can be considered without allowing weight to this
factor.[14]

An even more recent interpretation of Luddism has suggested
that Luddism was not the work of the Nottingham framework-
knitters but of those of the industrial villages, especially to the
west and north of the town. In Nottingham there was a strong
tradition of constitutional activity in a favourable political
atmosphere and the men acted in a sophisticated manner, with
petitions to Parliament under the protection of the magistracy.
By contrast the men of the villages had a record of violence,
thought that the town men neglected their interests, and resorted
to frame-breaking when the town leadership of Henson and his
associates failed to satisfy them. This contrast between town and
country, previously suggested between Leicester and the villages
of that county, was noticed at the time, but the authorities had
a simpler explanation than the economic and geographical
structure of the industry. They knew that the problem of maintaining law and order in straggling villages was infinitely greater
than in the town. It was the county magistracy who took all
the kicks throughout the Luddite period and the town ones who
received the praise, but the latter were under no illusions about
their superiority or there being a lesser danger in the town.
Frames might be brought into Nottingham from outlying districts because the town was safer, but it was safer only because
of the great number of troops stationed there and the relative
ease of devising an effective police system. The town authorities
never underestimated the dangers facing them. Nor is it true to
say that few frames were broken in Nottingham itself. The town
was supposed to be a main centre, probably the main centre, of

[14]Felkin, op. cit., p. 230; Parl. Debs., Vol. 57, 814, 14th February, 1812; Ne.C. 4919b,
op. cit.; *Nottingham Journal*, 23rd March, 1811; E. J. Hobsbawn, op. cit.; E. P. Thompson,
op. cit., p. 534.

the committees which organised the breakings, and many occurred inside the town. This is true of 1811, 1812, 1813, 1814,
1815, and 1816. Evidence simply will not support the contention
that the town itself was relatively free from Luddism, even if the
townsmen did like to pass on the responsibility for it to their
rough country cousins.[15]

Luddism was a complex and evolving phenomenon, by no
means static, complex enough in 1811 but infinitely more so
in 1816. These years undoubtedly saw a great diffusion of purpose amongst those involved in the outbreaks; and as Luddism
came to mean many things to many different people it lost much
of the 'purity of purpose' which might with some justification
have been accorded to it at the outset. Early fears expressed by
the Nottingham town clerk were that contributions levied by
the Luddites were causing their numbers to rise and men to
acquire the habit of supporting themselves without working.
The dissolute, the profligate, and the lazy were readily attracted
to this life, and systematic terror became another job to be done
for wages. By January, 1812, Coldham was describing what
amounted to a Ludding business, acts being perpetrated against
individuals who could be made to appear guilty of some trade
offence; the men were in employment and suitable victims were
found for them. It is possible to detect almost the build-up of
an industry. Success brought imitation. Workmen previously
unemployed were reported suddenly to be well-dressed and
paying for drinks with guinea notes. Ludding had become their

[15]R. A. Church and S. D. Chapman, 'Gravener Henson and the Making of the English
Working Class', *Essays in honour of J. D. Chambers*, ed. Mingay and Jones, 1966; A. T.
Patterson, 'Luddism, Hampden Clubs, and Trades Unions in Leicestershire', *English
Historical Review*, LXIII, 1948; H.O. 42/117, T. Wright to H.O., 11th November, 1811,
Coldham to H.O. (December) 1811, Middleton to H.O., 12th December, 1811. Examples
of the many complaints made against the country magistrates include H.O. 42/117, S.
Smith to H.O., 28th November, 1811, Newcastle to H.O., 2nd December, 1811; H.O.
42/120, J. Spencer to H.O. 8th February, 1812; H.O. 42/117, Conant's Memo, 4th
December, 1811; H.O. 42/121, Coldham to H.O., 12th March, 1812; Felkin, op. cit.,
p. 231; H.O. 42/117, Loughborough Magistrates to H.O., 8th December, 1811; H.O.
42/120, Coldham to H.O., 26th February, 1812; H.O. 42/121, Coldham to H.O., 12th
March, 1812. The town clerk, George Coldham, the most regular H.O. correspondent
from the area, was under no illusion about the strength of Luddism in Nottingham, 1811-16,
and reported many town breakings. Throughout these years he and his successor, Henry
Enfield, repeatedly begged the Home Secretary not to withdraw military forces from the
town.

existence and a vested interest was created; with the willingness of those in employment to subscribe, either through fear or sympathy, to the maintenance of Luddites, frame-breaking became a well-paid job. When it was a question of frame-breaking, wrote Felkin later, it was done for hire, and he reckoned that £140 had been offered for the Loughborough job, of which John Blackburn admitted to having been offered £40, though not to having received it. Money kept frame-breaking going, wrote J. R. Sutton; without the financial incentive there would have been little Luddism, and the attractions of quick, relatively easy money must have been great. An interesting side-light on this question of vested interests was thrown by the confessions of James Towle, who alleged that even the police officers were anxious to perpetuate the system to remain in a job and so refrained from making any important arrests in case Luddism came to an end. The confessions of arrested Luddites strongly suggest that they were almost pure professionals.[16]

Another allied aspect of Luddism to be remembered is that it gave opportunity and some cover to many wrong-doers to break the law and commit acts of theft in the turmoil. This was realised at an early stage. The *Journal* distinguished between 'true Luddites' and 'Ned Lud's men', who were simply criminals who exploited the situation. Lord Middleton's pheasant poachers of 1812 gave way to virtual gangsterism by October, 1814, and apparently meaningless frame-breaking was accompanied by stealing or some form of destructive behaviour. If motives were 'pure' at the outset, they became sordid as Luddism developed, and the reckless heroism of the early enterprises gave way to a calculated commercialism and systematic plunder. The gangs recruited for the later jobs contained a ruthless, thuggish element and it is difficult to find men of heroic stature amongst them. Blackburn in his confession said that the same spirit was not there which had been present in earlier times, and it was observed that

[16]H. O. 42/117, Coldham to H.O. (December) 1811; H.O. 42/119, Coldham to H.O., 14th January, 1812; Nottingham Borough Records M.429, Fol. 26; Accounts of subscriptions to be found in H.O. 42/117, Newcastle to H.O., 30th November, 1811, Wright to H.O. 1st December, 1811, Newcastle to H.O., 2nd December, 1811, Coldham to H.O. (December) 1811; H.O. 40/3(1), Confession of John Blackburn of Nottingham, January, 1817; Felkin, op. cit., p. 240; Sutton, op. cit., p. 334; H.O. 40/9 (5), J. Towle's Confession, 20th November, 1816.

machine-breaking had been replaced by a general crime-wave.
Nor must it be forgotten that many individuals probably turned
Luddite during the turmoil to settle an old score, and George
Coldham felt sure that many of the examples of frame-breaking
in the town were distinct cases of private and personal resentment
against individuals and their property.[17]

Again, it can hardly be ignored that many hosiers who escaped
the visits of the Luddites must have experienced a certain satisfaction at seeing the discomfiture of their rivals. After all, the
trade was grossly over-stocked with frames. It was commonly
agreed that after the breakings there would be more than enough
left for the needs of the industry; the breaking of judiciously
chosen frames was not necessarily a bad thing for those not personally involved. No one tried to blame the mass of the outrages
on the manufacturers themselves, but a challenging accusation
appeared in the *Review* some years later. This was a suggestion
that the Loughborough job, the destruction of Heathcoat's lace-
machinery in June, 1816, was the work of his trade rival Lacey.
Heathcoat, it was suggested, had gone to Loughborough in the
first place not because he was afraid of men pulling down his
machines in Nottingham but because he feared that they would
try to put them up. He wished to retain an exclusive use of his
patented invention for manufacturing bobbin-net. When he
tried to move even further away, to Tiverton, as he planned in
the early part of 1816, Lacey, a former partner, organised the
destruction before the machines could be carted off to the West
Country. It was a case of trade jealousy and the work of frustrated
rivals. The assertion, never repudiated through the press or
through a libel action, is at variance with the more popular version that Lacey's hands had financed the venture, in co-operation
with some of Heathcoat's own men and warp-lace hands from
Nottingham, because Heathcoat was paying his men less than
standard rates. The truth is probably beyond recovery, but it is
interesting that there was a readiness to advance an argument

[17]H.O. 42/119, Brief Statement of Transactions in the County and Town of Nottingham; *Nottingham Journal*, 10th January, 1812; H.O. 42/141, Coldham to H.O., 15th
October, 1814; H.O. 42/153, Enfield to H.O., 14th October, 1816; *Nottingham Journal*,
31st August, 19th October, 1816; H.O. 40/10, Blackburn's Confessions before Lancelot
Rolleston, 9th January, 1817; H.O. 42/117, Coldham to H.O., 13th December, 1811.

G

involving the manufacturers themselves in the perpetration of Luddism.[18]

The extent of trade union involvement in Luddism has always been a matter of dispute. It has recently been suggested that constitutional and Luddite activities were simultaneously employed by the framework-knitters and that the trade unions could well have directed both types of operation, at least until 1814, when the union was prosecuted and collapsed. It is suggested that the change over from illegal to constitutional action in February, 1812, was so sudden that it is impossible to believe that the same men were not involved in leading both movements. After the 1814 prosecution under the Combination Laws the Luddites, it is claimed, continued to be paid by underground trade union lodges. These ideas are feasible, and always with Luddism the problem is to find a feasible interpretation that fits all the facts. The weakness of this interpretation is not the association of trade unionism with Luddism but the dating of the association. The activities of the 1812 Union Committee represented the purest form of constitutional activity; but in 1814 the case against the trade unions was very strong, though not provable.[19]

When Gravener Henson and a few associates began in February, 1812, to organise an approach to Parliament for legislative regulation of the hosiery and lace trades, they aroused some doubts in the minds of Messrs. Conant and Baker, the Home Office representatives in Nottingham assisting in Luddite detection, but none in the minds of the local magistracy. Through the ensuing six months their conduct was open, their meetings public, their purpose publicised, and the magistracy consulted at all times. These were the very opposite of Luddite methods. The latter were at all times bitterly condemned by the constitutionalists and were seen as the biggest single threat to the successful completion of the approach to Parliament. The correspondence and papers of the Union reveal very clearly their antipathy to Luddism and its methods. Their only common factors were the grievances producing the two movements and the mass support for both, which would have gladly accepted from either a solution to the

[18]Ne.C. 4919b op. cit., *Nottingham Review*, 28th August, 1829; H.O. 40/9 (5), Towle's Confession, 20th November, 1816.

[19]S. and B. Webb, op. cit. p. 88; F. A. Wells, op. cit., p. 113; J. L. and B. Hammond, op. cit., p. 264; E. P. Thompson, op. cit. pp. 535, 556, 574.

problems of the trade. Luddism was indeed largely held in abeyance whilst the constitutionalists made their bid from February to July, 1812, but this was not the result of a change of tactic but rather a result of a general rise in wages, the more effective policing of the area, and the Bill to make frame-breaking a capital offence. And when the attempts of the constitutionalists failed, there was no immediate and general return to frame-breaking. This was resumed in the Spring of 1814, and it is on this occasion that the case against the trade unions was strongest. There is very good reason to suppose that now, probably for the first time, the trade union of the framework-knitters began to see the value and use of limited, selective frame-breaking for the achievement of certain industrial ends. The situation prevailing in 1814 was in many ways quite different from that in either the earlier or later periods of Luddism.[20]

On 16 November, 1813, a resident of Mansfield sent the Home Secretary some hearsay, but substantially accurate, information about the powerful build up of a trade union organisation inside the county. The Home Office prodded the town clerk of Nottingham, and he promised to infiltrate a few men into the organisation. The magistrates had not feared the union in 1812 and they had evidently no fear now. Coldham happily reported that trade was reviving wonderfully, which, he believed, would take away all occasion for combining. But instead of following the usual pattern and disappearing, the Union Society now began to launch a novel tactic of exploiting a favourable economic situation to press wage demands. For perhaps the only time in half a century the men really felt that they had a strong bargaining position. The correspondence of magistrates and manufacturers over the next weeks indicates a real apprehension that trouble could be expected from the men, and when a new series of frame-breakings began in April, they had no hesitation in laying the troubles at the door of the Union. Their views now were not dependent on the reports of informers, though these were uniform in their allegations, but on the emergence of a clear pattern in which a great succession of frame-breakings occurred after disputes between the Union and various employers, who appear to have been marked down for further treatment. This time it

[20]H.O. 42/120, Conant and Baker to H.O., 16th February, 1812; Framework-knitters' Papers, 1812-14, Fols. 19, 23, 33, 79, 85, 127.

seems to have been less a particular type of frame that was marked for destruction than particular men who were to be punished for offences, real or alleged, against the Union Society. One master, John Bullock, quarrelled with the Union over the amount of subscriptions to be paid from his workshop, and had his frames broken shortly afterwards. Another, Simon Orgill, of Castle Donington, related that the Union had attempted to make trouble for him by trying to persuade his men to leave; this effort failed as his employees were a contented body and so he lost his frames instead. Orgill accused John Blackner, by this time working on the *Nottingham Review*, of having given the order, and the established personal hostility between the two men and the close association of Blackner with the Union go some way to lending credibility to Orgill's version of the truth. Three more hosiers, Needham, Nixon and James Hooley, were associated with each other in a common stand to resist Union demands for a rise; all three had their frames broken. And equally interesting is the fact that Ray Brothers, who were attacked by the more orthodox strike weapon, in June, 1814, were not susceptible to coercion by frame-breaking since they worked entirely on independent frames, not ones owned by themselves, which was the usual position with hosiers. It appeared to the town clerk, George Coldham, that the Union selected the means appropriate to the victim. All these circumstances add weight to the accusations of magistrates and hosiers that the Union was itself now using selective frame-breaking as a technique of collective bargaining, attempting to raise wages by pure intimidation. But the charges were never proved, and posterity has tended to believe the leaders of the men, such as Gravener Henson, who denied Union involvement and who claimed that Luddism was at best the work of misguided workmen who renounced trade union methods, at worst a put-up job by the government to give them an excuse for further repression. Henson was himself widely believed to be King Lud and there is no modern agreement on this issue.[21]

[21]H.O. 42/135, William Woodcock to H.O., 16th November, 1813; H.O. 42/137, Coldham to H.O., 20th February, 1814; H.O. 42/138, Coldham to H.O., 4th, 7th, 13th April, 1814; Norton to H.O., 8th April, 1814; Allsopp to H.O. 3rd May, 1814; H.O. 42/139, Coldham to H.O., 8th, 10th May, 21st June, 1814; J. T. Becher to H.O., 14th May, 1814; *Nottingham Journal*, 23rd April, 7th May, 1814; *Nottingham Review*, 29th April, 20th May, 1814; *Report of Select Committee on Artizans and Machinery*, 1824, V. pp. 281-2. For further discussion of Henson's role see, M. I. Thomis, *Old Nottingham*, op. cit., ch. 12.

The more extensive frame-breaking that began after the invoking of the Combination Laws and the break-up of the Union Society seems to suggest the withdrawal of the discriminating power which had wielded the weapon with precise and careful selection. From this time onwards there is no clear evidence to suggest that frame-breaking was carefully controlled by a trade union type of organisation which employed it for bringing direct pressure to bear upon masters. There were repeated allegations that the unions continued to organise breakings in an underground capacity and that Henson was heavily involved. It may be that between his constitutionalist phase and his later role as friend and adviser to manufacturers and governments he did experience a period of disillusionment with conventional and legal methods and flirted with the illegal schemes, industrial and political, that the informers laid at his door. This is a matter for speculation. By the end of 1814 Luddism had acquired a shapeless form, in which the idealist phase and the trade union phase had been left behind and the movement became a heterogeneous mixture of numerous interests, some identifiable, some not, who were able to exploit Luddism for their own particular purpose.[22]

It was in its final stages that Luddism, although culminating in a great industrial coup at Loughborough, came to be associated, in the minds of the authorities at least, with politics. Indeed, any dissociation of Luddism and politics can be achieved, it has recently been suggested, only by special pleading, since the connection between frame-breaking and politics was assumed on every side. Certainly there were from the onset people who saw the Luddites as intending revolutionaries. Letters poured in to the Home Secretary from Nottingham implicating Cobbett, Cartwright, or French agents in the work of sedition, and little reassurance, in these trying times, could be derived from Nottingham's reputation for dissent and protest movements. The officer who commanded government troops in the area suggested that the Luddites were armed and that a thoroughly disaffected population was ready to support them in anything they attempted, but evidence was never produced to support these wild allegations. Official investigations made by local and central

[22]H.O. 42/144, Coldham to H.O., 3rd June, 1815; H.O. 42/152, Enfield to H.O., 10th August, 1816.

authorities all concluded that Luddism was industrial not political in cause and intent; a matter of trade, wrote county magistrate Becher, not of politics.[23]

This was in the period when Luddism appeared a spontaneous eruption of discontent against particular men and techniques. And the same was true of most of 1814, when there was some reason to suppose that Luddism was adopted by the Union Society as a means of applying pressure. Only the extremist *Nottingham Gazette* associated Luddism with 'Jacobinism' though it failed to show any connection between the two.[24] It was in the final stage of Luddism, after the prosecution of union leaders, when Luddism took on its most amorphous shape, that beliefs of political purpose began to be widely expressed. It was when the union was driven underground, when the local magistracy aligned so unmistakably with the employers, when Luddism degenerated into general lawlessness and violence, and the pattern became thoroughly confused, that political mutterings were reported and almost certainly heard.

Between the collapse of the Union Society in July, 1814, and the Pentrich rebellion three years later the authorities, local and central, were totally incapable of distinguishing clearly between the Luddism they had experienced and talk of the coming revolution, which did materialise in June, 1817. The evidence has become little clearer with the passage of time, though certain points can be made. The informers at all levels did supply stories of suspected Luddites who talked of and planned revolution, and the authorities did believe that revolution was in the air. The town clerk of Nottingham really did fear, in June, 1815, that the magistracy was threatened and that law and order could be preserved only if substantial troops were restored to Nottingham. Luddism had frightened him and he was ready to believe those who now said that the Luddites had turned to other than industrial designs. It can also be reasonably assumed that there

[23]E. P. Thompson, op. cit., pp. 577, 587; H.O. 42/117, Munn to H.O., 4th December, 1811; H.O. 42/119, J. Boultbee to H.O., 1st January, 1812; H.O. 42/120, Conant and Baker to H.O., 6th February, 1812, R. A. Fletcher of Bolton to H.O., 25th February, 1812; H.O. 42/121, Major General Hawker to H.O., 12th March, 1812, N. T. Haines to H.O., 22nd March, 1812; Nottingham Borough Records, M.429, Fol. 26; *Nottingham Review*, 23rd January, 1818; Ne.C. 4919b, op. cit.

[24]*Nottingham Gazette*, 9th September, 1814; with somewhat different sympathies E. P. Thompson, op. cit., similarly claims, but fails to show, a connection, e.g. p. 494.

was much loose talk of revolution and that the informers were not left short of quotations to pass on. It would have been surprising if the great crowds who gathered at Jem Towle's funeral in November, 1816, had not, in that emotional setting, muttered revolutionary talk, and our knowledge of the plans laid, however sketchily, in the Spring of 1817, suggests that some of the participants then must have mingled with the crowds and been Luddite sympathisers earlier.[25]

This general picture is feasible. What are less acceptable, because they are not in accord with the rest of our knowledge about the people concerned and because they are so very much hearsay evidence that the authorities never verified, are the supposed detailed plans and activities of men like Gravener Henson and Francis Ward, who were alleged to be both unscrupulous Luddite organisers and thorough-going revolutionaries, plotting and planning revolution from 1814 and indulging in every type of lawless and subversive activity. The details are unlikely. The general desires of men who had been Luddites or had supported them were very probably in accord with the general picture given to the authorities. But those who were revolutionaries were not Luddites by this time, just revolutionaries; Luddism was limited in aim and was concerned with frame-breaking; governments could not be overturned by broken frames. Similarly, men who had been Luddite sympathisers would undoubtedly join the Hampden Clubs, but this is not to say that the Hampden Clubs were an extension of Luddism. Blackburn in his confession said he knew of no connection between the Luddites and the Hampden Clubs. They were separate movements with different ends, though there must have been some continuity in their sympathisers, even membership. Doubtless former Luddites were engaged in 'politics and poaching' by 1817, and in other things too. But they were Luddites only whilst they were breaking frames.[26]

The true political significance of Luddism was realised by George Coldham almost at the outset of the movement, when

---

[25]In this period informers' reports were passed on to the H.O. indiscriminately. H.O. 42/144, Coldham to H.O., 29th April, 1815; H.O. 42/155, Enfield to H.O., 23rd November, 1815.

[26]H.O. 40/10 (1), Blackburn's confession, op. cit.; H.O. 40/4 (1), Mr. Lockett, Derby, to H.O., 12th January, 1817.

it anticipated the 1816-17 revolutionary movement and contributed to it in political theory rather than in techniques or
personnel. Coldham was not only worried that men were living
without working, unforgivable in Luddite or sinecurist, but also
that people were accomplishing their wishes by the use of force.
If Luddism succeeded, he wrote, the workmen would proceed
further and there was no telling who would be the next object
of their vengeance. This clearly revealed the limits of Corporation Whiggery. Becher wryly noted that the Nottingham reformers were having their just reward when the 'jacobinical
principles with which the inferior orders have been sedulously
inoculated' were now working against the inoculators. He was
wrong to see the Whigs as propagators of 'Jacobinism', but he
was right to see that Luddism was driving a political wedge
between the working classes and their Whig patrons. The town
clerks, George Coldham and Henry Enfield, who had to cope
with Luddism, seem like different men through the Luddite
period. Coldham before and Enfield afterwards were spokesmen
for the reforming Whigs of the Corporation, and Coldham had
barely escaped the 'Jacobin' taint in the 1790s, yet in the 1811-17
period they were apparently transformed into collaborators
with their traditional foes as they communicated with the Home
Office authorities and urged them to vigorous action. The Whigs
were badly shaken. They had had their fill of Luddites and
Radicals, at least for the time being. When war came again
with France in May, 1815, and the inevitable protest meeting
was held in Nottingham, the Corporation Whigs, intrepid and
tireless petitioners and demonstrators in the past, remained aloof
and saw behind the meeting the frightening designs of Radicals
and revolutionaries. Whatever the economic consequences of
Luddism, its political results were to ensure that Corporation
Whiggery remained very firmly on the side of law and order,
and moderate reform, along constitutional lines, became even
more certainly the limit of its ambitions.[27]

The question of why Luddism came to an end can be answered
only by a discussion of when it ended. It has been suggested that
the chronological division of Luddism into its separate phases
has so far been insufficiently brought out. 1811-12 might be

[27]H.O. 42/117, Coldham to H.O. (December), 1811; Ne.C. 4919b, op. cit.; H.O.
42/144, Coldham to H.O., 10th May, 1815.

termed the classical period of Luddism, when workmen organised themselves and broke frames in accordance with their own idealistic view of how the trade ought to be operated. This period closed with the new law making frame-breaking a capital offence, the greater efficiency of the policing system, and the general, if temporary, raising of wages. In 1814 there was the trade union phase, which closed when the union was attacked under the Combination Laws. The final phase began soon afterwards and did not end until seven men were caught and hanged for the Loughborough job, at the end of 1816 and in early 1817. This last was a confused period. It might have had its idealists, it certainly had its gangs, its thieves, and its murderers, and at the end it merged imperceptibly with the revolutionary phase of 1817. Luddism died out, it was widely believed, because many of its leaders had been caught and hanged and those remaining were frightened to continue. It did not die out because the economic conditions which had produced it were ameliorated. The wilder spirits turned to thoughts of revolution, the milder to Parliamentary reform, and many hoped that with the ending of the widely-blamed war conditions would begin to improve. It is not suggested that the three periods were separate and distinct but that each had a characteristic of its own along with the characteristics common to all.

The achievements of the Luddites cannot be assessed purely in terms of their willingness to act illegally; against their supposed heroic stature must be placed their measured ability to reach a 'realistic assessment' of the situation confronting them. It is doubtful if the Luddites took the right decision, and it is certain that the benefits gained from Luddism were almost nil. Any short-term gain, such as the two shillings per dozen rise suggested by Felkin, was quickly lost and any temporary success in coercing particular employers into prohibiting cut-up manufacture was similarly lost when the terror was lifted. Most contemporaries, even when they sympathised with the Luddites, thought that they were unwise and were bringing down the greatest suffering upon themselves. It is difficult to resist this conclusion. The stagnation of trade and the over-stocking of the market meant that the sales profits of the manufacturers were not much affected, though their property was destroyed. The owners not personally involved saw a reduction of the number of frames in the industry, a useful thing for themselves, but even those who lost frames, the *Journal* argued, were temporarily relieved of the need to produce goods which they could not sell. Pressure is best put on when trade is good, and it is hard to see how the creation of more unemployment amongst the workmen benefited any stockingers other than those who were actually paid to break frames. The cut-up workers whose frames were destroyed lost their good wages, and even had cut-ups been eliminated, which they most certainly were not, that would not have solved the problem of lost markets which cut-ups had been introduced to recover. The Luddites had even, argued some, caused the workmen of Nottingham and district a loss of some £10,000 per year in wages, and Felkin quoted the case of Heathcoat's removal to the West Country, with his 600–700 lace machines, after the Loughborough job. Yet Heathcoat himself admitted that his decision to move had been taken before the attack and even explained the attack as a consequence of his decision. Another manufacturer quickly moved into Heathcoat's vacated premises and by May, 1818, the *Nottingham Review* was applauding the healthy expansion of the lace trade in Loughborough and arguing that there was no question of distress through the removal of capital.

The later history of the hosiery and lace trades suggests no grounds for arguing that the Luddites drove away business from Nottingham and district.[28]

And the continued enterprise of local workmen in the field of invention and the total absence of attempts to destroy new machinery after Luddism, confirm that Luddism neither continued nor inaugurated an anti-machinery tradition. The problems of the hosiery trade deriving from obsolete technology and organisation must be blamed not on reactionary workmen but on the vested interests of manufacturers in frame-renting in conditions of over-abundant labour supply. It was not the Luddites who kept the hosiery trade in the home and out of the factory.[29]

[28]E. P. Thompson, op. cit., p. 592; Felkin, op. cit., pp. 242, 439; *Nottingham Journal*, 16th March, 1811; J. L. and B. Hammond, op. cit., p. 243, quote a letter from H.O. 42/156 in which Heathcoat explains the attack in terms of the offence given by his decision to remove to Tiverton; *Nottingham Review*, 8th May, 1818.

[29]See list of inventions in Hosiery and Lace, 1589–1843, compiled by Gravener Henson, in *Report of Royal Commission on Condition of Framework-knitters*, 1845, XV, pp. 21–4.

Trade problems were neither solved nor created by the Luddites whose impact, except in the very short term, was slight. The supposed villains of the piece, the manufacturers who were producing cut-ups and other cheap articles, were making a much more imaginative contribution.

6

TRADE UNIONS AND POLITICS

'That no political discussion be allowed any time it may be necessary for the Trade to meet together. Any person intruding himself on such a meeting and introducing politics . . . (shall be) admonished from the Chair . . . and . . . shall be expelled.'[1]

This was a resolution unanimously carried at a meeting of framework-knitters in Nottingham in February, 1821. Clearly, there was to be no mixing of trade union affairs and politics. There was no party allegiance felt by the trade unions as such, and political discussion was felt to be dividing in its effect, perhaps even irrelevant to such matters as concerned workmen. It is unlikely that there was any fear of being accused of dabbling in politics at this time; more likely that the game of politics was not one which the framework-knitters wanted to play. It must not, however, be thought that the trade unions never involved themselves in politics. They did on rare occasions, such as the Parliamentary reform crisis of 1831-2, take a specific line. In addition, they were quite prepared to pronounce on political questions which concerned them as workmen, such as the Dorchester Labourers of 1834. Above all, they were at all times very ready to employ the techniques of political behaviour, the public meeting, the petition to Parliament, and attempted legislation, to further their ends. If they affected to avoid politics, they were nevertheless ready enough to act politically, though their purpose was almost always industrial in intent.

[1] *Nottingham Review*, 2nd March, 1821.

Their greatest campaign was the attempt to secure Parliamentary regulation of the hosiery and lace trades. The nineteenth century efforts were preceded by an attempt in 1777-9, which, according to Henson's account, revealed a greater degree of political consciousness and a greater willingness to use political power than the attempts of the early nineteenth century. Henson wrote that the Midlands Stockingers' Association of these years was so powerful and influential in Nottingham that it had complete control over returning Members to Parliament and that notwithstanding the party spirit that prevailed in the town all parties united to return members favourable to their trade. In 1778 the Association proposed a Whig, Abel Smith, of the local banking firm, as their candidate, and he was returned unopposed as their champion. On his death in 1779 his brother Robert was proposed by the Association and elected without opposition, and in the following year, at a general election, the Association also caused Daniel Parker Coke, a Tory, to be returned as Smith's fellow member, on account of his services during the applications to Parliament. Henson suggested then that both sitting M.P.s in 1780, one Whig and one Tory, owed their places to the Stockingers' Association.[2]

This story of its political power was repeated by Felkin, and has remained unchallenged, though Henson's account was highly misleading and mainly myth. Abel Smith was chosen by a conventional meeting of the Nottingham Whigs at Thurland Hall, where he gave the usual vague promises of all prospective M.P.s that he would work to preserve burgess rights. He showed great sympathy with the framework-knitters and their cause and became an honorary member of the Framework-knitters Company, but there is no reason to suppose that he owed his existence to the stockingers or that his brother's election in 1779 followed anything but standard procedure. After all, the family regularly supplied M.P.s to Nottingham and elsewhere. Similarly, Coke, whatever his sympathies with the framework-knitters then or later, was not their creature but chosen because of his general popularity, as M.P. for Derby, and the absence of a viable alternative.[3]

[2]Henson, op. cit., pp. 383-394.
[3]Felkin, op. cit., p. 115; Sutton, op. cit. pp. 122, 126-7, 142; *D.N.B.* Vol. IV. When John Smith was elected M.P. for the Cities of London and Westminster in 1965 he became the thirtieth M.P. from the family, *The Observer*, 24th October, 1965.

With the assistance of these sympathetic Members, the Association petitioned Parliament in 1778 and again in 1779 to raise wages, lower frame-rents, and prevent abuses of their Charter, which had crept into the working of the hosiery trade. The hosiers formed a counter-association to resist the men, who had a supporting committee representing many major interests in the town, and the proposed Bill of the framework-knitters was defeated in 1779 in spite of Robert Smith's efforts. This was followed by a week of rioting in the town. Unlike the nineteenth-century endeavours, this one was evidently mismanaged financially. In April, 1785, debts of almost £240 still remained unpaid, which the framework-knitters attempted to clear up by contributing one shilling per frame.[4]

In 1812 a further attempt was made. The occasion for this was the national publicity that the hosiery trade had received because of Luddism. Questions were asked at the Parliamentary level about the causes of Luddism and the grievances of the men in the trade, and the enterprising Gravener Henson, along with a few other hosiery and lace workers, seized the opportunity to provide an answer. In the somewhat clumsy wording of the *Review*: 'This disposition of our legislature to enquire ... the framework-knitters are about to take legal advantage of.' Their ostensible purpose was, at the outset, to supply information, their real ambition to secure Parliamentary intervention in the affairs of the trade to eliminate the grievances and abuses of which they complained. This was Henson's first well-documented effort at trade union organisation, and his ambitious plan involved not only the mobilisation of the local lace and hosiery trades but the organisation, from Nottingham headquarters, of all provincial centres of the hosiery trade in England, Scotland, and Ireland, for a period of about six months. Such a scheme was more ambitious in conception than effective in practice, but a national campaign was mounted and Henson's achievement was no mean one.[5]

The scope of the 1812 programme is interesting. 'The laws of England', wrote a London frameworker-knitter, 'are able to

[4]Henson, op. cit., pp. 394-404; Sutton, op. cit., pp. 127-131; *Nottingham Journal*, 2nd April, 1785.

[5]*Nottingham Review*, 14th February, 1812. The campaign can be followed in detail from the correspondence and documents in Nottingham Borough Records, Framework-knitters' Papers, 1812-14.

render us Justice as well as others', but when the London Committee expressed surprise that the Nottingham men had evidently no intention of trying to advance wages through Parliament, they were quickly put in their place. Thomas Latham replied to them:

'It is well known that governments will not interfere with the regulation of the quantum of wages which shall be paid for a certain quantum of labour; because the thing in itself would amount to the odious practice of fixing a maximum and minimum upon our article, which fluctuates as does our national prosperity and adversity . . . the writings of Dr. Adam Smith have altered the opinion of the polished part of society on this subject. Therefore, to attempt to advance wages by parliamentary influences would be as absurd as an attempt to regulate the winds. . . .' The men were aware of prevailing economic ideas and knew that wages could be approached only indirectly, but they were challenging the rising school of economists by demanding Parliamentary control of other aspects of their trades, evidently unaware that all aspects of regulation would be seen in the same light.[6]

Apart from their demand for an ending of truck payments, something more difficult to achieve in practice than in law, the men's major requests were that employers should be obliged to publish and adhere to agreed wage rates and that they should be prohibited from manufacturing certain categories of articles which the men alleged to be inferior products. The workmen's case was impressively handled by Henson, who spoke to the Parliamentary Committee appointed to hear evidence at great length and in comprehensive detail. The Committee appears at first to have accepted the arguments, especially concerning fraudulent production and its effect on trade, but was later persuaded to change its views by the opinions of the hosiers, who belatedly organised resistance to the proposed legislation. The House of Commons tore the heart out of the men's bill and the Lords rejected it completely.[7]

Quite apart from the workmen's lack of experience and finesse in the handling of their case and the administrative weaknesses that impeded their progress, the insurmountable obstacle was the fact that their basic principle, the need for Parliamentary regula-

[6]Ibid. F.7, W. Nicholls to G. Henson, 24th February, F.19, T. Latham to W. Nicholls (March), 1812.
[7]First and Second Reports of Select Committee on Framework-knitters' Petitions, 1812, 11.

tion, was unacceptable either to Parliament or to the employers. When the workmen demanded schedules, the hosiers demanded the preservation of their liberty as employers and showed why they regarded the proposed schedules as an intolerable interference. When the men sought to determine the quality of goods made, the employers demanded their freedom to make what they wanted when they wanted, with faith in economic laws and enlightened self-interest to prevent harm being done. The replies of the hosiers that they would not produce what they could not sell, and that production varied according to demands, coming from the employers, carried greater weight. The workmen were asking for interference in the laws of trade, and Parliament's replies read as if this were already the hey-day of *laissez-faire* and non-interference.

An interesting commentary on the question of Parliamentary regulation was provided at this time by the Rev. J. T. Becher, the Southwell magistrate, when he favoured the Home Secretary with his intelligent views on the causes of Luddism. Becher admitted his awareness of 'the delicacy attaching to any interference with the regulations of trade', but he saw, quite correctly, that one of the great evils in hosiery was frame-renting with its tendency to proliferate frames. He did not propose the abolition of the system but suggested that Parliament might prescribe fixed sums to be charged on particular frames and also make it illegal to collect full rent on frames not working full time. He justified his suggestion in part by saying that Parliamentary action would show the framework-knitters that Members were not unmindful of their distresses. His idea would have produced only a slight improvement in conditions, but it is of interest that he should have proposed any interference. Later he indicated the gap separating his views from those of the men when he wrote:

'The lower orders cannot generally be made to understand the impossibility of limiting the application of any manufacturer's trading capital by legislative restriction or of controlling the privilege which every man claims of manufacturing with the materials and machinery best adapted to his own notions of personal emolument.'[8]

[8]H.O. 42/120, Becher to H.O., 11th February, 1812; Ne.C. 4923, Becher to Newcastle, 10th April, 1812.

There were several other minor attempts to secure Parliamentary regulation. In June, 1816, the framework-knitters tried again and were praised for their constitutional behaviour and their denouncing of continuing frame-breaking. In March, 1818, a further attempt was made to prohibit the manufacture of articles 'made with Scissors instead of Selvages', and a Leicester effort in 1819 was backed by Nottingham but thrown out by the House of Lords. On this occasion the two Nottingham M.P.s earned themselves condemnation for their failure to help the stockingers; in 1812 the sitting Members, especially Coke, the Tory, had taken great trouble to give the men every assistance.[9]

In 1823 was advanced the most ambitious scheme to date. Gravener Henson, in campaigning for the repeal of the Combination Laws, proposed to replace them with a whole code of protective legislation for the workmen. This time the former emphasis on faulty production was replaced by concentration on workers' rights. The culmination of Henson's campaign, the political intrigue and manoeuvre by Joseph Hume, allied with and prompted by Francis Place, by which Henson was thwarted, have been described by Wallas in his biography of Place. The issue is portrayed as a matter of political manipulation in which Place was able to outwit Henson, whose extravagant schemes would have alienated so many that no part of his plans would have been achieved. In fact it was more than a matter of politics; it was one of belief. Hume had revealed the hand of the philosophic radicals back in the 1812 debates. He had then declared himself against the use of trade societies for supporting strikes; he wanted 'to allow the labour of every class to come to market with free and open competition, by which labour in every instance would find its proper and fair level'. Francis Place was then in 1823-4 not concerned to protect labour but to remove a main obstacle against the free operation of the economic laws in which he believed. He wished to remove the Combination Laws and put nothing in their place. Henson, on the other hand, believed that the framework-knitters were susceptible to forces and pressures from which only direct interference and legal protection could defend them. In co-operation with George White, a House

[9]*Nottingham Review*, 14th, 21st June, 1816, 25th June, 1819; *Nottingham Journal*, 14th March, 1818.

H

of Commons clerk, he prepared a charter of labour rights which
was designed to give workmen the sort of guarantees and safe-
guards in their employment which were not in fact to come for
another century.[10]

Henson's bill was mainly concerned with giving workmen
security in their employment, guarding them against sudden,
wanton dismissal from their jobs, and to keep them from being
exploited whilst they worked. To this end he proposed work
contracts in writing, binding on both parties, forbidding dis-
charge before the agreed time, and establishing the right of workmen to fourteen days' notice. The contract was to specify the
wages, hours, and work agreed to, and no workmen could be
compelled to work overtime or accept wages in kind rather than
money. Where the circumstances applied, and here Henson was
clearly thinking of hosiery and lace, no workman was to be given
work without a ticket specifying the quantity and quality of the
raw materials handed to him, the work to be done, and the price
to be paid for it. The hosiery and lace workers had long complained
and would long complain of the arbitrary deductions and
exactions made by employers as a result of argument over loss of
materials or variations in styles. To deal with any disputes arising
Henson put forward very detailed plans for compulsory arbitra-
tion. Perhaps mistakenly, he filled out his bill with a number of
marginal matters such as the right of a workman to be rewarded
for improvements to machinery and provision against criminal
activity, a matter already covered to a large extent by the law
of the land.

Henson apologised for omitting the question of apprenticeship which was, he said, too technical a matter for the bill, but
his proposals were nigh comprehensive, and they horrified Place.
'A mass of absurdities', he wrote, 'a beautiful scheme of legislation, as complicated as two such ill-instructed men could well
contrive', drawn up by people 'not conversant with business.'
But Henson was only too well aware of the businesses which
prompted his action, and there could be no greater contrast than
the idealised employer who appears in Place's accounts and those
who are described by the framework-knitters before various

[10]G. Wallas, *Life of Francis Place*, (1898), pp. 207-18; Parl. Debs. Vol. 59, 1177, 21st
July, 1812; Copy of Henson's Bill, with Place's comments, in Place MSS., B.M. Add.
MSS. 27800.

nineteenth-century Commissions. Place imagined a natural harmony to exist in industry. Henson knew that it did not. Place demanded for the employer the right to dismiss a man when he wanted to without recourse to the magistrates. Let there be free association on both sides. Avoid legal formalities which would bring litigation and produce hatred between masters and men. The specifying of work conditions would breed loss of confidence, the best guarantee of good conduct. Rely on men's honour, said Place, and they act honourably. His faith in human nature seems boundless, his assumption of bargaining parties of equal strength complete. But all employers were not as humane as Place himself and Henson tried to provide against the unscrupulous. Workmen were not simply counters of value in an economic game; some were very poor men in a very depressed industry and they could hope for very little from their freedom to strike an independent bargain. In his own view, Henson's bill was not just a matter of industrial regulation, or even of economic philosophy; it was a morality that he advanced, contrary to the prevalent individualism of his day, the 'Every one for himself and the devil take the hindmost' attitude which he abhorred. 'Our object', he said, 'was not to attack any man or body of men, but to attack principles, which we conceived to be wrong in governing society.' But he was outmanoeuvred. Place's scheme for a straight repeal of the Combination Laws was successful and the sort of guarantees that Henson envisaged for the workman had to wait until the next century for fulfilment.[11]

Not all the workmen saw the issue in terms of morality but were just concerned with practical aids to better conditions. Frustrated in their support for Henson's Bill in 1823, they petitioned again in 1824 for the repeal of the Combination Laws. In November and December, 1830, there was widespread agitation on behalf of Littleton's Bill for the abolition of truck, which received wide support. Within 4 days over 8,000 signatures were collected for a petition, and these included over 100 manufacturers, the Mayor, and magistrates of the town. Again in 1833 the framework-knitters petitioned Parliament to consider their distress and do something to ameliorate their suffering, and they

[11]Place MSS., B.M. Add. MSS. 27800, 5, Place to Hume, 13th May, 1823, and Place's comments on Henson's Bill; G. White and G. Henson, op. cit., pp. 140, 141.

followed this with yet another series of petitions for Parliamentary regulation of the trade.[12]

All the grievances covered in Henson's abortive Bill of 1823 were still being voiced in 1845, but the validity of some of the points remains open to question. The efficacy of selective prohibition as a means of raising standards and thereby improving trade must remain in doubt, though many of the points raised, such as schedules, were purely administrative and could have been implemented, if with difficulty, to give the framework-knitters greater guarantees and make their payment less arbitrary. Even with the great variety of production involved it should have been possible to fix specific rates for specific jobs and reward greater skill by employment on the more skilled work. Whether it was practicable to keep labour supply as constant and protected as Henson wished, in view of the highly fluctuating nature of local trades is, however, open to considerable doubt. Parliamentary interference might have secured greater rights. It is doubtful if it could have revived the hosiery trade. A more effective and fundamental attack could have been directed against frame-rents, which remained only a subsidiary part of the framework-knitters' programme and did not even feature in Henson's scheme. The retention of frame-renting was one of the central factors behind the failure of the industry to move into factories and over to steam power, the only salvation open to it. The developments which were eventually to lift the depression which had hung over the town's major industry since the early part of the century were in no way anticipated in the proposals of the men, who were seeking to legislate for a domestic industry.

On these occasions the working classes of Nottingham were using political processes to further their industrial programmes only as petitioners to Parliament. They were not using their potential political strength as voters to try to control political machinery in order to promote some particular economic programme. They were not interested in power, yet over half the voters in any Parliamentary election in Nottingham in the period 1785-1835 were always framework-knitters because of the burgess franchise. This should have enabled some connection to be established between trade union grievance and political activity. In fact the

[12]*Nottingham Review*, 2nd April, 1824, 26th November, 17th December, 1830, 15th February, 8th March, 15th March, 1833.

relationship between the two capacities of the working man, as a worker and possible trade unionist and as a voter, has in this period continued to perplex historians, with Nottingham adding particularly to the confusion. It has been suggested, for instance, that in Coventry a broad franchise, taking in the ribbon workers, enabled political and industrial relations to be peaceful and harmonious; conversely a narrow franchise in Nottingham led to violent industrial relations, Luddism, and violent politics, the Reform Bill riots. This breaks down because Nottingham had a broad franchise and violence in spite of it, which suggests that more than the broad franchise is needed to explain the peace and calm of Coventry. It has elsewhere been similarly suggested that the 'violent tradition' occurred north of the Trent, where a narrow franchise prevented Radicals from making use of electoral processes. Nottingham was, in this period, north of the Trent, and it had the 'violent tradition', but it did not have the narrow franchise. The right to vote was evidently not a sufficient guarantee of good behaviour, in spite of the claim made by one of Nottingham's M.P.s in 1821 that the responsibility felt by men possessing the elective franchise had a tendency to promote the tranquillity of the place and that Nottingham was perfectly tranquil because of the working class franchise there. This was complete and demonstrable nonsense, as every riotous election in Nottingham showed, for whatever the consequences of the possession of voting rights in Nottingham they were not pacific behaviour in politics or passive behaviour in industry.[13]

At the height of the Luddite troubles, in December, 1811, Major Cartwright visited Nottingham, an old stamping ground, and vainly tried to persuade the magistrates to allow him to hold a public reform-meeting there. He had to be content with addressing letters to the working classes through the press, in which he denounced the frame-breakers as the worst enemies of the working classes because they added to the government's powers of mischief and gave them an excuse for using the sword. Instead of supporting the Luddites the working classes should turn to Parliamentary reform, for they would enjoy prosperity only through full representation and annual elections. Cartwright's

[13]See Poll Books for the period; J. Prest, *The Industrial Revolution in Coventry*, 1960, pp. 138-9; E. P. Thompson, op. cit., p. 471; Parl. Debs., Vol. 81, 1075, Thomas Denman, 2nd March, 1821.

appeals seem to have made little impact. In 1816 William Cobbett made a similar attempt in his 'Letter to the Luddites' to attract the working man of Nottingham to the cause of Parliamentary reform. And again in April, 1821, in his Political Register he condemned the stockingers' folly in attempting to maintain statement prices in hosiery when demand was poor; their distresses, said Cobbett, resulted from excessive taxation and the only remedy was Parliamentary reform. On this occasion he was answered by one of the leaders of the men, R. Hall, who rejected Cobbett's belief that wages must be allowed to find their own level, denied that high taxation was the cause of their troubles and showed that their troubles, being confined to their own industry and not general, could be answered only by action pertaining to that industry. He showed a total lack of interest in the political solution that Cobbett offered and his attitude fairly well represented that of the Nottingham working classes generally. Possession of the franchise had not rendered them a satisfied group; it had simply brought them no particular benefits and no particular grounds for believing that political power was a means to economic emancipation.[14]

Rightly or wrongly the leaders of the men evidently regarded the industrial struggle as independent of the political one, or, at any rate, saw no prospect of furthering their economic and industrial aims by mobilising their followers on behalf of Parliamentary reform. When the *Review* was offering Parliamentary reform as a panacea for all ills in the 20s, the trade unions were heavily involved in their own activities. It is certain that many of the leaders were supporters of reform. Henson's political activities in the Luddite and post-Luddite period leave no doubt about his hostility to the unreformed Parliament, but he was quite prepared to work through it to achieve his industrial programme. Parliamentary reform was a secondary rather than a primary consideration for him, just as later the Chartists were a nuisance because they distracted attention from his industrial schemes and gave people the idea that political reforms were a short cut to economic

[14]H.O. 42/117, Coldham to H.O., 28th December, 1811; *Nottingham Review*, 27th December, 1811; *Nottingham Journal*, 17th January, 1812; Political Register, 30th November, 1816, in H.O. 40/9; Political Register, 14th April, 1821; R. Hall, *A Reply to the Principal Objections advanced by Cobbett and others against the Framework-knitters' Friendly Relief Society*, 1821.

rejuvenation. Inevitably, when the reform movement reached a climax in 1831-2 the trade union organisations, like just about all other organisations in Nottingham, were mobilised on behalf of reform. In March, 1831, 300 cap and drawer hands who were on strike went in procession to sign a petition in favour of the Reform Bill, and the various trades' societies were active in petitioning against delay in passing the Bill. One alleged reason for the decline in Nottingham's support for the National Association for the Protection of Labour in February, 1832, was the fact that the late Special Commission for trying the Reform Bill rioters had totally engrossed the whole attention of the town, including former members of the Association. But this was exceptional. On the whole the political enterprises of the trade union organisations were involved with matters of intimate concern to the unions as such, wages or conditions of work, and the disillusionment of the post 1832 period was such as to destroy any faith that some trade unionists and working men might have had in politics as a means of salvation, at any rate Whig politics.[15]

An example of trade union disillusionment in this period was the reaction to the sentence on the Dorchester Labourers in 1834. On 31st March a crowd of over 2,000 trade unionists met to protest against the sentences. A committee was elected to promote petitions on behalf of the men and over 7,000 signed the Nottingham protests. A further petition to the King demanded the dismissal of the ministers of the day as ultimately responsible for the sentence. One speaker recommended a 'universal strike' if the demands of the men were refused, perhaps evidence of a growing sense of power but, significantly, an industrial solution to a problem that would eventually have to be tackled by political means.[16]

It would be surprising if the great mass of practical detail produced by Henson and other leaders throughout their long campaigns for Parliamentary regulation to improve conditions in their industries had fallen into some great pattern, that emerged as something akin to a 'philosophy of labour'. On the other hand it would be surprising if these multifarious details had not occasionally been cited as illustrations of some higher principle

[15]*Nottingham Journal*, 2nd September, 1842; *Nottingham Review*, 31st March, 1831, 24th February, 1832.

[16]*Nottingham Journal*, 4th April, 9th May, 1834.

or with reference to the achievement of some larger purpose. Occasionally such a notion breaks through, and it was Henson who seemed most capable of expressing his thoughts in a larger setting than that provided by his immediate industrial environment. In 1823, for instance, in language anticipatory of Marx as well as reminiscent of Locke, he wrote that 'the value of every article arises from the labour or skill bestowed upon it', and his whole scheme of that year was a projected charter of labour rights rather than a simple statement of grievances and suggested remedies. The ideas were echoed elsewhere. 'Labour ... all the property we possess' was the expression of one framework-knitters' petition in April, 1827; 'our labour is our capital' an expression of February, 1834.[17]

In 1833 a framework-knitters' petition from Basford on the north-western fringes of the town contained the following passage:

'The war of labour against property has not yet commenced, but there arrives a moment when endurance reaches its utmost point. It is in vain for you to repeat the old threadbare declaration that "you can do nothing for us"—"that our distresses arise from causes beyond the reach of Parliament" ... that "trade must find its level" ... "that all interference of Parliament in the regulation of trade and manufactures is improper" and the like statements. We have heard these things again and again, along with millions of our fellow-workmen besides, until we can no longer admit their validity; as we have learned, by woeful experience, that they mean nothing more, than that we should live contentedly in poverty, and disgracefully in a workhouse, in order that capitalists may inhabit palaces, and live in luxury.... Your petitioners ... have nothing but their labour which requires protection, and for it, they demand protection ... not as favour but as a right ... a right due to them not less as citizens than as men. Property they have none to protect.'[18]

This is the most poignant, bitter, and suggestive statement that appeared on behalf of the framework-knitters in this period. It makes unambiguous reference to 'class-war', it rejects totally the ideas of *laissez-faire* as a rationalisation of inequality, and it

[17]G. White and G. Henson, op. cit., pp. 24-5; *Nottingham Review*, 27th April, 1827, 28th February, 1834.
[18]*Nottingham Review*, 15th March, 1833.

asserts rights, not of a political kind such as the Corporation Whigs loved to enunciate, but of workers, as men, to tolerable living standards. It represented the thoughts of one man rather than the programme or collective outlook of hosiery workers; it was not a rallying cry immediately taken up and followed by industrial or political action of a kind presaged in the opening sentence. Nor were these lines from the pen of a framework-knitter. The *Review* hinted strongly that they were composed by Thomas Bailey, a substantial local tradesman, philanthropist, and later historian of the county. This was quite probable, since Bailey, who was no part of the local Corporation establishment, was in 1844 to produce a forward-looking essay on 'The Rights of Labour' in which he proposed the payment of retirement and sick pensions from money obtained through death duties and income tax. Like the 1833 declaration it was a scathing attack on *laissez-faire* and its alleged failure to confer substantial benefits on the workers.

The irony of the 1833 statement is that it serves to substantiate the claim that there emerged in the period 1830-4 'a consciousness of the identity and interests of the working class . . . as against those of other classes' but was not itself an example of working-class consciousness. Whilst Thomas Bailey was breaking with the Whigs, beginning to call himself a Tory, and writing on behalf of working-class interests, Gravener Henson was quitting political radicalism, abandoning trade union organisation, and advocating class co-operation as the only basis for future progress. The experiments in general union in the period 1831-4 did contain some suggestion of working-class self consciousness, but not until Chartism was there any carry-over into politics. Henson was hostile to Chartism, and its leaders locally were mostly 'new men' who had played no part in the earlier period.[19]

[19]E. P. Thompson, op. cit. p. 807; Full Report of Speech on Corn Laws delivered by Mr. Bailey at a Meeting of the Nottingham Town Council, 19th February, 1838. For fuller details of Thomas Bailey see M. I. Thomis, *Old Nottingham* (1968), Ch. 8.

7

THE STRUCTURE OF
LOCAL GOVERNMENT AND THE
RELIGIOUS BASIS OF
NOTTINGHAM RADICALISM

The governing portion of Nottingham Corporation was, in the words of the 1833 commissioners, 'a close and self-constituted body'. The Corporation's principal members were the Mayor, who was one of seven Aldermen, who also acted as town magistrates; the Aldermen were themselves chosen from eighteen Senior Councillors. The election of the latter was theoretically in the hands of the burgesses as a whole, who numbered approximately 3000 in 1833, but in practice contested elections were rare by this date. The only people eligible for election were members of the 'clothing' or 'livery'. These were people who had served in the office of Chamberlain or Sheriff of the town, both of which offices, light in the duties they entailed, were in the gift of the current Mayor. It was this power of the Mayor, and the charter-provision restricting Senior Councillors to the 'clothing', which ensured the closed nature of Nottingham Corporation. It was strengthened by the fact that the 'clothing' also elected the Aldermen from the ranks of the Senior Councillors. Because of the small size of the 'clothing' group, estimated at around seventy, it was usually possible to ensure that only as many candidates emerged as there were vacancies to fill. Occasionally, a member would not wait his turn to get on to the Senior Council or would quarrel with those who had given him his status, and then a contested election for a Senior Councillor would take place and the burgesses as a whole would be given a limited power of choice. Usually, however, the circle of relatives and friends granted promotions amongst themselves untroubled by such untoward occurrences.[1]

The stranglehold of the oligarchy described by the Corporation Commissioners had not been built up quickly and had not been in existence long in 1833. The system of co-option and promotion on which Nottingham operated involved nomination by the Mayor on to the 'clothing', election from the 'clothing' to the Senior Council, election then to the rank of Alderman, and the Aldermen became Mayor in turn, thereby acquiring the right to nominate to the 'clothing', thus setting the whole process again in motion. It might take many years for a man to work through this sequence, and an indiscreet nomination to the 'clothing' might threaten the harmony of the ruling group many years later. There is plenty of evidence to show that the ruling group moved only slowly and hesitantly to its commanding position. In 1787 the election of John Collishaw to the Senior Council was contested by Samuel Heywood, a 'clothing' member who had defected to the enclosing party and forced his former friends to an election. The following year a more ominous contest occurred. The Mayor's nominee to fill a vacancy was defeated by Henry Green, who proceeded to celebrate his victory with an 'elegant dinner' at the White Lion Hotel. This was the customary headquarters of the Nottingham Tories, and the 'clothing' should have taken the hint. Instead, Green became an Alderman, in 1793 Mayor, and in 1794 emerged as a rabid anti-Jacobin Tory, the most notorious Mayor in Nottingham annals since the Jacobite Hawksley had drunk to the "King across the water" in 1715. In 1790 George Burbage, the editor of the *Nottingham Journal*, was elected to the Senior Council, and he was soon to be the principal spokesman for Tory views in Nottingham. More care was now evidently taken with nominations to the livery after this, though in 1819

[1]*Report of Commission on State of Municipal Corporations*, 1835, XIII, Appendix to First Report, Part III, p. 2005. Burgesses might inherit the right to be a freeman, earn it by serving an apprenticeship within the town, have it bestowed upon them by the Corporation for services rendered, or purchase it with a money payment.

the system again showed that it was not complete. Thomas
Richards, a 'clothing' member, turning renegade, attacked the
extravagance and corruption of the Corporation and demanded
its reform. He was elected by 360 votes to 220, by a mixture of
Tory and Radical voters; the former, glad to embarrass the
Corporation oligarchy whenever they could, were wished joy with
their new champion.[2]

Over the final decade and a half of the old Corporation's
existence oligarchical control was virtually complete. Elections
to the Senior Council in this period illustrate the fulness of control
eventually exercised by the ruling group. Elections became pure
formalities and members of the 'clothing' were simply nominated
by their fellow members for elevation. In September, 1821, as
many as four of the eighteen positions became vacant simultaneously; they were filled by the nomination of just the right
number of candidates from the 'clothing'. So smooth was this
process that the expression 'elected' was often replaced by
'received the appointment'. In May, 1823, Alfred Thomas
Fellowes was elected a Senior Councillor to replace his dead
father, and in August of the same year Mr. Kirke Swann took the
place of his deceased brother, Edward A. Swann, in the select
body of Senior Councillors. In 1835 the commissioners remarked
on the achievement of four families, the Allens, the Wakefields,
the Fellowes, and the Swanns in holding down three-quarters of
the positions in the governing body. Those not related could usually
be relied upon for they would never otherwise have penetrated
the ranks of the livery. They were products, said the *Journal* in
1825, of a system of favouritism long acted upon which produced
aspirants 'all of one party and ready for the purpose'. And further
incentives could sometimes be added. John Collishaw, elected
Senior Councillor in August, 1787, was, in the December, given
a newly created post of supervisor of Corporation workmen,
which brought him forty guineas per year, 'the price of a servile
vote', in the opinion of the *Journal*, 'the price for which the choice
of the people is sold'.[3]

[2]*Nottingham Journal*, 25th August, 1st September, 1787, 13th, 20th September, 1788;
Blackner, op. cit., pp. 388-91; Sutton, op. cit., p. 185; *Nottingham Review*, 9th April, 1819.

[3]Sutton, op. cit., p. 366, *Nottingham Review*, 23rd May, 29th August, 1823; *Report of
Commission on State of Municipal Corporations*, 1835, XIII, Appendix to First Report,
Part III, p. 2005; *Nottingham Journal*, 26th February, 1825, 22nd, 29th, December, 1787.

The remaining members of the governing part of the Corporation were the Junior Councillors, six in number, who, like the rest, sat for life or until retirement, but who, unlike the others, required only the qualification of burgess to be eligible for election. It was only after a long struggle to enforce the terms of the Charter that the Senior Council were forced in 1776 to accept Junior Councillors into Common Hall as part of the Corporate body. This background to their arrival, against the wishes of the established body, ensured that the Junior Councillors would play an opposition role from the start. They were almost entirely chosen at contested elections, though very occasionally an unopposed return would be made. The Junior Councillors appear to have been the 'democratic', popular element inside the governing body, but they were, as the Commissioners pointed out, too few to have much influence. Also they were not eligible for senior positions.[4]

The Junior Council was the only means of access to Corporation business, though not power, for those outside the magic circle. Contestants for membership tended to call themselves, or be called, Tories, though they were also discontented Whigs and men fighting under the 'Radical' label. All those elected in the period 1785-1835 were Tories, though the policies they pursued were anti-Corporation oligarchy rather than specifically Tory. It was the Junior Council who took the lead in resisting the growing power of the oligarchy. In 1777, soon after their admission to the Council, the Junior Councillors had attempted, unsuccessfully, to usurp the traditional right of the Mayor to nominate to the livery. Had they succeeded, Nottingham might have had a Tory oligarchy in 1833. In October, 1789, it was the Junior Council who successfully invoked the Test and Corporation Acts against Mayor Smith, who, unlike most of Nottingham's Nonconformist Mayors, was unwilling to make his token act of conformity. In 1807 Lewis Allsopp on his election as Junior Councillor refused to take the Corporation's oath of secrecy on the grounds that it was part of his mission to expose Corporation misgovernment; the Corporation were eventually directed to admit him in spite of his refusal. Some gestures succeeded; others failed, such as the attempt in January, 1803, to prevent the town magistrates from defending themselves at the public expense against charges

[4] D. Gray, *Nottingham through 500 Years* (1960), pp. 120-1.

of improper electoral conduct, under the pretence, said the Junior Councillors, of 'supporting the honour and dignity of the Corporation'.[5]

What the commissioners, and later observers, failed to notice is that the Senior Council, knowing the powerlessness of the Junior body, made no attempt to control its composition. There is no reason to suppose that elections to the Junior Council could not have been manipulated, like any other Nottingham event, by the Corporation. In fact the Senior Council remained aloof, allowing Tories, Radicals, or anyone else to contest the representation, so that the Junior Councillors became virtually a tolerated, official opposition. In the period 1785-1835 Tories won every election to the Junior Council. In January, 1794, when anti-Jacobin feeling was nearing its height, John James was returned unopposed, but this was unusual. In 1798 Richard Hooton, a Tory, defeated Robert Brown, a framework-knitter, who stood as a Radical In 1801 the magistrates intervened firmly to ensure the peaceful, as well as comfortable, return of Charles Twells, an attorney, again a Tory, which suggests a certain disinterestedness in the outcome. One of the classic contests for the Junior Council occurred in 1815 when James Dale, a Tory, beat Richard Bonnington, a Whig. This was in no way a Corporation defeat, for Bonnington had mobilised on his side support and ideas which the Corporation could not tolerate. Robert Denison advocated the right of burgesses to have more influence in Corporation affairs, whilst Thomas Richards, proposing Bonnington, attacked the degenerate Corporation as unfit for the nineteenth century. Two other contests of interest occurred in this period. In August, 1832, Richard Sutton of the *Nottingham Review* stood as a Radical and was defeated by Samuel Roberts, a Tory, and in January, 1835, there was a lively contest between two Tories. The issue on this occasion was enclosure, and the supporter of enclosure was, almost inevitably, defeated.[6]

It is clear that, although in many of these contests the good name of the Corporation Whigs was at stake, their electoral management was not in question. They were content that

[5]Sutton, op. cit., p. 117; *Nottingham Journal*, 31st October, 20th November, 1789, 2nd May, 1807; Corporation Hall Books, 1802/3, pp. 17-18, 6th January, 1803.

[6]*Nottingham Journal*, 18th January, 1794, 3rd March, 1798, 26th December, 1801; *Nottingham Review*, 18th, 25th August, 1815, 30th January, 1835; Sutton, op. cit., p. 438.

Tories should fight it out with Radicals or Whig malcontents for positions which, when attained, gave members no practical control or influence over affairs of the town. They were evidently considered worth having from a prestige point of view since bribery went on extensively on these occasions. William Parsons, for instance, the defeated candidate in 1835, believed that his father had spent about £1,400 on the campaign.[7]

The powers and privileges of the governing group, on occasions challenged by members of the Junior Council, were also widely resented in the town at large and sometimes challenged by groups from the body of burgesses as a whole, but two test cases in 1807 and 1809 served only to reinforce and formalise the powers which opponents sought to undermine. In November, 1807, John L. Darker challenged the exclusive right of the 'clothing' to present candidates for the Senior Council; though not a member of the livery himself, he offered himself for election and proceeded to campaign for burgess support. When the day of the poll came, however, he was simply declared ineligible by the presiding official, and he could do little to take the matter further. In 1809 a more spirited resistance was made by a number of burgesses who challenged the exclusive right of the 'clothing' to elect the Aldermen of the Corporation, which had been unsuccessfully questioned previously in 1791. Having elected their own rival 'Aldermen', the burgesses secured the central government's support for their case, and the Mayor was compelled to defend his interpretation of the Charter against the Crown. He won his case, and the burgesses continued to be excluded from all choice of Aldermen. It was argued, in defence of this, that to allow the burgesses at large any say in the matter would bring inconvenience and the possibility of disorder upon the town; the Aldermen were in any case town magistrates also, and popular election of magistrates was not a notion to be encouraged.[8]

This repeated and comprehensive refusal to advance burgess participation in the political life of the borough, together with the completeness of control that the oligarchy exercised, suggests

[7]Any generalisations about Corporation intervention in Municipal elections, such as R. A. Church, op. cit., p. 168, require considerable qualification; Diaries of William Parsons, 1830-71, 15th February, 1835.

[8]*Nottingham Journal*, 26th December, 1807; *Nottingham Review*, 28th July, 4th August, 1809.

that any interpretation of local political life which is based on the idea of a Corporation commanded by burgess votes or acting in deference to the views of the freemen is unacceptable. The Corporation oligarchy owed nothing to the burgess at large for their hold on political power in Nottingham. They exercised power in spite of burgess demands rather than because of them.[9]

If the governing oligarchy of Nottingham was a politically uniform and compact group, it also possessed strong social cohesion. Few would have denied that the City Fathers represented the most prosperous families in the town and were men of high social standing. The radical Blackner revealed very snobbish views on the question of social eligibility for Corporation office. Though himself a strong advocate of working man's rights, he condemned occasional attempts made by the working men to become members of the Corporate body; this, he argued, caused the whole body, which had the guardianship of burgess interests in its hands, to fall into disrespect and might even provoke a demand for a narrowing down of the franchise if working men had such pretensions. He evidently favoured the right of the social élite to govern locally, as long as their general political outlook was in accord with his own. Sutton's Date-book names the occupation of thirty-four men who attained at least the rank of Senior Councillor in the period 1785-1835. Of these, thirteen were hosiers, a group who had risen quickly to social pre-eminence in the second half of the eighteenth century through their economic power, three lace manufacturers, and two cotton manufacturers. There were also thirteen who belonged to the tradesman-shopkeeper category, including a silversmith, a brewer, a wine-merchant, ironmonger and grocer. There were two professional men, a surgeon and an attorney, and one 'Gentleman' of independent means. It was clearly the world of business which dominated the Corporation, the main trades of Nottingham and the trades to be found anywhere. The great gap was the relative absence of professional men and the so-called 'gentlemen'. It was this that caused the 1833 Commissioners to remark on the omission of many whose standing in the town entitled them to share in its councils; these excluded groups tended to be Tory in politics. The governors of Nottingham,

[9] J. D. Chambers, *Modern Nottingham in the Making* (1945), p. 21; R. A. Church, op. cit., p. 163.

though not possessing titles or long pedigrees, were sufficiently wealthy through their businesses to have the necessary status inside the town to spurn with impunity the aristocracy or gentry of the county who opposed their political views. Inside Nottingham they ruled and the Duke of Newcastle was tolerated. And something which promoted their social cohesion as much as their common economic interest was the significant fact, noted by the Corporation Commissioners, that three chapels practically accounted for the personnel of the Corporate body, the political significance of which will be examined shortly.[10]

Apart from the recurrent criticism of the oligarchical nature of Corporation rule and the limited range of political opinion represented by it, the other major attack on the Corporation focused on its alleged mishandling of financial affairs. The Corporation had the responsibility of administering a large amount of property, and the Corporation Commissioners showed that over a twenty-year period an income of over £67,000 had been received from the Chamber Estates. It was a serious complaint that details of the yearly budget were never supplied to the public at large; the annual account, said the *Journal*, in April, 1820, 'is composed of gross sums and general terms, that we might be nearly as wise if we had none'. On January 28th, 1822, a public meeting of burgesses was held to attempt to force the Corporation to give a public account of their disposition of public property, which they were exercising without check. The meeting formed itself into a 'permanent' committee to work towards this end, but its efforts failed. As long as accounts were kept secret, people would continue to believe the worst, that members were corrupt in their administration, that favouritism prevailed in administering charities, and that the ample moneys of the Corporation were frittered away on improperly high salaries and undeserved entertainment allowances instead of being applied to the welfare of the town. One thing was evident and incontrovertible, that the Corporation had progressively increased the town rate that it had been entitled to levy since 1795 to a point at which it exceeded that of any comparable area in the country, and this when, according to many, there was already provision made

[10]Blackner, op. cit., p. 306; *Report of Commission on State of Municipal Corporations*, 1835, XIII, Appendix to First Report, Part III, p. 2005; J.D. Chambers, *Modern Nottingham in the Making* (1945), p. 21.

I

from Corporation funds for the purposes for which the special
rates were raised. And in spite of the large income from the Estate,
the money raised in rates, and the sale of Corporation property
to the value of almost £30,000 in twenty-six years, the Corporation had managed in that time to incur a debt of almost £19,000.
It was these failures, imprudence, extravagance, and total failure to
show any adequate recompense to the town for moneys expended,
of which the Corporation Commissioners complained in 1833.
They noted the self-indulgence of members at their meetings at
the public expense and their failure to throw open contracts to
public tender, but it was folly rather than sin that offended them.
Thomas Bailey, for a long time a leading critic of the Corporation, emphasised the 'great want of prudence and sound econ-
omical management in the disposal of funds—and recklessness in
expenditure', but rejected the charges of 'systematic peculation
or plunder indulged in or tolerated.' The *Review*, opposed to the
principle of self-election, was nonetheless ready to admit that the
Corporation was as free from corruption as any in the kingdom,
and there were many declarations on the Whig side that no one
need fear for the results of any investigation, whatever feelings of
shame might be prompted by the revelations.[11]

But of all the issues raised about the conduct of the Corporation
at the time of the 1833 Commission the one of most importance
for the development of the town was not the exclusion from power
of some political group or some petty malversation of finances but
the whole question of the physical growth of the town. The
Commissioners made their personal recommendations that
enclosure of the common lands around the town, over which the
burgesses exercised rights, should go ahead. They listed the disadvantages in terms of housing and the town's economic growth
arising out of the failure to proceed with enclosure, but they did
not attempt to allocate responsibility for this state of affairs.[12]

The issue of enclosure was in fact the most consistently recurring
theme of all Nottingham elections, local and parliamentary,

[11]*Report of Commission on State of Municipal Corporations*, 1835, XIII, Appendix to First
Report, Part III, pp. 2006-7; *Nottingham Journal*, 15th April, 1820; 28th January, 1823,
30th October, 1824; *Nottingham Review*, 1st, 8th February, 1822, 28th January, 18th
October, 1833; Bailey, op. cit., p. 389.

[12]*Report of Commission on State of Municipal Corporations*, 1835, XIII, Appendix to First
Report, Part III, p. 2001.

throughout the whole of the period 1785-1835. In 1787, at an
election for the Senior Council, one candidate, Samuel Heywood,
advocated extensive improvement schemes for the town, to be
assisted, and in part financed, by the enclosure of the common lands
and the Corporation's realising the value of its own share of the
lands. This scheme produced, in Heywood's words, 'an uncom-
mon Union of the Lower Orders' against him. An unprecedented
number of people turned out to vote, and there were stirring
declarations of burgesses' being unwilling to barter away their
rights for gold. From this time forward candidates for any office
fell over themselves to swear their opposition to enclosure and
their determination to preserve the rights of the burgesses in-
violate. And the burgesses remained resolute in their opposition
to enclosure because of their hope of one day acquiring a 'burgess-
part' of land for their own private exploitation which they might,
until death, turn into a steady income, and because of their
ironical concern for the health of the town.[13]

What is also ironical is that the burgesses themselves have been
allocated so much blame for the town's failure to take the needful
political decision to go ahead with enclosure when the burgesses
were so evidently rendered increasingly powerless and politically
innocuous through this period. It is true that election candidates
appealed to the burgesses and promised them freedom from
enclosure in return for their support. It is not, however, true that
the support of the burgesses was necessary for the holding and
retention of power inside Nottingham. The corporation oligarchy
treated the burgesses with sufficient contempt throughout this
period to leave beyond doubt their lack of need to cultivate the
favour of the burgesses. The latter could, if able to resist the
pressures and temptations placed upon them, act as a political
pressure-group of some importance at Parliamentary elections.
In local elections, however, their assent or dissent was a purely
nominal thing. The ruling oligarchy was self-perpetuating and
needed no popular sanction to retain control. 'The power of the
burgesses within the closed Corporation' was only a power to
exercise common rights in the fields, not power to control the
Corporation. The rulers certainly found it expedient to please
the burgesses over the question of the lands and affect to be the

---

[13]*Nottingham Journal*, 1st September, 1787.

guardian of their interests, for the continued existence of the common lands allowed the Corporation the further power of jurisdiction over them. If any right of property be in the burgesses, said the town clerk ominously in 1793, the Corporation are their legal representatives and the repository of their rights. But the Corporation's need of the burgesses was slight. It might even be concluded that the blowing up of enclosure into the bogey it became and the identifying of the Corporation with the popular burgess opposition to it was an act of Machiavellian politics to share blame and responsibility for the selfish and harmful policy for which Councillors and Aldermen were themselves entirely responsible. The burgesses were certainly obstructionist and hostile to change, but it is quite erroneous to maintain that they held a 'stranglehold' or that they maintained this through their powers of electing members of the Corporation. The power of election was purely illusory, and so it is hardly possible to maintain that their exercise of it had disastrous effects upon the town's developments.[14]

In October, 1806, the Corporation swore to oppose enclosure to the utmost of their powers, and they kept their resolution with good heart. The reasons why they were willing to act the role of champions of the burgesses cannot lie in the power structure of Nottingham's local government, in which the burgesses had an insignificant part, but must lie in the selfish interests of Corporation members who used the known resistance of the burgesses as an excuse for holding back a development of vital necessity to the town's well-being which they in fact opposed because of private, vested interests in the status quo. A later government commission in 1844-5 exposed some of these private interests, the ownership of slum property in the town centre, which might lose its monopoly value if alternative, better accommodation were offered through new building developments, and the wish to keep artificially high property and site values in the town, which could only be done if the town's expansion were restricted. Probably the wealthiest of the slum-property owners was Alderman Thomas Wakefield, the leading member of the old Corporation and the first Mayor of the new one, a philanthropist in some fields but a resolute opponent of enclosure, whose opposition alone was

[14]J. D. Chambers, *Modern Nottingham in the Making*, (1945), pp. 20-24; R. A. Church, op. cit., p. 163; *Nottingham Journal*, 9th March, 1793.

believed sufficient to stop the cause from making progress. Another factor behind Corporation attitudes was that the common lands had been for many years a source of financial relief to harassed administrators who were in the habit of alienating a small piece of property to clear up a pressing debt, a practice that would have to cease once the land had been formally apportioned and ownership clearly determined. It is clear, too, that the Corporation had, in its control over the commons, a source of patronage and power which could be exercised over the burgess body. Beside such factors as these the wishes of the burgesses were of little significance.[15]

In taking a comprehensive view of the effect of Corporation rule on Nottingham before 1835 it is difficult to agree with the Review's verdict that although members were improperly installed in positions of power their conduct was good and beneficial to the town; or to be satisfied with the 1835 Commissioners who attacked Corporation members for their imprudent stewardship but almost allowed them to escape the charge of false stewardship in connection with the town's real welfare. They remarked on the absence of great public works and improvement schemes to explain the enormous revenue that the Corporation had managed to consume, but they failed totally to allocate guilt for the criminal omission of enclosure.[16]

It would be convenient, having blamed slum-property owners for the failure to enclose, to accept the thesis that enclosure was advocated by the working classes, that 'the nascent equalitarianism of the working class', through Jacobinism, Pentrich, the Reform Bill riots, and Chartism worked towards this end, and that in resisting these movements the Corporation was defending its own and burgess privileges 'against the rising tide of political equality'. This is not, however, a thesis that can be substantiated. Even assuming a working-class consciousness that had existence and continuity through these movements, it is difficult to show the Corporation in perpetual and direct opposition to it and quite impossible to show that enclosure was a theme of working-class

[15]Corporation Hall Books, 1806/7, p. 15, 13th October, 1806; Appendix to First Report of Royal Commission on the State of Large Towns and Populous Districts, 1844, XVII, p. 145; S. D. Chapman, 'Working Class Housing in Nottingham during the Industrial Revolution', Transactions of the Thoroton Society, 1963.
[16]Nottingham Review, 1st November, 1833.

political agitation, even ignoring the fact that the burgesses who opposed enclosure were very largely working class. The rather sad truth is that the enlightened policy was just as much dictated by selfish, economic interests, those of the freeholders in the common fields who wished to sell their freeholds for building land, as the unenlightened policy of the burgesses and the Corporation. William Parsons was persuaded by his father to stand for election to the Junior Council in 1835 in order that he could advocate enclosure policies on the Council. The family owned seven acres in the Sand Field which, as building-land, was expected to fetch 20/- to 30/- per square yard; father Parsons was 'very liberal with money for the voters', but in vain. There had been men who advocated enclosure for the town's good from the beginning of the period, such as the doctors and clergymen of the 1786-7 Committee for Improvements, but they were very few in number and were not necessarily to be found in working-class or Radical politics. The *Review*, which had strong sympathy with such politics, unhappily formed part of the general chorus in defence of 'the traditional rights and privileges of the burgesses'.[17]

It is somewhat surprising that a body of men so clearly concerned with the preservation of their own exclusive control as were the ruling oligarchy of Nottingham could have been united by anything other than pure self-interest. They did in fact possess clear ideological ties which were widely recognised and proclaimed on the national stage. It would doubtless be possible to trace political radicalism in Nottingham back to Civil War days when the town, after first providing Charles I with a setting in which to raise the royal standard, performed notably on the Parliamentary side. Thomas Denman, one of the town's M.P.s, related in 1825 that Nottingham Corporation had been the first to congratulate King William on his arrival in 1688. Blackner thought that radicalism could be traced back at least to 1715, when Jacobite Mayor Hawksley went down on his bare knees to toast the absent Stuarts only to be apprehended by his fellow-magistrates and thrown into jail. Though he became the hero of the High Tories he succeeded in delivering a death-blow to the influence of his

[17]J. D. Chambers, *Modern Nottingham in the Making* (1945), p. 30; Diaries of William Parsons, 1830-1871, 16th October, 1834, 26th January, 1835; *Nottingham Journal*, 9th September, 4th, 11th November, 1786.

party in the Corporation. Nottingham reacted violently against him, showed a great loyalty to the Hanoverians in 1745 when Charles Edward reached nearby Derby, and invariably championed radical and popular causes until the years 1793-4. In 1738-9 the burgesses of the town were active in rallying their M.P.s to the support of Pension Bills to limit the number of placemen in Parliament and were quite uninhibited where politics were concerned. The American War of Independence aroused a great public interest in the question of popular rights and following Yorktown people would come to blows when they met in public places, so high did feeling run and so great was the political consciousness of the town. A publican could with impunity swing a picture of Bunker's Hill above his inn-door during demonstrations against the government, echoing the rejoicings that had taken place in Nottingham in 1770 on the release of John Wilkes from prison. And when the Rev. George Walker arrived in Nottingham in 1774 to become Minister of High Pavement Presbyterian Chapel he found 'by happy accident', said his son, a Corporation which acted upon 'the same liberal and enlarged principles as himself'.[18]

Lord Holland, when granted the freedom of Nottingham in 1807, paid tribute to a Corporation 'long distinguished for their attachment to the pure and genuine principles of Civil and Religious Liberty'. This was an echo of Charles Fox's sentiments of 1803 that the town was under the government of 'some of the most enlightened men in the country'. During the Revolutionary and Napoleonic Wars their 'enlightenment' had been clearly shown. They had conspicuously opposed Britain's entry into the War in 1793 and in 1795 petitioned the King to dismiss the government. The *Journal* blasted them for this, for the 'impropriety and partiality of their public conduct' in 1795, and again in 1798 for refusing by a large majority to subscribe to a voluntary collection for national defence, on which it was said, they should have been setting a better example to the people. Throughout this period the Corporation devotedly followed the lead of Fox, and on his death in 1806 the Mayor and town-clerk

[18]Parl. Debs., Vol. 90, 361, 4th May, 1825; Blackner, op. cit., pp. 379, 338; W. H. Wylie and J. P. Briscoe, *A Popular History of Nottingham* (1893), pp. 98, 102-3; Bailey, op. cit., p. 109; Memoir of the Rev. George Walker, by his son, in G. Walker, *Essays on Various Subjects* (1809), pp. 82-4.

attended the funeral. Later a bust of him was acquired for the municipal buildings. Like Fox many years earlier, the Corporation left themselves open to 'Un-Whigging' when they protested in January, 1811, against any diminution of the royal prerogative when exercised by the Prince Regent. During the reform movements of the 20s and 30s the Corporation was prominent in its advocacy of and petitioning for Parliamentary reform and all measures to relieve religious minorities and earned tributes from the sometimes critical *Review* in 1828 for being a 'foremost advocate of liberal measures'.[19]

George Walker also found on his arrival in Nottingham in 1774, that the Corporation members who happily shared his politics were also in large measure members of the religious community over which he was to preside. This was a vital aspect of Nottingham's liberal politics, their association with certain kinds of religious dissent. Nottingham, it was said, was ruled by a 'body Corporate of Civil and Religious Dissenters', and a correspondent commented in 1827 that but for Occasional Conformity and Indemnity Acts scarcely an individual in the Corporation would hold his gown for another year, for they were almost all Dissenters. The 1835 Commissioners were to confirm this opinion. They reported that despite the Test and Corporation Acts a large proportion of members had always been Dissenters; the town-clerk had claimed that so too were a large proportion of the town and he had denied that the Corporation had specifically aimed at a Dissenting majority; they had sought people 'whose principles they thought to be wise and good' and these had, naturally, turned out to be Dissenters.[20]

Tories and opponents of the Corporation had no doubts that radicalism in religion and politics went together. When one was mentioned so too was the other, just as 'civil and religious liberties' were always classed together by the reformers. Nottingham, 'this reputed stronghold of dissent and radicalism' was ruled by

[19]*Nottingham Journal*, 7th November, 1807, 19th December, 1795, 2nd January, 1796, 10th March, 1798, 5th January, 1811; Parl. Debs., Vol. 36, 1236, 29th April, 1803; Corporation Hall Books, 1797/8, p. 23, 6th March, 1798, 1805/6, pp. 65-6, 24th September, 1806, 1810/11, pp. 19-25, 2nd January, 1811; *Nottingham Review*, 28th June, 1828.

[20]Memoir of the Rev. George Walker, op. cit., p. 84; *Nottingham Review*, 17th October 1812, 9th March, 1827; A. Lincoln, *Some Political and Social Ideas of English Dissent, 1763-1800*, (1938) p. 45; *Report of Commission on State of Municipal Corporations*, 1835, XIII, Appendix to First Report, Part III, p. 2005.

'a motley assemblage of infidels, Socinians, revolutionists, and political Dissenters', and when the Corporate body went electioneering it did so 'in combination with the Socinians, infidels, Papists, and a large section of Dissenters'. Indeed, so bitterly were the Dissenters denounced for their politics at one stage that their chapels were said to be more like political houses than places of religion. When Archdeacon Wilkins wrote to Lord Grey in 1834 he protested that Nottingham was sound in its support of Church and State save for a small group of 'ultra-radical dissenters' and the *Times* also paired together 'mischievous political and theological dogmas'. This association emerged very clearly in the Parliamentary election of 1803. Daniel Parker Coke's Tory victory was acclaimed by the ringing of church-bells and his victory toasts included one to the religion of the country. Whilst the Tories championed the established religion, their opponents were castigated as haters of prelates, men of no religion, or, what amounted in their eyes to much the same thing, Dissenters. The Nonconformists, faintly praised and damned as the 'respectable part of the Jacobin Party', received harsher treatment in one election squib:

'Ye new-coin'd Methodists with oblong chin,
Ye Presbyterian Saints—and Quakers prim;
Ye sage Dissenters, of all germs and classes,
Who strive to undermine Church, State and King,
And guide the Mob as pedlars guide their asses,
To you great Sirs!—The Muse directs her strain,
Exulting in your fall with stern disdain'.[21]

For their part the Whigs and Radicals made no attempt to deny this identification of themselves with religious nonconformity but made it one of the main features of their appeal. Religious liberty was one of their foremost rallying cries and the repeal of the Test and Corporation Acts one of their main aims. Parsons they classed with dukes and lords. Nor were the Dissenters themselves

[21]*Nottingham Journal*, 28th February, 1834, 22nd, 15th December, 1832, 24th January, 1834, 11th June, 1803; G. Wilkins, *Letter to Earl Grey on the subject of Ecclesiastical Reform*, 1832; W. Howitt, *The Three Death Cries of a Perishing Church* (1835), p. 27; *The Times*, 25th December, 1852, quoted by W. H. Wylie, *Old and New Nottingham*, (1853), p. 300; *Paper War carried on at the Nottingham Election of 1803*, pp. 223, 69-70, 313.

reluctant to agree to the association. The widow of the Rev. Joseph Gilbert, Minister at Friar Lane Independent Chapel throughout the second quarter of the nineteenth century, writing of her late husband, said that 'as a consistent dissenter he espoused the liberal side in politics'. It was evidently natural for him to do so. Nonconformist Sunday Schools were accused of teaching political radicalism in 1819 when the Rector of St. Peter's complained in a sermon that in some Sunday Schools children were being instructed in politics instead of the Bible. And when the Dissenters were contending for their rights they could rarely resist the sort of argument employed by William Howitt, a Quaker, in 1834. In advocating the disestablishment of the Anglican Church, as a Dissenter, he argued, as a reformer, that not only was the presence of bishops in the House of Lords unjust but also that their political influence was pernicious, as evidenced by their recent opposition to Parliamentary reform.[22]

High Pavement Presbyterian Chapel, which the Corporate body attended so numerously, traced its history back to Restoration days, and the ejection of the ministers in 1662. It was one of the oldest and certainly the strongest of the religious bodies outside the established church in Nottingham throughout the eighteenth century, and its own struggle for survival in the seventeenth century fitted it for the role it it was to play in radical leadership in Nottingham, even through the years of the Evangelical Revival which largely passed it by. Carpenter, the historian of the Nottingham Society, was concerned to show the importance of nonconformist activity in promoting social progress, and he emphasised the factors which permitted the Presbyterians to take a lead in social and political matters. Through the course of the eighteenth century the Presbyterians dropped the form of church government with which they had originally been associated and became independent as far as organisation was concerned. They ceased also to require any confession of faith from their ministers at ordination, permitting them to pursue their theological studies at will, with the result that doctrinal preaching was no feature of church life and the ministers taught only the general principles of Christian belief and behaviour. People were left to form their own opinions and Presbyterians moved gradually

[22] *Accidents of the History of Daniel and Joseph in Ten Chapters* (1803), p. 35; Mrs. A. Gilbert, op. cit., p. 77; *Nottingham Review*, 4th June, 1819; *Nottingham Journal*, 3rd January, 1834.

away from orthodox Christianity, from Trinitarianism, through Arianism, to Unitarianism, which was definitely established at High Pavement by the beginning of the nineteenth century. This liberal approach to theology, the spirit of inquiry, and absence of authoritarianism, almost inevitably led to a similar approach to politics. But it was not only this. The Presbyterians owed their very existence to their successful struggle for the principles of civil and religious liberty and felt conscious of their trust to uphold and develop these principles. As a result they sought high office in local affairs and used their authority and influence to promote their principles.[23]

It was then to be expected that when the High Pavement community received an outstanding leader they would blossom forth politically, and this is what happened with the arrival of George Walker, F.R.S. in 1774. This man, said his friend the classical scholar and pamphleteer Gilbert Wakefield, possessed the greatest variety of knowledge of any man he ever knew. As mathematician and poet, philosopher and divine, he had talents way out of the ordinary and was well equipped to lead his congregation and to play an active part in the political life of the town both in his own right and through his influence over those to whom he ministered at this time of great political ferment. He is recognised by all local historians as the local leader of the 'civil and religious liberty' campaigns, which principles he 'long thundered forth', according to Blackner. Ten years after Walker's arrival there returned to Nottingham the Rev. Gilbert Wakefield, a son of the former rector of St. Nicholas' and himself an ordained, though now non-practising, Anglican clergyman. Wakefield quickly developed a great admiration and friendship for Walker, shared his religious views and political outlook, and the partnership raised High Pavement's intellectual leadership of Nottingham to new heights. 'The residence of two such distinguished men, united by friendship, as well as by congenial pursuits and opinion, in a provincial town' wrote Carpenter, 'must have formed no unimportant feature of its society at that day'. Amongst other things they formed a literary club which met at members' houses. Above all they directed political expression in Nottingham along radical lines. In spite of the personal gentleness and tender-hearted nature of both men, in matters political their blood was

[23]B. Carpenter, *Early Presbyterianism in Nottingham* (1862), Preface, p. iii, pp. 162-4.

hot, and there are several testimonies to their vehemence and fanaticism when their political beliefs were at stake. Whilst Walker remained a provincial figure during the Revolutionary War years, Wakefield, from London, was to acquire national fame, notoriety, and a two year prison sentence for his bitter attack on the government in his 'Reply' to the Bishop of Llandaff in 1798. Yet it was Walker who, through his sermons, his essays, and his political work, was to provide posterity with the clearer statement of the contemporary radical, nonconformist case, and he was closer to being a political philosopher than any Nottingham citizen in this period.[24]

For George Walker political life was not an addition to his religious work but an extension of it, for politics, he wrote, 'is founded in moral principle, it is a branch of morals, it involves the character and the happiness of a people, and to think and to act aright in it must for ever be a serious duty of man'. And behind all political behaviour was the religious sanction, for 'no duty calls, no obedience is due where God forbids'.[25]

Fundamental to Walker's political philosophy were his ideas on equality and the rights of men. In language strongly reminiscent of Locke, Walker stated that political society was for the good of all, that civil allegiance entitled a man to the protection of and accessibility to all the advantages and privileges of a citizen. The guiding principle of the English constitution, he said, was public good, universal and individual good. Whilst it recognised distinction of rank, it knew no distinction of right. All were under an equal protection. Governments and their agents were set apart only to serve the people and provide for their happiness; they held 'a generous trust, a sacred deposit of dignity and power to be returned with blessing to them all'. Governments could not grant rights; religious toleration was no grace or favour over which a discretionary power could be exercised. Again, on Parliamentary reform he spoke of legislation as the equal and

[24]Quoted by the Rev. J. Tayler in Sermon at High Pavement on death of George Walker, Nottingham, 1807; Blackner, op. cit., p. 107; Carpenter, op. cit., p. 167; C. Brown, *Lives of Nottinghamshire Worthies* (1882), p. 271; Bailey, op. cit., pp. 130, 229; Correspondence of G. Wakefield with C. J. Fox, 1796-1801 (1831), p. 69.

[25]Letter to an M.P. quoted in Memoir of the Rev. George Walker, op. cit., p. 186; Sermon on 'The Duty and Character of a National Soldier', *Sermons* (1790), Vol. 2, p. 437.

common right of all, something 'inherent in the very idea of an English freeman'.[26]

It is not possible to say whether Walker's ideas on human rights led to or arose from his great concern for the free exercise of full religious and civil rights by Dissenters. This was his most important political campaign. The principle he propounded was that religion was not within the jurisdiction of the civil magistrate; it concerned man and God alone. Consequently, no difference of religious faith and worship should exclude a citizen from any of the rights and privileges due to him as a citizen. The emphasis was all the time on rights; toleration he believed to be an invidious term. Nor could there be exceptions where rights were concerned, and he wrote 'we have committed the great principle of religious liberty to the Churchman, to the Roman Catholic, and to the world'. As an apologist Walker produced his famous tract 'The Dissenters' Plea', rated by Charles Fox the best pamphlet on the subject of the Test Acts. As an organiser he brought together the Presbyterians, Independents, and Baptists of Nottinghamshire and Derbyshire and strongly advocated the union of all Dissenters in the country to work for the repeal of the Test Acts.[27]

It would probably be true to say that George Walker spoke the political philosophy of John Locke and in practical politics was a Foxite Whig. In this latter respect he was at one with most members of the Corporation of Nottingham, for whom Fox was both hero and patron. And Walker's was the voice of the local Establishment, politically radical but socially rather conservative. When praising the British Constitution for knowing no distinction of right, he had acknowledged the distinction of rank that it preserved. And his sermons on 'The Excellence and Blessedness of Charity' confirm this trend of thought. We should reconcile ourselves, he said, to the inequalities of human life, for these very inequalities seem to have been designed by God himself to give scope for human benevolence and to be a continual prompter to it. These arguments were to be heard many

[26] G. Walker, *The Dissenters' Plea* (1790), pp. 3, 19, 21; *Sermons*, op. cit., Vol. 2, p. 424; Memoir of the Rev. George Walker, op. cit., p. 126.

[27] *The Dissenters' Plea*, op. cit., pp. 3, 21; J. Tayler's Sermon, op. cit.; Memoir of the Rev. George Walker, op. cit., pp. 158-172; Minutes of High Pavement Vestry Meetings, 1777-1812, 4th May, 1787.

times in various forms through the nineteenth century from the opponents of social reform.[28]

This social conservatism is also in harmony with what is known about the economic ideas of Walker and the High Pavement Unitarians. Walker was himself a partner in Major Cartwright's cotton mill at Retford, and one of his essays on diverse subjects concerned the application of the steam-engine. Walker's interest in manufacture and his acceptance of Adam Smith economics probably helped to attract the great number of cotton manufacturers, such as Denison and Wakefield, who worshipped at High Pavement, and attention has been drawn to the influence of High Pavement Chapel in the economic development as well as the political control of Nottingham in the late eighteenth and early nineteenth centuries. The Whiggery and political radicalism of its members touched on social questions only when they concerned the general humanitarian causes such as the slave trade and slavery. They were essentially the product of the exclusion of Dissenters from full civil and political rights and as such could have no answer to many of the questions to be raised in the nineteenth century.[29]

A recent verdict on George Walker is that he kept Presbyterian influence high in local affairs at a time when the Evangelicals were taking over the religious lead. Almost alone of the religious communities in Nottingham the Presbyterians, or Unitarians as they were becoming, failed to increase in numbers during the religious revival of the early nineteenth century. An old member of the congregation later recalled how newcomers were put off by the frigid and distant manners that greeted them and how they seemed to be regarded more as intruders than anything else; there was no spirit of evangelism and no apparent wish to make converts. More important than this aloofness was the thorough antagonism between the beliefs and methods of the Evangelicals, with their emphasis on piety and the Scriptures, and the rationalism of the Unitarians, and it was the Evangelical approach that was making the appeal amongst Nottingham's growing numbers. Whereas during the last quarter of the eighteenth century twelve of the fifteen men to hold the office of Mayor had worshipped at

[28]Sermons, op. cit., Vol. 2, pp. 424, 14.
[29]S. D. Chapman, *The Early Factory Masters* (1967), pp. 104, 108, 188-9, 197; G. Walker, *Essays on Various Subjects* (1809).

High Pavement, during the first thirty-four years of the nine-teenth century six Evangelicals were Mayor for half of those years. Castle Gate Congregationalists and George Street Particular Baptists were fast undermining the paramountcy of High Pave-ment by the time of the 1833 Commission, though the power of the Unitarians remained disproportionately great. Attacks were still being made on the 'Arian Dissenting Body Corporate' in 1825, and 'King Wakefield', the leader of the Corporation Whigs before and after 1835, ensured High Pavement's continu-ing influence. In fact, the Nottingham Constitutional Club could report in 1833 that High Pavement still provided the town clerk, twenty other members of the livery, and four or five of the officers of the Corporation, though its entire congregation at this time was no more than a two-hundredth part of the town's population. It was believed to have been a sixth part at the beginning of the previous century.[30]

The political influence of Methodism and the later Evangelical Revival has always been of great interest to historians. In Notting-ham the Methodists outstripped all other Nonconformist groups and equalled the Anglicans in number by 1833, though, signific-antly for their political role, they refused throughout the period 1785-1835 to regard themselves as Dissenters. Under the leader-ship of Wesley himself the movement played politically a conservative role. Some Nottingham Methodists were con-cerned by the pro-Government line adopted by the leadership over the American War of Independence, and it is not surprising that in the years following Wesley's death Nottingham should have played such a prominent part in the events concerning the split of 1796, when the followers of Alexander Kilham broke away from the parent body over the question of Church govern-ment and formed the New Connexion. The division between the Wesleyan Methodists and the New Connexion Methodists in Nottingham is very clear in a political sense as well as in matters of church organisation. Not for the first time in Nottingham

[30]J. C. Weller, The Revival of Religion in Nottingham, 1780-1850, Nottingham University B.D. Thesis, 1957, p. 36; Carpenter, op. cit., p. 178; S. D. Chapman, 'The Evangelical Revival and Education in Nottingham', Transactions of the Thoroton Society, 1962; A Report of the Evidence given before the Commissioners, etc., printed for the Nottingham Constitutional Club, 1833, Appendix, p. 1; Address to the Citizens of Nottingham, Anon. (1825), p. 6; J. D. Chambers, Nottinghamshire in the Eighteenth Century (1932), p. 313.

affairs did a liberal, democratic approach to Church government help to produce political liberalism. A contemporary claim that the New Connexion included 'most of those that were of the Mercantile class' need not be taken too literally, for the 'mercantile class' were the backbone of all Nottingham's Nonconformist bodies.[31]

When Alexander Kilham died and was buried at Nottingham in 1797 a monument was erected in the New Connexion Chapel which described him as 'a zealous defender of the rights of the people against attempts to force on them a Priestly domination'. Indeed the whole of the New Methodist case against the Wesleyans contains as much political comment as anything. Their cause was 'the cause of the people', their enemy 'a priesthood bearing rule over the people, exercising an usurped and degrading tyranny, of which we have no other examples in modern times, nor any precedent since the dark ages of popery'. The authors of these sentiments could hardly fail to make a contribution to political radicalism, and, predictably, the New Connexion included Charles Sutton. An Evangelical convert from High Pavement's growing Unitarian outlook, under which he might have joined the great throng of High Pavement public figures who ran the Corporation, Sutton joined the Methodists in 1783, a body never represented on the old Corporation, and was one of the seceders with Kilham in 1796. His great influence came through the weekly newspaper, the *Nottingham Review*, which he began in 1808 and which he used for spreading his liberal political creed. Sutton remained largely apart from the Corporation oligarchy, probably because of his religious history and also because his political views were often too strong for the City Fathers. He showed what many considered to be an unnecessary sympathy with the Luddites in 1811–14 and his ideas on reform took in municipal a well as central government. His son Richard, who followed his father in religion and politics, used the *Review* to advocate manhood suffrage and annual parliaments. In 1832 he made an abortive attempt to secure election as a Junior Councillor, and it is indicative of the Suttons' separation from the Corporation oligarchy that Richard's chosen means of access was not

[31]For full discussions of the Evangelicals see Muriel Jaeger, *Before Victoria* (1956) and Ford K. Brown, *Fathers of the Victorians* (1961). *Nottingham Review*, 13th December, 1833; J. C. Weller, op. cit., p. 95; W. Salt, *Memorials of the Methodist New Connexion* (1827).

co-option into the Senior Council but election into the ranks of the opposition.[32]

The parent body, the Wesleyan Methodists, involved itself little in the political affairs of the town during this period, and what political influence the Wesleyans had was believed to be exercised on the conservative side. Refusing to recognise themselves as Dissenters, the Wesleyans did not co-operate with the Unitarians, Baptists, Independents, Quakers, and New Methodists in their campaigns against the Test Acts, and for disestablishment in 1834 and, being in many cases Anglican communicants, they had not the political grievances which turned the other groups to political radicalism. Their theology, too, placed them firmly on the conservative side. Gravener Henson, who was not without admiration for their work in education and other fields, was less content to observe that 'they invariably inculcate the doctrine of passive submission to events as happening according to the fore-knowledge of the deity; that man, in this world, is in a state of preparation for another, and that his only care and object ought to be submission and resignation to the will of heaven'. Their passive approach made them, in the eyes of Francis Ward, a political activist, 'an accursed set', proverbial among Dissenters for their loyalty. For the Tories they were the one non-Anglican group from whom they expected to receive support; they were also, according to the *Journal*, the honourable exception amongst non-conformists 'leagued in common band with the Papists'.[33]

There is no more characteristic figure of the Wesleyan Methodists in Nottingham than Mrs. Mary Tatham, whose daughter married Richard Oastler, and her diaries give clear indication of the Wesleyan attitude to the social and political problems of the day. During 1800 she was worried about the prosecution of the war and the scarcity and dearness of food; whilst the Unitarians were blaming these evils on the war and the government and agitating for changes, Mrs. Tatham saw the explanation in the wrath of God which hung over the nation and she called for the emergence of a Moses to avert the Almighty's anger. This is in line with the Rev. Joseph Beaumont's explanation of the

[32]Salt, op. cit., pp. 41, 136; J. T. Godfrey and J. Ward, *History of Friar Lane Baptist Church* (1903), p. 196.

[33]Henson, op. cit., p. 253; *Nottingham Review*, 23rd January, 1818; *Nottingham Journal*, 15th December, 1832, 23rd October, 1835.

K

depression and misery he witnessed in Nottingham in 1829 in terms of the nation's failure to learn righteousness. Again, in the year 1819, a time of the most intense depression in Nottingham, Mrs. Tatham lamented the spirit of the common people, condemned their abuse of liberty, and demanded its punishment. 'Disaffection and rebellion', she wrote, 'must have a scourge and be put under control'. Rightly or wrongly, the Wesleyan refused to seek the causes of distress around him and their remedy through political action. In the 30s, through the marriage of her daughter to Oastler, Mrs. Tatham had a unique opportunity to witness the movement for factory reform at close quarters; on December 27th, 1831, she wrote to her daughter that there seemed to be little interest in the question of child labour in Nottingham and district since the factories in the area were better conducted than those in the West Riding. She lamented this lack of interest, not because she shared Oastler's regret at the sufferings in the West Riding but because 'much of the defection in morals among the lower classes of society may be traced to this source in every place where the mill-system has been supported'.[34]

Other sects which expanded rapidly during the period of the Evangelical Revival were the Congregationalists and the Baptists, Particular and General. These three groups, unlike the Methodists, were all very active in political affairs. During the early decades of the nineteenth century they broke the monopoly of High Pavement Unitarianism in local affairs, and it was an oligarchical control of Baptists, Congregationalists, and Unitarians that the Corporation Commissioners found in Nottingham in 1833.

The Congregationalists, praised by Blackner for their liberality and charity to the poor, provided an outstanding leader in Joseph Gilbert, Minister of Friar Lane Independent Chapel from 1825, who was to be prominent during the Reform Bill controversies and other struggles. Wylie records that Gilbert, both by pen and in addresses, advocated the reformers' causes of the day, repeal of the Test and Corporation Acts, Catholic Emancipation, abolition of slavery, free trade, and 'many other great and beneficial measures'. The *Journal* believed Gilbert to be a prime source of sedition in the town, a fair testimony to his success. The editor

[34]Rev. J. Beaumont, *Memoirs of Mrs. Mary Tatham* (1838), pp. 127, 220, 324-5; J. Beaumont, *Life of the Rev. Joseph Beaumont, M.D.* (1856), p. 105.

was to recall how he had in 1831 condemned 'the factious oligarchy' who opposed Parliamentary reform, and seconded a
resolution to stop supply until the Bill became law, conduct
which the *Journal* thought unbecoming in a Minister of religion,
whose duty was to teach respect for the constituted authorities.
Clearly Gilbert saw his functions otherwise. Members of the
Independent Congregation were also active in local politics, and
it is not without symbolic significance that in October, 1831,
Mayor Wilson had to hasten from Castle Gate Congregational
Chapel to deal with the multitude assembling in the Market
Place after the ill news had been received concerning the fate of
the Reform Bill in the Lords.[35]

The Baptists also provided a goodly share of Corporation
dignitaries and men prominent in the political life of Nottingham.
In the 1780s they acted in close co-operation with the Independents and Presbyterians in the organising of campaigns against
the Test and Corporation Acts. Friar Lane Particular Baptists
must have exercised a very powerful influence through the public
figures in their ranks. Alderman Joseph Oldknow, a Particular
Baptist, was Mayor of Nottingham in 1792 and 1799, whilst his
son, Octavius, held that office in 1822 and 1829, before serving
on the new council for six years after 1835. It was Octavius
Oldknow who presided over the public meeting in 1830 at which
the citizens of Nottingham expressed their admiration for the
revolutionary enterprises of their brother Frenchmen in that year.
Alderman John Barber, three times Mayor of Nottingham in
the early nineteenth century, had as a member of Friar Lane taken
upon himself the task of raising funds for a new Baptist Chapel in
George Street, where he was to serve as Deacon and which was
to be one of the chapels of undue influence named by the Commissioners. Another well-known representative of Friar Lane in
public life was Absolem Barnett, a former hosier who became
St. Mary's Overseer in 1819 and who was to give detailed evidence
and informed recommendations to successive government commissions on working class conditions, the state of housing, and
especially the operation of the Poor Laws in Nottingham. And
the continued importance of the Evangelicals inside Nottingham

[35]Blackner, op. cit., p. 107; W. H. Wylie, op. cit., p. 201; *Nottingham Journal*, 14th
March, 1834; A. R. Henderson, *History of Castle Gate Congregational Church, Nottingham*
(1905), p. 174.

public life and in the Corporation was characterised by the career of Baptist William Felkin, Nottingham's leading citizen during the middle years of the nineteenth century, businessman, administrator, and historian.[36]

The tradesmen, hosiers, lace-manufacturers, and cotton spinners who acquired power in Nottingham during the eighteenth century patronised or even formed their own religious establishments outside the Anglican Church, which continued to look to the aristocratic patrons, Newcastle or Middleton, whose political power inside Nottingham the newly-rich were gradually usurping. The social tensions created by new wealth and influence are probably enough to explain the dominance of Nonconformity in Nottingham as it became a commercial and industrial centre without any need to enter deeper into the connection between Protestantism and capitalism. The implications of this dominance of religious nonconformity for the politics of Nottingham were very great. The ruling classes were associated politically with the Whigs rather than the Tories, for religion was one of the few issues which gave party labels any meaning in the eighteenth century, and their political campaigns were certain to be concerned with religious issues such as the Test Acts, Church Rates, disestablishment, even Catholic Emancipation; 'Civil and religious liberty' was their twin programme. They were never noticeably anti-monarchy, though anti-aristocracy, and their loyalty to the person of the monarch survived the French Revolution and the French Wars, even if it was to be shaken somewhat by the Reform Bill crises. During the French Wars, the threat to Nottingham's economic interests and the strength of the Unitarians ensured that Nottingham Corporation remained anti-government, pro-reform, and Foxite-Whig, which position was about the limit of its political radicalism.

Religious nonconformity gave direction to political radicalism in Nottingham but it also kept it within certain bounds. The High Pavement Unitarians, though champions of religious and civil liberty, accepted the need for a social hierarchy, though one to be ascended by successful business enterprise rather than one fixed by birth and a natural order of things. The influence of the Unitarians remained strong in Nottingham in spite of the

[36]J. T. Godfrey and J. Ward, op. cit., pp. 207, 170-1, 175-6; *Nottingham Review*, 27th August, 1830.

Evangelical Revival, and the latter, even with its greater contact with the masses, failed to graft onto the already thriving stock of nonconformist radicalism any new life of social reform. The Evangelicals, with their emphasis on prayer and personal salvation of the individual soul, were concerned with moral reform. In economics they were *laissez-faire* Liberals and in politics Utilitarians. They accepted Chadwick and the 1834 Poor Law and became the New Establishment. Nonconformity, a radical force as long as the aristocracy and Church of England were the enemies, became a conservative one when the immediate political reforms had been achieved. The eminently respectable manufacturers and tradesmen who controlled the Corporation and the forces of law and order in Nottingham patronised reform and put it on a firm and respectable footing, but they also put a limit to its scope. The hand of friendship managed also to hold in check and ensure that reforming energies were directed only towards the removal of certain political abuses. Such distinguished patronage was bound to leave many social and economic problems untouched. Significantly, it was the Tories and Anglican parsons who took the lead on both factory reform and agitation against the new Poor Law in Nottingham in the 1830s. This helps to explain why the political movement in Nottingham never came together in this period with the great protest movements of the framework-knitters, which were conducted largely on an industrial basis and only occasionally overlapped into politics. Chartism, which did bring the two together, was not a Corporation cause.

And so the role of the Corporation and its influence on political radicalism becomes clear. Corporation leadership constituted both the strength and weakness of radicalism in Nottingham. Initially it strengthened the radical movement, which was itself a source of strength to the Corporation in giving it leadership, even control, of any possible 'popular' movement. The Vicar of Arnold might condemn public meetings on the grounds that the inhabitants of his village were not sufficiently intelligent for such assemblies, but the Corporation of Nottingham never underestimated their value, if well organised. Through the French Revolution period 'Jacobinism' never became a popular force but always remained under the control and patronage of the Corporation. But Corporation radicalism was also an incentive to more thorough-going radicals. When the Luddites began to break stocking-frames it served the Whigs right, said the Rev. J. T. Becher, for their own pernicious doctrines were now being thrown back at them. And at the end of the war a weak revolutionary radicalism did emerge for a short time beyond the control of the Corporation and strongly opposed by local as well as central authorities. The history of political radicalism in Nottingham during this period is the history of an attempt made by a reforming Corporation to lead and give expression to radical movements and to resist any attempts of more thorough-going reformers to take over. To a very large extent the Corporation was successful. It was threatened only at odd moments; Luddism, Pentrich, and the Reform Bill Riots were its crisis points, but it was generally successful in preventing the emergence of any popular radical front. This came later after the death of the old Corporation and in the time of Chartism.[37]

---

[37] R. W. King and J. Russell, *A History of Arnold* (1913), p. 122; Ne.C. 4919b, J. T. Becher to Newcastle and H.O., 12th February, 1812.

8

THE PARLIAMENTARY BOROUGH

In pre-1832 Parliaments, Nottingham was a large borough with an extensive popular franchise. Voting rights rested in part with the burgesses, or freemen, of the borough, an open group which could be entered by serving an apprenticeship in the town, and this permitted the framework-knitters, the main element in Nottingham's working class, to acquire the vote through serving their trade. In addition, the vote was also possessed by the 40/- freeholders, since Nottingham was 'the town and county of the town of Nottingham'. The electorate was then mainly a mixture of property-owners and industrial workers, supplemented by any who became burgesses by other means, gift, purchase, or inheritance, though the heirs to the rights would also, in most cases, be framework-knitters. The stockingers were the largest single component group, constituting a half to two-thirds of the people voting on any single occasion. In short elections as few as 700 might decide the issue. In long ones, when a candidate hesitated to concede defeat, as many as 4,000 might vote. Control of such a seat would not fall easily into any hands, and the right to sit as its representative would be a prize of some value.[1]

In the year 1785 Nottingham was far from being the pocket-borough under the control of the Whig Corporation that it was to become after 1818. The Corporation as such had little concept of the power and influence it could wield in determining the nature of the town's Parliamentary representation, and the closing decades of the eighteenth century must later have seemed, in retrospect, times of Corporate innocence and goodwill. There appears to have been bilateral agreement between the Whigs and the Tories to share the town's representation, and when Captain

[1]See Poll Books for the period.

William Johnston was nominated by the Tories in 1790 to try to oust Robert Smith, the sitting Whig, this move was widely frowned upon and proved unsuccessful. People chose to cast one Whig and one Tory vote, Johnston came a very poor third, and Smith and Daniel Parker Coke continued to share the representation of the town as they had done for a decade. Until 1818 it was always possible for the well-known and well-liked figure to build up something of a bi-partisan following. Coke, for instance, a Tory, currently popular in 1785 because of his resistance to Pitt's commercial proposals concerning Ireland, found himself listed along with 1688, King William, and Charles James Fox, amongst the toasts drunk by a meeting of supporters of 'freedom of election'. In 1812 John Smith, a Member since 1806, survived two conversions, from his early Whiggery to French War Toryism and back again to a Whig outlook, to emerge comfortably at the top of the poll in 1812 on Whig and Tory votes. Similarly, the Whig, Joseph Birch, was believed in 1818 to have had the support of moderate Tories on the strength of his being well-known to them, to put him at the head of the poll.[2]

It is a false account which portrays Nottingham Corporation at work to secure the election of suitable men as early as 1753 and arriving at a state of such dominance by the end of the century that there was only a sprinkling of Tories left to upset the Whig harmony. Until 1796 the Tories had one of the two Members. In that year they gained them both. Smith defected to the Tories as a result of the French Revolution and in time to receive a peerage from Pitt, and the Whigs found themselves without a Member, which state of affairs lasted until 1812. In 1797, when Smith moved to the House of Lords as Lord Carrington, Sir John Borlasse Warren, a Tory and a successful naval figure, was returned unopposed.[3]

It was in 1802 that Whig members of the Corporation first used to any great effect the power which their official positions gave them. The Parliamentary Committee chosen to try the subsequent election petition found that the returning officer and magistrates had been very negligent in the performance of their duties, that

[2]Blackner, op. cit., p. 300; Sutton, op. cit., p. 185; Nottingham Journal, 26th June, 1790, 26th March, 1785; Sutton's Poll Book for 1818, p. IV.

[3]D. Gray, Nottingham through 500 Years (1960), pp. 117, 141; Nottingham Journal, 11th November, 1797; Sutton, op. cit., p. 232.

the poll had been improperly prolonged whilst the Whigs searched for a candidate, and that the town authorities had given no protection to Tory candidate Coke and his supporters against the violence of their opponents, concluding that without Parliamentary interference in the affairs of the borough there could be no reasonable hope of a free election in the future. This interference came in the shape of a Bill extending the jurisdiction of the county magistrates to Nottingham itself, a Bill supported by Coke and hotly opposed by the Corporation, which was now clearly committed to continuing its opposition to Coke to clear itself of the findings of the Parliamentary Committee and to repay Coke for the insulting Bill for which he was held responsible. At the time of the election petition, the young poet, Henry Kirke White, who was training in the solicitors' office of Coldham and Enfield, one the present incumbent, the other his successor as Town Clerk of Nottingham, wrote that his masters were working day and night in preparing the defence of Birch, the Whig candidate. A complete and unashamed entry of the Corporation into electoral politics had now taken place. At the 1803 election a resolution was passed in Common Hall declaring Corporation support for Birch, the Whig candidate, and informing burgesses that Coke could not be supported without violence to the conscience in view of the violation of his burgess oath involved in the late Bill. On Coke's side the battle was joined enthusiastically. The Corporation were charged with every conceivable abuse of their authority, charges investigated in 1833, and Coke swore his resolution to bring these trustees to account for their false stewardship. In this way the Corporation were brought into the forefront of Parliamentary contests and there they remained. In 1806 they circularised all Corporation tenants and holders of leases, urging them to vote for the Whig nominee, and they offered homes to anyone evicted by a Tory landlord for voting Whig, yet despite their strong campaigning the Tories won both seats. It is clear that the Corporation had not yet realised how its power could be used to turn defeat into certain electoral victory.[4]

[4]*Report of the Select Committee, 1803, to try the petitions on the Nottingham Election of 1802,* 1803 (43 Geo. III) C45. 'An Act for the more effectually preserving the peace and securing the freedom of election in the town of Nottingham and county of the said town'; MSS. relating to the County of Nottingham in the possession of Mr. James Ward, p. 164; *Nottingham Journal*, 14th, 21st May, 1803; Corporation Hall Books, 1896/7, p. 19, 3rd November, 1806.

The fusion of Whig and Corporation interests was clearly seen at the start of 1809 when a Whig candidate, John Wheatley, was chosen by 'a select meeting of the Corporation and Whig interest', and from this time onwards Whig candidates were invariably thought to represent the Corporation. With the return of John Smith to the Whig fold and the retirement of Coke in 1812, there was a strong danger, the Tories believed, of giving the Corporation a second Member. Ideas of divided representation, in practice suspended to the advantage of the Tories under the impact of the French Revolution, were not now acceptable to the Whigs. For the first time for many years, wrote Bailey, the Whigs held both seats in 1812, and the large manufacturing town was being turned, in the eyes of the Tories, into a close borough at the disposal of the Corporation. The double triumph of 1812 in fact occurred as much by Tory ineptitude and the initiative of John Blackner and some enterprising friends as by Corporation design, but in 1817 the Corporation took the decisive step in establishing its own control.[5]

In that year it totally abandoned any last remaining pretence to neutrality in Parliamentary contests and perpetrated what the Corporation Commissioners were to call 'so gross a perversion' of its power, the creation of honorary burgesses for electoral purposes. There had been some few complaints about the creation of non-resident burgesses in 1802 and these had become more common at the 1812 election. Coldham, the Town Clerk, did not bother to deny the charges and simply pointed out that the Corporation was acting within its rights to bestow honours upon whomsoever it pleased. In 1817 the number of such creations began to rise steeply and in 1819-21 there were almost 600 compared with the usual handful per year. One M.P. alleged, in 1826, that Nottingham had made over 1,200 freemen unconnected with the place; Parliament was also informed that the town of Leicester had contributed many non-resident voters to Nottingham's Whig ranks just as the town of Nottingham had helped to swell the Tory ranks controlled by the Corporation of Leicester. These creations were within the powers of the Corporation but they were undertaken, and this was not denied, in order to bolster

[5]*Nottingham Journal*, 7th January, 1809; Collection of Addresses etc. concerning the Election of 1812, p. 23; Bailey, op. cit., p. 259; *Nottingham Journal*, 31st October, 7th November, 1812.

up the Whig vote. It was claimed that it was done to counteract the devious schemes being carried out on the Tory side to produce 'mushroom freeholds', begun as early as 1812. Clubs had been established to erect buildings and create freeholds in the names of tenants of the local aristocracy. Once established as voters, the tenants were recalled to their farms and the properties were re-let. In this way, it was said, the number of freeholders had risen from 383 to 534 in the period 1818-20, and the Corporation had acted in order to preserve the 'independence' of the town. The Whigs had established their building clubs too, but these contributed little in comparison with the Corporation, which could manufacture votes at will. And the Corporation seems to have succeeded well. The *Journal* claimed that out of 527 honorary burgesses who had voted in 1826, all but ten or twelve had voted against the Tories. One national newspaper believed that the Corporation achieved its success by choosing its nominees particularly from the members of Unitarian congregations in neighbouring towns. Whatever the principles of choice, the Corporation succeeded in turning an ultra-marginal seat, where in 1818, even with the spurious creations under way, the Whigs could muster a majority of only eighteen, into a seat which the Tories did not bother to contest, and this in the space of twelve years. Compared with this misapplication of power, other techniques employed by the Corporation to influence elections were insignificant, though the Municipal Corporation Commissioners were also regaled with dark stories of Corporation members who had given bribes indirectly through agents known to witnesses.[6]

The war of the honorary burgesses against the mushroom freeholders was the struggle, at a technical level, between the Nonconformist businessmen and tradesmen who controlled Nottingham and their enemies, the Anglicans and Tories, who were politically excluded inside the town and looked to the local gentry and aristocracy who had themselves been gradually pushed out of influence during the second half of the eighteenth

[6]*Report of Commission on State of Municipal Corporations*, 1835, XIII, Appendix to First Report, pp. 1993, 2005; *Nottingham Journal*, 21st May, 1803, 24th, 31st October, 1812; Parl. Debs., Vol. 93, 1209-1217; A. T. Patterson, *Radical Leicester* (1954) pp. 146, 154; *Nottingham Journal*, 4th October, 1st November, 1833; W. H. Wylie, op. cit., p. 317; *The Record*, quoted in *Nottingham Journal*, 15th December, 1832.

century and cast in the role of villains, wishing to take over the town and destroy its independence. Namier's analysis of Nottingham politics in the 1750s shows the Duke of Newcastle in the position of Recorder of Nottingham and he and Lord Middleton aspiring to lead respectively the Whigs and the Tories of the town, contesting supremacy with each other. But even at this time the noble lords could never hope for control, rather than influence, over the affairs of the town. As Nottingham's population and industries grew and its leaders became wealthy hosiers, cotton manufacturers, or substantial tradesmen, men who had the wealth and influence locally to give them near parity with the old county families, so did Nottingham cease to be a centre of aristocratic society and under aristocratic patronage. The fine eighteenth-century houses were divided up and made to take several families, and Nottingham became an industrial community, which the aristocrats visited only on special occasions and over which they came to have less and less influence. The wealthy rulers of Nottingham were Dissenters in religion and in politics they remained Whig-Radical, even through the period of the French Revolution, when the old Whig patrons, the Dukes of Newcastle, were moving over to the other side. Their choice of Lord Holland as Recorder of Nottingham on the death of the Duke of Portland in 1809 was to be a symbolic rejection of the local aristocrats and an assertion of the right to choose whom they pleased.[7]

In these circumstances, Coke's Bill of 1803, throwing open the town to the jurisdiction of the county magistrates, was a bitter blow. The Bill had come from the Tories, their rivals inside the town, men much better disposed to the pretensions of the local aristocracy, and power and influence were now being restored to the county aristocrats through their stooges, the county magistrates, at a time when the town was feeling itself independent of the county. In fact the county magistrates did not interfere much in the life of the town, and the great praise won by the town magistrates for their handling of Luddism, contrasting with the condemnation given to the county magistrates, went far towards eliminating the impression of 1802-3 that the town was not fit to look after itself. At the same time as the town magistrates were winning national approval, the town for the first time secured in

[7] L. B. Namier, *Structure of Politics at the Accession of George III* (1957 edit.), pp. 91-4; Sutton, op. cit., p. 287.

1812 two Whig Members of Parliament in a result always re-called as 'the victory for independence'.

It is impossible to say how resentful neighbouring peers were at their exclusion and how concerned they were to restore their former position. There was no prospect of breaking Corporation control, and a recent study of the 4th Duke of Newcastle, the Corporation's favourite bogey, has concluded that he had no serious pretensions or ambitions to exert influence there and that he went no further than acting as patron of the local Tory associations such as the Pitt Club. Tory candidates in the borough were almost certainly chosen with Newcastle's blessing, but the latter had neither the prospect nor the hope of a prominent voice in borough affairs. A recent impression of Nottingham in the early nineteenth century as a town under the thumb of the local aristocracy is totally mistaken.[8]

The Duke of Newcastle did, of course, serve an admirable purpose for the local Whigs as permanent whipping-boy. Thomas Wakefield could tell the election crowds in 1826 that the Nottingham Whigs had rescued the town earlier from the arbitrary yoke of a county aristocracy and they would, by the blessing of God, do the same again, but Wakefield must have known that the danger was long since past. With the Duke as their public enemy, the Corporation Whigs could act the part of popular egalitarians, which they were not. They also secured a moral advantage over the Nottingham Tories, who always found it necessary to state that their conduct was not being influenced by the Duke of Newcastle, as in the anti-reform petition of 1831, and that they were as much in favour of an independent Notting-ham as the Whigs were.[9]

The Whig image of an independent Nottingham proved somewhat difficult to realise in terms of Members of Parliament. It is ironical that control of the representation of the town, which came to the Corporation after the Napoleonic Wars, meant in practice the virtual abandonment of the custom of having local men to speak for the interests of Nottingham. The firmer Corporation control became and the greater their ability to assert independence, the more representation passed into outside

[8]J. M. Golby, 'The Political and Electoral Influence of the 4th Duke of Newcastle', p. 131, M.A. thesis, University of Nottingham, 1961; J. Prest, op. cit., pp. 138-9.

[9]Nottingham Review, 9th June, 1826; Nottingham Journal, 1st October, 1831.

hands. Of the ten men who represented Nottingham in the period 1785-1835, all were rather curiously cast to portray the characteristics that its leaders seemed to want to show. Coke, 1780-1812, a Derby lawyer, was a local man with good local knowledge and very ready to help his constituents and consult their views, but he was a Tory. Robert Smith, 1779-97, and John Smith, 1806-18, were members of a local banking firm, and were both men of independent views, so much so that, though nominally Whigs, they had defected to the Tories and allied with Coke during the Revolutionary and Napoleonic Wars, later returning to the Whig side. Sir John Borlase Warren, 1797-1806, was wrong in every respect; he was a country gentleman, a naval man, and a Tory. Lord Rancliffe, 1812-20, 1826-30, was a country gentleman and an Irish peer, though his views were radical enough, for he ended up as a supporter of O'Connor. Joseph Birch, 1818-30, a Liverpool merchant from Preston, had the right political views, but he was totally unconnected with Nottingham until first brought in as a candidate in 1802. Thomas Denman, 1820-26, 1830-32, was a lawyer of national standing, a moderate Whig, whose local connection was his defence of the Pentrich rebels in 1817 and who welcomed the prestige that a large, populous borough gave its member.

The last three in the period had not the least connection with Nottingham until introduced there to be its Members of Parliament. After their long struggle to free themselves from Tory members and to escape the disturbing effects of the French Revolution on the Smith family, the Nottingham Whigs found themselves, by 1830, under the need to bring in as candidate General Ferguson, a Scottish Member with no local claims, reputedly disowned by his own borough. In 1832 they accepted Lord Duncannon, an Irish peer who was recommended to them following an application to the Prime Minister for a suitable candidate. This produced a not unmerited charge of 'political coquetry between two noble Lords and the electors of Nottingham', and when Ferguson was replaced, following promotion, in 1834, by John Cam Hobhouse, a further government nominee, the local Radicals could hold back no further and put up a candidate against him.[10]

---

[10]*Nottingham Journal*, 31st July, 1830, 1st December, 1832, and Poll Books for 1830.

And so the period closes with the Nottingham Whigs, who had proudly championed the town's independence against outside interference, selling out to the government and admitting into the town's representation men without the local specialised interests and knowledge which had so long been deemed essential. It is something of a reflection on the Corporation oligarchy and Whig businessmen that outside the Smith family they could find no one within their own ranks of sufficient stature to take on the responsibility of Member of Parliament for the town. Not surprisingly, this development caused the Tories to revive a demand, which they claimed as a right, to share the representation of Nottingham with the Whigs. Ignoring the fact that the unscrupulous manipulation of the right to create burgesses had shown the Corporation totally unwilling to compromise on control, they revived the demand, reiterated at intervals since they had been edged out in 1812, for a resumption of their natural right arising from the respectability and number of their members. The right was denied and no local Tory candidate could be found to attempt to enforce it, and Nottingham continued to be represented by outsiders whose political views were in general accord with those of the Whig Corporation and who were glad enough to have the chance to represent a large and important borough.[11]

There had always been evidence that some were not willing to accept the reforming ideas of the Nottingham Whig leaders as the limit of their ambitions. Back in 1780 Major Cartwright had contested Nottingham as a Radical, receiving 149 votes, against 341 for the Tory and 569 for the official Whig candidate. His programme had been almost exclusively one of Parliamentary reform, the need to cut down government opportunities for bribery and corruption, the abolition of the small boroughs, and the need for annual Parliaments. He had remained vague on the franchise issue, and his radicalism was in no way egalitarian. He was concerned purely with the reform of the political system and there was no radical social or economic programme attached to his political one. Indeed, his country gentry background and speculations as a mill-owner made this highly improbable.[12]

[11]*Nottingham Journal*, 22nd September, 1832.

[12]F. D. Cartwright, *Life and Correspondence of Major Cartwright*, Vol. 1 (1826), pp. 121-34; Sutton, op. cit., p. 142; S. D. Chapman, 'The Midlands Cotton and Worsted Spinning Industry, 1769-1800', p. 266, Ph.D. Thesis, University of London, 1966.

Dr. Peter Crompton, of Derby, who had almost risked his life by opposing the war-party in 1796 as the only man who could be found willing to stand, was, by the time of his next candidature in 1807, employing his fire indiscriminately against Whigs and Tories alike. He stood, according to Blackner, 'on the pure principles of electioneering', which meant that he was not prepared to spend money on buying votes and bribing people. Blackner commented, with no little irony, that on the existing system of representation and in a town with more than 1,000 outvoters such a system could not possibly be attended with success; these were not the ways of the Nottingham Whigs. At the 1812 election Crompton again expressed his dislike of both Whigs and Tories, the latter for their principles of passive obedience and non-resistance, the former, in spite of their admirable principles, for their support in practice of standing armies, their taxes, their corruption, and the wicked Septennial Act, still a grievance a hundred years after its passage. At the same time, Robert Denison, a former cotton-manufacturer, said that he found the conduct of the Whigs in power most detestable in spite of his admiration for them out of office. He launched a devastating attack on the House of Lords, demanding that the 56 members who shared an income of £250,000 per annum from the government should hand over their money to the starving poor, an idea not likely to be well received inside the Corporation. He also attacked the distribution of wealth and places amongst the Commons, and, like Crompton, felt no great faith in the Whigs to reform this situation. The following week the breach in the Whigs was confirmed when Crompton declared that he would be a traitor if he cast a vote for John Smith, who on two occasions had combined with Coke and the Tories in support of the war. Again, the complaints of Crompton and Denison, like those of Cartwright earlier, were little concerned with social or economic ideas. They attacked the Whigs for not being good Whigs, for their proneness to corrupting influences, their inconsistencies, and their weakness in pursuing the causes in which they claimed to believe. Cartwright, returning to Nottingham at the end of 1811 at the height of the Luddite troubles, believed the Corporation Whigs to be a half-hearted, spineless body of men since the departure of the Rev. George Walker from Nottingham in 1798.[13]

[13]Sutton, op. cit., p. 225; Blackner, op. cit., pp. 300, 302; *Nottingham Review*, 9th, 16th October, 1812; F. D. Cartwright, op. cit., Vol. 2, p. 19.

The feeling that there were in practice few basic differences between Whigs and Tories produced an independent candidature from Thomas Bailey, the historian, in 1830. Believing that the town's representation had become 'reduced to the chance of a scramble among adventurers', he offered himself as 'a decided and determined Whig according to the original intentions of that term'. His opposition was primarily to Ferguson, who, as a military man, a complete stranger to the town and the habits of commercial life, seemed to him totally unsuited to represent Nottingham. An ardent supporter of Parliament's reform and opponent of contemporary corruption, he also condemned the Corporation of Nottingham. His attack on Corporation abuses caused great indignation inside that body, to be increased when he later gave evidence before the Corporation Commissioners, and won him the support of many Tories. But without the Corporation he was bound to fail. Only reform which left the Corporation unreformed was likely to have official support.[14]

Yet the greatest manifestation of non-Tory discontent was still to come. John Cam Hobhouse, coming to Nottingham in July, 1834, was described as 'the rejected of Westminster, invited by the Corporation without consulting the electors of Nottingham'. When George Gill proposed a rival candidate, William Eagle, a Norfolk barrister, he told how for thirty-five years he had fought 'battles for freedom' alongside the Corporation and how painful his course of action was to him. Benjamin Boothby, seconding Eagle, said that the time had come to show whether they were real or sham reformers; Hobhouse, as the First Commissioner of Woods and Forests, a choice sinecure, and supporter of Irish Coercion Bills and other measures of government betrayal, was guilty of the 'grossest acts of political apostasy of any public man of the day'. Against Hobhouse Eagle offered the secret ballot, complete abolition of pensions and sinecures, shorter Parliaments, a free press, reduction of the standing army, repeal of the Corn Laws, and the abolition of tithes, the malt-tax, and military flogging, to which the *Review* mildly added that the Radicals had for some time been dissatisfied with the slow progress made by the government towards reform.[15]

Though Eagle received only a quarter of the votes cast, this

14*Nottingham Review*, 30th July, 1830; Poll Book, 1830.
15*Nottingham Review*, 25th July, 1834.

L

was more than 500 votes. The way seemed now open for a new alignment of forces in Nottingham, for the traditional Whig-Radical alliance had collapsed. Though the emphasis during the actual election campaign was on political questions, the need for more radical political reform and the behaviour of the Corporation, the men who backed Eagle during the election, former members of the Political Union and future Chartists, were broadening the scope of their thoughts and activities. Radicalism was no longer simply the impatience of gentleman or manufacturer with official leadership on reform policies, but an outlook geared more to the needs and aspirations of the working-classes. What the Radicals had to beware of was that they did not become simply rallying points for anti-Whig Tories rather than for people who really shared their sentiments, for both in 1830 and 1834 many local Tories were believed to have voted Radical, even been urged to do so by their leaders. And this initially unholy association was to be part of a take-over bid, by the Tories, of the social policies which were emerging as part of the new radicalism.[16]

It would be tedious to list the elections of the period 1785-1835 and to note the many issues on which each was fought. The Whig case was mostly predictable and varied only according to the pressure of national events which forced particular points into prominence. Elections at the end of the eighteenth century were dominated by the issue of the French Wars, on which the Corporation took a strong line of opposition. Political and humanitarian reform, reform of Parliament, penal reform, and the campaigns for the abolition of the slave-trade and slavery and for full religious liberty all passed temporarily into the background as the Nottingham Whigs concentrated on exposing the evil economic consequences of the French Wars. Pressure for peace and demands for government economies dominated the early campaigns of the nineteenth century. After the war, opposition to the Corn Laws, a symbol of aristocratic government, and a growing demand for Parliamentary reform became important. Traditional Whig causes, opposition to standing armies, defence of Habeas Corpus, freedom of press and assembly, also featured in the period 1815-20. In the 20s Catholic Emancipation and repeal of the Test and

[16]R. A. Church, op. cit., p. 141, wrongly suggests that the alliance between Whigs and Radicals was never disturbed between 1818 and the Chartist era; Poll Books, 1830; *Nottingham Review*, 25th July, 1834.

Corporation Acts were causes successfully pursued; Parliamentary reform and free trade in corn remained to be achieved. These causes represented Corporation orthodoxy through this period and in so far as Parliamentary elections represented contests between rival ideologies, they constituted the ideology of the Whig/Corporation party.

There were, of course, other factors in the elections. The most characteristic feature of any Nottingham election, Parliamentary or local, was the discussion of enclosure of the common lands around the outskirts of the town. This issue was not introduced for the purpose of discussing the merits of enclosure and the benefits it might bring the town but always for the purpose of smearing opponents. Ever since the notorious Council election of 1787, no candidate dared to be associated with the idea and each one dreaded that his opponent would manage so to associate him. The best example of the role of the enclosure issue was the 1806 election. Coke's running-mate, John Smith, had a brother who had been indiscreet enough to sign a declaration in support of enclosing the common lands. This caused Smith to be at the centre of a passionate storm such as this question could always arouse. The brother withdrew his name, but the damage had been done; the Smith family, it was alleged, stood to gain £10,000 from enclosure and this was the main motive behind their campaign. Smith got himself elected because his supporters were able to cast an almost equal amount of doubt upon the intentions of the Corporation and, therefore, the integrity of their candidate. The preoccupation of both sides with dissociating themselves from enclosure, which was never even considered on its merits, caused them to omit almost totally other, more real, issues which might have been put to the electorate. And enclosure remained the perennial bogey with which to frighten the burgess voters, certainly until the Municipal Corporations Act. It is ironical that the Whigs, in winning eventually the battle of abuse and being accepted as the anti-enclosure party, achieved their popular appeal through the most disastrous policy-decision that the town's governors ever took.[17]

It would be a mistake to expect to find much social content

[17]Sutton, op. cit., p. 168; J. D. Chambers, *Modern Nottingham in the Making* (1945), p. 17; *The Paper War during the late contested (1806) Election at Nottingham*, pp. 3, 8, 10, 15 25-6, 32, 41-4, 47.

and precise economic policies in the statements and schemes of the Nottingham Whigs, though they often hinted at them. One of the most consistent themes on the Whig side was that they, as champions of civil and religious liberty, were the representatives of the little man, struggling to be independent of the oppressive rule of squire or parson, the poor, struggling to remain un-corrupted by the rich or simply down-trodden by them, and the working class of electors, oppressed, presumably, by an employing class who were Tory. The claims and accomplishments of Joseph Birch and Lord Rancliffe illustrate the 'working class' theme in Whig propaganda.

On the day of his nomination in 1803 Birch said that the forth-coming election was nothing more than a contest between the rich and the poor. He and some of his supporters went to great lengths to emphasise this aspect of their case, and the term 'working class' cropped up frequently in their propaganda. Birch allowed himself to be proposed and seconded by workmen, and one apprehensive supporter noted this 'dangerous activity on the part of the labouring class of the community' as a frightful omen. The language on the Whig side was that of class-struggle, if not of class war. It was a question, the voters were told, of whether rich men or poor men should weigh down the scale, for the whole mass of the aristocracy was arrayed against them. Coke was the poor man's foe, and the cause of Birch was that of the working class of electors.[18]

There are, however, certain reasons for doubting the reality of this presentation. The City Fathers, for instance, propertied and prosperous, seem cast in a strange role and appear to be fighting on the wrong side, for the Corporation made no secret of its support for Birch. Coke, the poor man's foe, was to receive official support from the framework-knitters in 1806, and in 1812 was to be their staunchest ally. Nor was Birch's election programme designed to appeal primarily to the working classes. Abstract concepts of freedom and liberty were no substitute for encourag-ing words on wages, poor relief, cost of living, or opposition to the Combination Laws, yet social questions had no place in Birch's appeal. And if this were really the class struggle that Birch

[18] *The Paper War carried on at the Nottingham Election, 1803*, p. 252; Asa Briggs, 'The Language of Class in Early 19th Century England', p. 52, in *Essays in Labour History* (1960); *Paper War, 1803*, op. cit., pp. 267, 96, 109, 271, 274.

said it was, and if he really were the champion of the working classes, some evidence to support these claims should have appeared in the polling statistics. The framework-knitters, who should have been particularly susceptible to Birch's argument, tended to support him; 615 voted for him, yet 454 voted for his opponent, a sizable minority. And if Birch's predictions were to be borne out, the hosiers should have lined up solidly against the workmen; in fact, 58 hosiers voted for Coke whereas 67 voted for Birch. The class-struggle, described by Birch, had no relevance to the outcome of the 1803 election or to his later career. When he eventually became Member for Nottingham in 1818 he served in Parliament as an orthodox, well behaved, reforming Whig.[19]

Lord Rancliffe, who became one of Nottingham's M.P.s in 1812, always delighted in acting the part of champion of the oppressed poor. In that year the Nottingham Whigs, with characteristic lack of foresight, for they had earlier been caught unprepared in 1802, had no one ready to stand with John Smith when the election came. What happened then, according to Blackner, was that some eight or ten 'common working men', one a returned convict, meeting together at the Golden Fleece, decided to approach Lord Rancliffe, of Bunny Hall, seven miles out from Nottingham on the Loughborough road. These men, of whom Blackner himself was probably one, clubbed together so that three of the number could take a post-chaise and deliver a personal invitation to Rancliffe. This incident has been adjudged of great importance in marking the first effective entry of working men into local politics. The story of Rancliffe's appearance was politically of great value. Rancliffe himself never tired of referring to the humble men at whose appeal he had come forward, 'called forth by the voice of the poor'. Yet the episode's importance has probably been overrated. If Rancliffe enjoyed his pose as the man of the workmen rather than the creature of the Corporation, he nonetheless shared the latter's views, sponsored their causes, and joined in their rallies. His programme remained unexceptional and nothing came of his much-vaunted reliance on the support of the poor working men. He championed no social programme on their behalf, and when unemployed framework-knitters applied to their two M.P.s in 1828 they never even received an answer from Lord Rancliffe. In later years he dabbled in Chartism,

[19]*Paper War, 1806*, p. 35; Poll Book, 1803.

but in his years as M.P. he was ineffective, enabling the *Journal* to dismiss him as a rake, who divided his time between Newmarket and Paris.[20]

In fact neither Birch nor Rancliffe nor any other Whig candidate or M.P. suggested any social programme to alleviate working class conditions in the period 1785-1835 or any measure of specifically working class appeal. Parliamentary reform was invariably offered as a panacea for all their trouble, and their own specific interests were not catered for. Ironically, if one Member of Parliament in this period was associated with the interests of the stockingers it was Daniel Parker Coke, the Tory foe of 1803. When Coke's friends met in June, 1804, to celebrate Coke's 1803 victory they saw on view a 'handsome and costly flag', provided by the framework-knitters as a tribute to their Member. At the 1806 election a Whig supporter expressed surprise at the fact, but admitted, that the stockingers polled for Mr. Coke in great numbers; Coke even received a message of support from a general meeting of framework-knitters held at the Nag's Head during the course of the election, in which he was thanked for his 'repeated and unmerited kindness'. This kindness was repeated in 1812 when Coke supported their attempts to secure legislative interference in the hosiery and lace trades, an action described by his opponents as the 'most silly of his labours', a frank expression if an indiscreet one in view of the large number of enfranchised stockingers. That is not to say that the latter were solidly behind Coke; the effects of the wars caused a majority to oppose their local champion, but equally they showed no tendency to mobilize solidly behind the Whigs. As will be seen shortly, the social pattern of Nottingham polling statistics in this period is not a clear one.[21]

Incipient constituency party organisations were in existence throughout the last quarter of the eighteenth century to coordinate political activity. It is particularly difficult to separate the political from the social activites of the local party at this time since they were invariably based on public houses, such as the

[20]Blackner, op. cit., p. 303; *Nottingham Journal*, 7th November, 31st October, 1812, 22nd November, 1828; A. C. Wood, 'George, Lord Rancliffe', *Transactions of the Thoroton Society*, 1954.

[21]*Nottingham Journal*, 9th June, 1804; *Paper War*, 1806, pp. VII, 35; *Nottingham Review*, 6th November, 1812; *Collection of Addresses etc. concerning the Election of 1812*, p. 11.

White Lion or Flying Horse, and were as much wining and dining clubs as political organisations. With the coming of the French Revolution and war the Tory White Lion Club was supplemented by the Constitutional Association of loyalists, with an overlap of membership and providing further opportunities for social life, and by 1797 the White Lion was also being known as the True Blue Club, though the latter did not have its formal inauguration until 1803, at which time the Whigs took over the White Lion Hotel. By the time of its 14th Anniversary, in 1817, it had 325 members. From 1813 it worked in conjunction with the Pitt Club and at the election of 1818 both played a useful part. The Pitt Club seems to have been responsible for the raising of funds to promote a Tory candidate, but it was the True Blue Club which was said to have given dinner and drink to some 900 burgesses of the 'Blue Interest' (which was almost exactly the number of burgesses voting Tory in 1818). The Pitt Club's fortunes varied a lot. In 1816 its opponents were saying that it was defunct, and in 1821 the Annual Dinner was attended by a mere forty. This contrasts with the claims put forward the previous year that its membership exceeded 300, amongst whom were to be found 'the greater part of the Nobility and Gentry of our town and county'.[22]

During the clamour which preceded and followed the Reform Bill, the Nottingham Tories were again organised into a 'Constitutional' Club, in June, 1831, known to the *Review* as the 'Tory' or even 'Conservative' Club, as early as 1832, and claimed to be the first of its kind. It was very active throughout 1832. In the September Richard Oastler was elected as an honorary member and he addressed his new society on the subject of why he supported Tory principles. The Club grew fast in the following years of post-Reform Bill, anti-government reaction, and by the middle of 1834 it could claim 580 members. It took the lead in the organisation of registration associations through the town after the Reform Act, a lead quickly followed by the Whigs, and contests between the parties to register electors became as furious as elections themselves. The other important function of the Club was the holding of serious political discussions, for it

[22]*Nottingham Journal*, 27th August, 1797, 14th June, 1817, 30th May, 13th June, 1818, 3rd June, 1820; Sutton, op. cit., p. 265; Poll Books, 1818; *Nottingham Review*, 14th June, 1816, 1st June, 1821.

provided for its members a programme comparable to that which the Nottingham Political Union had been offering to those of opposite sentiments.[23]

The Nottingham Whigs, like the Tories, were ready to use any event, the return of an M.P. or a notable political triumph of another sort, as an excuse for an anniversary dinner, but they retained the title of 'Whig Club' throughout a period when the Tories changed theirs according to their current meeting place, their current favourite, or events of the time. It is likely that the existence of a Whig Corporation, the opportunities that this provided for social intercourse, and the organisation it gave to the causes that the Whig Club supported, rendered the latter almost dispensable though it had a long continuous history through the eighteenth century. Members of the Corporation always had some reservations about allowing complete identification of themselves with the Whig Club. They usually claimed to participate in politics only as individuals and not as members of the Corporation, and in 1804 an incident occurred which illustrates their hesitations. Prominent Corporation members had been invited by the Whig Club to join them at a dinner to celebrate the Prince of Wales' birthday and to commemorate a number of political causes. The Town Clerk and Chief Magistrate replied that although they would have great pleasure as individuals in dining with members of the Whig Club on any occasion if their purpose were 'the recognition of Whig Principles, and the late glorious struggle, in the person of Mr. Birch, for the Liberty and Independence of the Town of Nottingham', they thought it wrong as civic heads to celebrate these in association with the Prince's birthday, an official occasion. But with the great participation of the Corporation in elections only the theory of separation between Whig Club and Corporation could be maintained, as it was before the Corporation Commissioners in 1833, but the practice was known to be otherwise.[24]

Elections themselves seem to have been conducted with a purpose of obscuring rather than illuminating principles and

[23]*Nottingham Review*, 28th September, 9th November, 1832; A. C. Wood, 'Nottingham, 1835-65', p. 67, *Transactions of the Thoroton Society*, 1955; *Nottingham Journal*, 29th September, 1832, 6th June, 1834.

[24]Part of a letter in a collection of privately owned papers relating to Mr. Robert Davison of Arnold; *Nottingham Journal*, 1st November, 1833.

policies. Robert Denison, at the election of 1812, continued his traditional practice of subjecting all the candidates to certain stock questions at the hustings so that all people might have an opportunity to reach independent conclusions on their attitudes and principles, but there is little reason to suppose that decisions were reached so rationally. For one thing, the atmosphere at election times was rarely conducive to any rational disentanglement of the issues involved. Rowdy campaigns, perhaps the result of a working class franchise, were standard. An unfriendly M.P. claimed in 1803 that there could be traced a continuous history of riots going back through almost every election in Nottingham for 120 years, and even Charles James Fox, the Corporation's champion, was prepared to admit the existence of 'an uncontrollable spirit of riot' which had prevailed at most elections. When elections occurred, as in 1806, when ardour was not supplemented by outright violence, the phenomenon was sufficiently unusual to merit much contemporary comment and a record in the chroniclers' accounts. Usually a state of more or less disorder prevailed. In 1790, before the French Revolution had made much local impact, passions aroused in an election where the only issue appears to have been the attempts of the Tories to secure both seats, were sufficient to provoke, according to Thomas Bailey's mature judgement of such things, 'a more than usual amount of rioting'. Robert Davison was later to recall 'life lost and your infirmary crowded with wounded—lives of his (Smith's) adherents in imminent danger, their houses demolished as far as the mob could accomplish it, his own home attacked with such violence that scarcely a window or window frame remained, his property removed . . .'. The same tone continued in 1796. The magistrates were apparently powerless to prevent the occupation of all avenues of approach to the polling centre by wild gangs of partisans who assaulted those of opposite views to their own. The windows of two of the town's principal inns, the party headquarters, were completely demolished, and only the arrival of the military prevented more serious trouble. In 1802 the intimidation and riot reached new heights, when cobblestones were torn from the streets and hurled at opponents and candidates. This time there was Parliamentary intervention, and for the next two decades the County Magistrates joined the town ones in an effort to keep order. The more obvious, though not necessarily the most effective, means of intimidation were gradually restricted in these years, though it was only the un-opposed returns of the early 30s that restored anything like tranquility to the Nottingham election scene.[25]

When gang warfare was reduced other techniques of applying political pressure were strengthened and extended. Here the historian meets the almost impossible task of distinguishing between what people did and what their opponents said that they did. 'Thumbing' was the standard term for the application of pressure, and on all sides there were complaints of coercive action to determine the way a person voted. Men were to be deprived of their farms, homes, jobs, or stocking-frames, it was asserted in 1803, and offers came from some quarters to build houses for those ejected through victimisation. People were urged not to spend money at shops owned by their opponents, and the master of the Blue Coat Charity School, the Rev. Mathew Browne, apparently brought some very questionable influence to bear on his charges and their parents. The poll itself, though far more orderly than that of 1802, produced alleged incidents of Birch's supporters having vitriol thrown upon their clothes, this for the perpetrators a capital offence, and being given by their opponents gin mixed with jalap, a harsh purgative. The extent of such practices cannot be accurately estimated, but when Daniel Parker Coke, the Member for 32 years, publicly supported land-lord pressure on tenants as right and proper, it is reasonable to assume that many accusations of such pressures were true. During the course of this election a society was established by Charles Sutton, soon to start the *Nottingham Review*, to assist those oppressed as a result of having voted for particular candidates. And pressures were evidently still sufficient to convince Colonel Ferguson, M.P., a moderate Whig when he came to Nottingham in 1830, of the need to introduce a secret ballot.[26]

[25]*Nottingham Review*, 23rd October, 1812; R. A. Church, op. cit., p. 140; Parl. Debs., Vol. 36, 1240, 25th April, 1233, 20th April, 1803; *Nottingham Journal*, 8th November, 1806; Bailey, op. cit., pp. 221, 136, 167, 203; *Ten Letters principally upon the subject of the late contested Election at Nottingham*, 1803, p. 30; Sutton, op. cit., p. 226; *Report of Select Committee, 1803, to try the petitions on the Nottingham Election of 1802*.

[26]*Paper War*, 1803, pp. 32, 243, 76, 357-60, 290-1, 255-6; *Accidents of the History of Daniel and Joseph*, p. 33; *Nottingham Journal*, 30th April, 1803; Parl. Debs., Vol. 103, 627, 22nd November, 1830.

Apart from the 'thumbing', the threats and blackmail resorted to, other devices for the fixing of elections were, to judge by contemporary complaints, most numerous. The creation of honorary burgesses by the Corporation, the biggest and most successful swindle of them all, has already been noted. That this happened is certain. Charges were also made on both sides on most occasions of voting by paupers and other unqualified; dead men were 'resurrected' at polling time; some people voted several times over; and at the election of 1818, according to the *Journal*, the 'most despicable artifices' were resorted to. These included the prevention of legal voters from getting to the poll, as well as the acceptance of many not qualified to vote, and in view of the Corporation's willingness to enter so fully into the election struggles, there is little reason to suppose that the magistrates would not be willing to sanction, or at least to ignore, other improper procedures.[27]

If all this is to suggest that the wishes of the electorate were frustrated and controlled by the parties and their agents, it is necessary to remember that the electors themselves co-operated very largely in their own seduction and subjection. When the defeated Tory candidate of 1812 lost nearly £20,000 in his abortive attempt, that money had been very eagerly consumed. When Lord Rancliffe made persistent declarations against fighting an election if it meant paying out money, he was refusing to co-operate in the game. It is most unlikely that his conduct measured up to his protestations for everyone agreed on the inability to secure election in Nottingham in a contested election without vast expenditure of money. Peter Crompton tried to do this in 1807 and his candidature was held to be 'frivolous' because of it. For many poor people the vote was the most marketable thing they possessed and election times were their market-days. But the sale of their vote demanded a careful exercise of judgement. Prices rose as the election proceeded and were particularly high when the rival candidates ran each other close; should a voter, however, hold out too long for a high price he ran the risk of the polls being closed and his assets being rendered valueless.[28]

And so it is not surprising to find election times the scenes of

[27]*Nottingham Journal*, 4th July, 1818.
[28]Sutton, op. cit., p. 304; *Nottingham Journal*, 2nd, 23rd May, 1807; Blackner, op. cit., p. 302.

wholesale bribery and corruption, and debauchery. When asked by a Commissioner in 1833 if he thought the burgesses acted under the influence of political feelings, a witness replied: 'I think they are under no influence except liquor—a shilling will turn them any way, and half a crown will buy them.' Half a crown would not in fact have been considered a very good price to get for a vote. Wylie blamed the local aristocracy for introducing corrupting influences in the early eighteenth-century elections, and the Whigs were happy enough to leave the blame there. Such influences were, of course, present on all sides and elections were almost inevitably bound to end up in the electors capitalising on their assets. Bailey believed that the successive elections of 1802 and 1803 had disastrous effects on working-class morals through over-indulgence in election delights. 'The whole Winter and Spring', he wrote, 'was one continued scene of drunkenness, disorder, tumult, canvassings, dancings, processions, and the like; by which means scores of young persons, of both sexes, were brought to ruin, and those in more advanced life to poverty and destitution.' And this view of Parliamentary elections as an opportunity for disorder, feasting, or frivolity, is supported by accounts of virtually every election in the period.[29]

And if the voters saw them in this light, there is also some reason to suppose that the organisers and leaders, even the candidates themselves, were contributing to one gigantic release of passions which continued long after the vanquished had withdrawn from the contests and the last election petitions had been dismissed as frivolous. The contests were, in fact, conducted in such a way, involved such an amount of mutual slanging, distortion, slander, and libel that the serious intent of those participating must be strongly questioned. In 1803 Joseph Birch was charged with having a desire to overturn the legal government of the country, being a hater of kings and priests, favouring plunder as opposed to industry, being a slave-trader, having unpatriotically exported corn under another guise in time of national famine, having supporters who flogged naked workmen and women to ensure their backing, and approving all the sins of omission and commission of which the Corporation were accused. Out of all this the electors had to try and assess the candidate's worth, if this

[29]*Nottingham Journal*, 15th November, 1833; W. H. Wylie and J. F. Briscoe; *A Popular History of Nottingham* (1893), p. 100; Bailey, op. cit., p. 211.

was their wish. When the election was over the processions and celebrations would continue, spiced with further denunciations of the opponents over whom triumph had been achieved. Petitions to Parliament were the normal conduct of the defeated side, but in 1802 the victory of the Whigs gave rise to a highly imaginative and offensive pamphlet in which John Bowles, on the strength of an account supplied to him from Nottingham, wrote of the 'impiety' and 'abominable orgies' of Nottingham life, the desecration of churches, the trampling down of the national flag, the assaults on young women, all this behaviour culminating in a disgusting election victory march in which Jacobinical songs were sung, a liberty tree planted, and a nude woman represented the goddess of reason. The account was almost everywhere false, and the Nottingham Tories must have known it to be so. But it was just as important to them to denounce the Whigs as debauched revolutionaries as it was for the Whigs to denounce them as subservient tools of the aristocracy who were anxious to sell out the town's independence to the Duke of Newcastle and his kind. The Whigs persisted, in their days of grossest corruption and closest oligarchical control and unashamed political manipulation, in their claim to be fighting for the 'independence' of Nottingham and resurrected the many-times slain dragon of aristocratic domination to be killed anew at each fresh election. Differences between parties there unquestionably were, on such matters as Parliamentary reform or Catholic Emancipation, but these were almost submerged in the torrent of abuse which poured forth from both sides. Reputation was everywhere butchered to make a Nottingham holiday. It was almost as if the electors were not to be allowed to grow up. Both sides served up the most incredibly infantile diet for them, and it was not until after 1830, and especially in 1834, that the old fare was varied. It is not without significance that the *Journal* should lament the unopposed return of two Whig Members in 1830 as the 'dullest affair ever'. After the sport of the mock-elections came the dullness of the uncontested, which in turn gave way to a renewal of contests, but this time on a new basis. The Whig claims to be regarded as the popular party were at last being severely undermined.[30]

[30] *Paper War*, 1803, pp. 16, 39, 61, 70, 220, 261; J. Bowles, *A Postscript to Thoughts on the Late General Election as demonstrative of the Progress of Jacobinism*, pp. 109-19; *Nottingham Journal*, 7th August, 1830.

Against this background the poll books of the period must be treated with caution. They contain a great wealth of information, giving as they do the names, occupations, and voting records of all those who polled. The Nottingham poll books confirm, as might be expected, that Anglican parsons voted Tory and most Dissenting Ministers voted Whig. Their answers to the more difficult questions of how the main social and economic groups were aligned politically are not so straightforward.[31]

The framework-knitters, the largest single group at each election, making up at least half of the number voting, did not vote solidly as an economic group. In 1796, when the Whig forces were in disarray after the defection of Robert Smith, the framework-knitters divided 16 : 11 in favour of the Tory Coke against the radical Whig Crompton. By 1803 they were dividing 4 : 3 against Coke and in support of the Whig, Joseph Birch. And from 1803 until the end of the period they continued to divide in favour of the Whig side, in 1812 on a 7 : 4 basis, by 1818 in almost a 2 : 1 ratio, though much less strongly in 1826. This seems to suggest that after the exceptional period of pro-war fervour in the mid-90s the framework-knitters as a whole tended to follow the Whig lead, in spite of the fact that the Whig programme contained little for them and in spite of the better relations that their leaders had had with the Tory M.P. of long-standing, Daniel Coke. It is hard to see how their voting habits were determined by their work as framework-knitters apart from their evident acceptance of what they were repeatedly told, that their distress was caused by the evils of the wars and successive Tory governments. Rather higher up the scale it is possible to identify a group of engineers and technicians, dependent on the town's principal industries, who followed the occupations of framesmiths, needle-makers, sinker-makers, and setters-up. These more highly-skilled, better off workmen were more inclined to the Whig side than their poorer associates who operated the machines. Even in 1796 they divided evenly between the Whig and the Tory. By 1803 they supported the Whigs in a 5 : 2 ratio, a voting record which remained remarkably steady through successive elections. It would be interesting to know if the tendency of better-off workmen to support the

[31]The following analysis is based on poll books available for the elections of 1796, 1802, 1803, 1806, 1812, 1820, 1826, and 1830.

Whigs was also present among the lace-workers as opposed to the stockingers, but, unfortunately, both groups appear simply as 'framework knitters'.

The hosiers themselves, apart from 1796, when they supported the Tory by more than 3 : 2, seem to have shown no great preference either way. Usually they divided almost equally between the two sides, with majorities going first one way and then the other. It is worth noting that most of the hosiers who came out into the open politically did so on the Whig side, the same as that of the municipal authorities, and that the hosiers were not, it seems, as ready to turn against the Tories during the wars as were their workmen. The lace-manufacturers were rather more inclined to the Whig side than were the hosiers. Not until the 1806 election did their numbers reach double figures in the poll books, on which occasion they voted 10 Whig and 5 Tory, and this 2 : 1 ratio remained fairly steady as more voters in this category appeared. It is very clear from the readiness of both employers and their workmen to support both sides in great numbers that party divisions did not represent any social distinction between bosses and workers.

A group of shopkeepers has been examined, containing inn-keepers, victuallers, butchers, bakers, grocers, druggists, hair-dressers, barbers, liquor-merchants, jewellers, fishmongers, and 'shopkeepers', and this group shows itself to have been strongly Tory throughout the period. In 1796 only 1 in 7 failed to vote Tory, and in the years of Whig ascendancy the shopkeepers remained Tory in a 2 : 1 proportion. Most remarkable were the butchers; they were commonly supposed, as a species, to be Tory, and examination reveals that the Whig butcher was almost a non-existent kind.

These figures are interesting but fail to leave any clear impression of economic groupings allied with particular political philosophies. To break the voters down into occupational groups seems somewhat unrewarding, and if patterns are sought they can be seen most readily by making the distinction that the compilers of the poll books were themselves concerned to make, the distinction between the burgesses and the freeholders. The burgesses, or freemen, of Nottingham, when it came to Parliamentary elections, voted Whig to a larger extent than did the electorate as a whole. When Corporation control was absent in

1796 they voted Tory, but not quite so readily as the rest of the electorate. When the Corporation was still weak but gaining strength, in 1806, they were dividing evenly, and by 1812, the first of many Corporation victories, the burgesses were moving strongly to the Whig side. The Whiggish tendencies of the burgesses were not, however, so strong as the Tory tendencies of the freeholders; nor did they harden so much. Whilst the burgesses, along with the whole electorate, were moving towards the Whigs, the freeholders were moving, more quickly, towards the Tories. Whereas in 1812 they had favoured the Tories only slightly, by 1820 they supported the Tory candidates by a vote of 534 to 232. Only the fact that the burgesses were twice as numerous as the freeholders, and sustained by the Corporation's doctrine of continuous creation, kept the Whig hold intact.

A likely conclusion that the poll-books offer is that even in Parliamentary elections the issue of real importance to people, apart from the Corporation's right to create votes and continue its hold, was the friction that dominated Nottingham life throughout the period, the friction between the burgess and his supposed enemy, the freeholder, over the question of enclosure. This is the shape that the voting figures take whatever the protestations of Tory candidates that they were the burgesses' friends. The Corporation Whigs succeeded in persuading the burgesses that they were the firmest opponents of enclosure and that the Tories, of whom very many were freeholders, were the people who had an interest in furthering enclosure. And the Corporation Whigs were probably correct in their assertions about themselves and their opponents. Where they were wrong, morally, was in allowing the vested interests of some burgesses and some slum property owners to compete against the vested interests of the enclosing freeholders in a political issue which had no ideological or moral basis and ignored the real interests of the town and welfare of its inhabitants.

9

NOTTINGHAM,
THE FRENCH REVOLUTION,
AND THE FRENCH WARS

James Orange, a local historian, wrote in 1840 that during the wars against revolutionary France Nottingham had been 'much agitated by political animosities'. His moderate words were given a lurid exposition some years later by the writer of a local guide who informed his fellow-townspeople that their grandparents had demonstrated in battalion formation in Nottingham Market Place in preparation for revolutionary action. His account was fanciful for the Market Place enterprises would never have passed unnoticed at the time. Yet an impression of Nottingham as a likely centre of revolutionary endeavour in this period has persisted, for only recently has it been described as having been an incurably Jacobin centre, marked down for special watch by the national authorities. This charge requires some investigation.[1]

There is little real evidence that the French Revolution in its early stages made much impact upon Nottingham. Blackner, in a somewhat melodramatic account, stated that the Revolution was an object of admiration to one part of the people and of terror to the rest, people dividing according to whether they were lovers of freedom or afraid of losing their property. This was almost certainly a rationalisation of the situation according

---

[1]Orange, op. cit., p. 868; J. Bramley, *Guide to Nottingham Castle* (1878), p. 46; E. P. Thompson, op. cit., p. 605. This account leaves an impression of Nottingham as a hot-bed of revolutionary activity for a quarter of a century.

M

to his own feelings on the matter. In similar vein a later historian was to repeat Blackner's claim that the Revolution evoked a great emotional response in Nottingham, 'filling men's minds with the most tumultuous and opposite emotions of hope or fear, of terror or delight', but when the *Journal* spoke in February, 1790, of the alarming crisis which existed and the need to defend the Constitution it was referring only to current attempts to repeal the Test and Corporation Acts. Bailey too seems to have been determined to anticipate the Revolution's impact locally. He claimed that it first began to stir men's minds in 1790 and used it to explain the riotous proceedings at the parliamentary election in that year, but contemporary accounts give him no support. The behaviour of the election crowds was in any case quite usual, and the *Journal*, never slow to detect 'Jacobins' on other occasions, blamed these troubles on 'several malignant and ill-disposed persons of the lowest description' who had no personal interest in the outcome of the election. So restrained, in fact, was reaction to the French Revolution locally that as late as June, 1791, there could still be reported as a straight news-item, meriting no comment, a meeting of the Manchester Constitutional Society, which had given its thanks to Mr. Paine for the publication of *The Rights of Man*. And even in November, 1791, the *Journal* was commenting on the 'liberality of sentiment' with which the Revolution had been received in Britain.[2]

Before the Summer of 1792 the temperature was beginning to rise. In April there were attacks on the Nottingham mill of Benjamin and Charles Morley and the home of Alderman William Smith; these people were Unitarians, and the incidents are in line with the experiences of Priestley in Birmingham at the same time and Robert Denison in Nottingham two years later. A further manifestation of division occurred when Mrs. Carter, the hostess of the Sun Inn, received a letter threatening that her house would be burned if she continued to harbour democrats, which suggests that supporters of the French Revolution were using her establishment for their political discussions. In June, a body of men, leading Tories according to most accounts, appealed to the Mayor to requisition a town-meeting that Nottingham might send its reply to the King's proclamation

[2]Blackner, op. cit., p. 300; Carpenter op. cit., pp. 165-6; *Nottingham Journal*, 13th February, 4th September, 1790, 4th June, 5th November, 1791; Bailey, op. cit., p. 136.

against seditious writings. The Mayor refused. A meeting was privately organised and some 500 'principal inhabitants' of the town signed the first of the loyal addresses from Nottingham. The *Journal*, previously uncommitted politically, now took up the cry against 'Clubs, Correspondencies, and Associations', though it found none to identify locally. Those favouring 'levelling principles' and feeling dissatisfaction with British government were recommended to leave for France or America, and readers were offered a choice between national tranquillity, with all its advantages, including security of property, and French anarchy. The deteriorating position of the French royal family also evoked strong comment. By the end of the year the *Journal* was happily reporting the emergence of a number of loyalist organisations in and around Nottingham. In the town itself a Constitutional Association sprang up, under strong Tory patronage, which swore loyalty to the King and a determination to suppress all who threatened to disturb the peace and good government of the town and neighbourhood. At nearby Stapleford the local vicar presided over an association for the preservation of 'Liberty and Property against Republicans and Levellers', but any such threats to date appear to have come from inside the loyalist ranks, and we know nothing of the identity of his supposed enemy.[3]

Throughout 1792 letters were beginning to reach the Home Office from troubled town-clerks and worried magistrates in provincial trouble-spots, and lists were compiled of disaffected persons throughout the country. The town-clerk of Nottingham wrote no letters and no Nottingham name appeared on the Home Office lists, though Leicester and Derby were already making their contributions. In November, 1792, Nottingham was first mentioned as a place where there was a sign of discontent, with the issuing of an address to the public by a society in the town. The only society known to have existed at this time which might have worried the authorities was the local branch of the Society for Constitutional Information. This was a relic of Major Cartwright's activity in the Parliamentary reform movement amongst the Nottinghamshire freeholders in the years 1780-85, in which

[3] S. D. Chapman, *The Early Factory Masters* (1967), p. 189; Blackner, op. cit., p. 386; Sutton, op. cit., p. 195; Bailey, op. cit., pp. 143-4; *Nottingham Journal*, 23rd, 30th June, 7th July, 4th August, 8th September, 13th October, 22nd December, 1792.

he was strongly backed by the Rev. George Walker of High Pavement. It seems likely that the branch was revitalised here, as elsewhere, by events in France and that Walker was responsible for pamphlet literature on its behalf in 1792-3 at the same time as he was organising petitions against the War, in 1793, along with the manufacturers and Corporation of Nottingham. That the Society made an abortive attempt to be associated with the London Corresponding Society in September, 1792, in an address to the French Convention, is indicative of current enthusiasms rather than any revolutionary intent.[4]

There were other broadsheets circulated in Nottingham at this time. The Friends of the People had an address to the inhabitants of the town and other, anonymous bodies published defences of the *status quo*, but all such publications were very general in tone and contained no details about events in the town itself. The only specific references came in an ironical statement, under the pen-name 'Ingenuitas', headed 'Seeds of Sedition', in January, 1793. This was addressed to the 'Honourable Committee of Sedition-Hunters' in Nottingham and lampooned their failure to find any sedition locally or even to define what they sought. The author mockingly offered the letters of the alphabet as the source of all trouble. The only work known to have achieved considerable circulation was *The Rights of Man*. Sutton admits that many hundreds of copies were sold in the neighbourhood, whilst Mary Tatham's biographer tells of Paine's work being extensively read in an area where revolutionary principles were propagated and animosity and discontent fostered. Against this it must be remembered that Paine's work had in no way excited the Tory *Journal* eighteen months previously and that Tatham and her biographer were leading Evangelical Wesleyans in the area, who were likely to take an extreme view of any politically radical ideas, especially when coming from a Deist. The only clear cases of anti-government sentiment so far revealed in the town had come from two official and highly respectable bodies, the Corporation, who had refused to join in the hunt for alleged

[4]H.O. 42/23, November, 1792; F. D. Cartwright, op. cit., pp. 121-34; Addresses to the Inhabitants of Nottingham in B.M. Collection of Broadsheets, etc., 1792-3; A. C. Wood, *History of Nottinghamshire* (1947), p. 280, quotes *Journal of House of Commons*, XIX, p. 603 and P. A. Brown, *The French Revolution in English History* (1918), p. 69.

sedition in June, 1792, and a delegate meeting of Baptist, Independent, and Presbyterian Churches in May, 1792, which had sent a message of sympathy to Dr. Priestley in Birmingham and condemned the attitudes which had caused his misfortunes. Apart from these events, there was nothing that could have worried the central government, which received no communications from Nottingham until May, 1794. This suggests a fairly trouble-free town, for it is certain that the County Magistrates would not have hesitated to write to the Home Office if their colleagues in the town had neglected their duty and failed to keep the government fully informed.[5]

What really seems to have produced the strong reactions and sharp divisions locally was not so much the French Revolution itself as the beginning of the French Wars in 1793. It was this development that prompted many of the leading men in Nottingham affairs to align and show their hands. And the most interesting aspect of the anti-war party is that it took its stand almost entirely on economic grounds, with practically no effort to comment on the rights and wrongs of the French Revolutionaries. There appeared, on the 23rd February, 1793, an address and petition, drawn up by the Rev. George Walker, which was to achieve fame and notoriety in Nottingham society and which was to be the starting-point of many a debate and discussion before peace came. The main arguments of the address, which was, significantly, to the 'manufacturers and other inhabitants' of the town and neighbourhood, were almost cynical in tone: if Britain remained at peace she could exploit the war situation; if she fought herself, increased insurance and freight rates would cripple her manufactures and no neutral navy would give her commerce access to foreign markets; France was no concern of Britain's and she must be left to her own vices or virtues whilst England pursued her own national self-interest, and that was peace. In the petition to Parliament the feasibility of total conquest of France was questioned and war's evil consequences predicted; they were the destruction of commerce, ever-increasing food-prices, higher poor-rates, and new taxes.[6]

The twenty-six signatories of the declaration were all substantial

[5]B.M. Collection of Broadsheets, etc., op. cit.; Sutton, op. cit., p. 197; J. C. Weller, op. cit., p. 58; *Nottingham Journal*, 26th May, 1792.

[6]*Nottingham Journal*, 2nd March, 1793.

local citizens, many of them Aldermen and Senior Councillors of the Corporation. They included hosiers, leading tradesmen, cotton manufacturers, like Robert Denison, worsted-spinning mill owner Thomas Hawksley, Francis Hart, the banker, and George Coldham, solicitor and town-clerk. They represented Nottingham's main economic interests and political strength. Immediately, they were answered. 'Veritas' was quick to point out that France, not Britain, had been responsible for the declaration of war and he reprimanded the signatories for their failure to hold a town-meeting, the customary procedure on such occasions. These relevant and moderate comments were soon superseded by the Secretary of the Constitutional Association, who put his own interpretation on developments. He prefaced his attack on the twenty-six by defining the purpose of his own organisation as the discouraging and prevention of seditious and alarming publications, which the petition and declaration were alleged to be. The signatories were now compelled to deny that they wanted a revolution in England similar to that in France and they protested their attachment to constitutional government and abhorrence of civil tumult. It is quite evident from their composition that they were the last persons to want revolution in England; they had not even expressed any opinion on that in France, but already there was developing that wartime phenomenon, very noticeable in England in 1914-18, whereby any deviation from the national line is crudely caricatured and all midway positions are to the majority quite unintelligible. Almost half a century later William Howitt was to write about how the British government had rushed to stifle liberty in France to avoid being annihilated by it in England, but in 1793 these were not the arguments of the Nottingham opponents of the war. They were not concerned with the rights of man in general but with their own economic prosperity as individuals. Such were the first Nottingham 'Jacobins'; it was fear of the war's economic consequences and resentment of the burdens that it actually produced that were the bases of Nottingham anti-war sentiment during this period. Disaffection came not from Jacobinism but from economic grievance.[7]

In the opinion of the Constitutional Association the town had

[7]*Nottingham Journal*, 2nd, 9th, 16th, March, 1793; see C. E. Playne, *Society at War, 1914-16* (1931); W. Howitt, *A Copious Historical Sketch of the Progress of Parliamentary Reform* (1840), p. 245.

been held up to ridicule. It recommended silent contempt as the best treatment for the anti-war group, but its own innuendos about their motives made this impossible, and 1793 was to witness more outbreaks of violence against supposed French sympathisers. Social undertones were creeping in. Attempts were being made, it was suggested, to rouse the 'vulgar against their superiors', hardly the social programme of the twenty-six signatories, who were required to answer, as 'democrats', the charges of favouring equality and despising kingly authority. Tom Paine, who had aroused no great anger earlier, was now being hanged and burned in effigy wherever two or three gathered together in the name of loyalty, and the crowds were encouraged to indulge themselves around his execution scene. By March the first news of victories was coming through, to be received by wild popular acclaim, and in November a society was established at the Crown and Anchor to make flannel waistcoats for soldiers. In October a man was sentenced to three months' imprisonment for damning the King, an offence at any time but a great one at such a time as this. The most menacing manifestation of feeling was, however, the beginning of military exercises by a number of loyalists. Encouraged in the belief that they were about to be threatened by insurrection on the French model, some had taken up arms and begun to drill. This had resulted in a number of clashes in the town and the magistrates were obliged to warn against such conduct. On the evening of July 24th feeling erupted into a serious political riot. Windows and shutters were broken and much damage done to the houses of persons thought to be sympathetic to the principles of the French Revolution, including the Mayor, Alderman Oldknow, who had himself signed the 1793 declaration; worse than this, a man was killed, an unhappy precedent for the following year. The army was called out and eventually the rioters were quelled.[8]

It was now freely stated, at least in the columns of the *Journal*, that there were 'Jacobins' in Nottingham and that they met at particular public-houses. Who exactly they were and what they were supposed to want no one bothered to define. It seems beyond doubt that a few men, almost certainly of humble social status, saw themselves, if only half-seriously, as 'freedom-fighters'. On

[8]*Nottingham Journal*, 16th, 23rd March, 4th May, 27th July, 19th October, 30th November, 1793; Bailey, op. cit., p. 151.

Blackner's admission, and he was a likely sympathizer, a few Nottingham 'democrats' formed a joint resolution to learn military discipline, engaged a retired soldier to instruct them, and paraded quite openly on the Forest on the edge of the town; for want of muskets they used sticks, sarcastically called 'wooden guns' by observers. Their behaviour in the circumstances, admitted Blackner, was indiscreet. They permitted their opponents to charge all opponents of the war with dangerous intentions, even if the men had been thinking more in terms of self-defence against those who had been under orders to arm on behalf of Church and State. Their efforts, it seems, were hardly a threat to peace and good order, but the response they evoked certainly was.[9]

A committee was now formed of those supporting the war, whose function was to collect money secretly for the purpose of hiring toughs, provided by the gangs of labourers then working on cutting the Trent Canal. They were to hunt out and man-handle those who were opposed to the war. The chief agent in these hirings was a man named Pilgrim, whose usual employment was writing lampoons and selling them on the streets. The 'navvies' might have provided the leaders, but there was also much popular support from a well-prepared section of poor people who, from June 2nd to the 6th, indulged in an outburst of pro-longed violence against supposed opponents of the war. Men were held under pumps and ducked in the Leen, 'sprinkled' and 'baptised' in the parlance of the time, and so savagely treated that one man died shortly afterwards. There were also damaging attacks on property. Out-buildings of a mill belonging to Robert Denison, a signatory in 1793, were set alight, and the property and persons of numerous others were violently attacked. This thuggery, once released, threatened to get out of hand. One eye-witness, a worsted spinning-mill owner, was later to claim that a general conflagration in the town was the aim of some of the trouble-makers and that water pipes had been cut to facilitate this, but military intervention saved the town.[10]

The most extraordinary aspect of this episode was the role of the magistrates, who were apparently content to let the riot proceed unchecked for a long time. Mayor Green, the 'Blue-

[9]This account is based on Blackner, op. cit., pp. 387-91, Rev. G. Walker's narrative in Sutton, op. cit., pp. 209-13, and *Nottingham Journal*, 5th July, 1794.

[10]R. Davison, *Ten Letters, etc.*, op. cit., p. 15.

Green Mayor', was actually to be seen encouraging the rioters and assisting them in their illegal entry into people's homes in an alleged search for hidden arms; and when a few of the chief offenders were later brought to trial their sentences were purely nominal. Blackner saw Green as the real villain and rejoiced that though he escaped the punishment of law yet was he marked out by the finger of heaven for divine retribution. From being a hosier he had risen to be a cotton-spinner, declined to the rank of brewer, gone bankrupt, and was finally shunned by everyone, dying of a broken heart when 'want and guilt haunted him like two spectres'.

The role of Henry Green and Robert Denison requires further consideration. Green, formerly a Whig, had moved towards the Tories as a result of the French Revolution, but it is possible that his failure to save Denison from the mob is to be explained in part by a personal animosity between the two men and the fact that they were both cotton spinners. Denison was so shocked by the treatment he received that he planned to leave the town and did in fact send his son to America away from the 'bigotry and Licentiousness'. He himself stayed behind and received £500 compensation but his mill remained closed from 1794 until 1801, in a period when lace was expanding, population increasing, and the main war difficulties were still ahead. And when Denison re-opened in 1801 he was in business for only a short time before his mill was completely destroyed by fire, with arson at least hinted at. Denison was certainly not an economic victim of the war in the normal sense, as Blackner suggested that he was. There is evidence that he had expected the attack before it came. An anonymous letter to the Home Office in May, 1794, told of cannons and balls being brought to Nottingham ostensibly for the defence of cotton mills but more likely for some evil design. The ostensible purpose was almost certainly the real one. When the mob attacked the mills they claimed to know of the existence of hidden arms, but Denison's only association with evil designs was his long-standing friendship with Major Cartwright and support for Parliamentary reform, his membership of High Pavement Chapel, and his signing of the 1793 declaration.[11]

[11]Sutton, op. cit., pp. 201, 211, 257; R. Denison to Boulton and Watt, 29th August, 1794, and James Watt Jun. to R. Denison (27th October?), 1794, Boulton and Watts Collection; *Nottingham Journal*, 20th February, 1796; Blackner, op. cit., p. 248; H.O. 42/30, Anon. letter from Nottingham to H.O., 22nd May, 1794; F. D. Cartwright, op. cit., Vol. 2, p. 42.

In 1815 Blackner said he knew the names of everyone involved in the 1794 outrages but refused to reveal them for the sake of avoiding further acrimony. John Sutton named many of the participants some forty years later. All who were interested to identify those responsible were agreed that they were the Nottingham Tories who had raised a mob, 'the friends of Mr. Coke', the 'Church and King crowd'. Certainly the events of 1794 were to take a prominent place in the annals of the Whigs and reformers of Nottingham; the Tories, whenever they complained later of their ill-usage were invariably reminded of 1794 and their unscrupulous exploitation of the war situation to terrorise their opponents on that occasion.[12]

The term 'Jacobin' was very much in vogue, a synonym for 'leveller' or 'democrat', having no revolutionary connotation in the Nottingham context but indicating simply that the person concerned was hostile to the war, or, at least, not prepared to join the crowds in pro-war demonstrations. Nowhere did anyone suggest that there was at this time in Nottingham any organisation that was planning revolutionary activity. The 'democrats' gave no indication that they were actively spreading democracy in England beyond giving general support to the idea of Parliamentary reform, and the 'levellers' neither spoke nor acted with apparently levelling-intent. All three terms were equally unsuitable for describing those men of Nottingham who were prominently following an anti-war line. And if they were suited to the fraternities who assembled at the Sun Inn and a few other smaller establishments, these groups were virtually silent worshippers of developments across the Channel, whose enthusiasm did not lead them into open proselytising activity. Some 'democratic prints' were circulated, said Blackner, but the only writer to be named by him and other commentators was one Henry Shipley, the son of a gardener. His ideas developed along unusual lines. At first an opponent of the Revolution, he later became one of its most enthusiastic supporters, joining every political society in Nottingham and developing an unsuspected literary talent which he exercised on its behalf. He was the author, said Wylie, of 'many fugitive pieces', and he appears to have been a man of little weight. He did move on to the fringes of higher society by his marriage to the sister of lace-manufacturer, Thomas Maltby,

[12]Blackner, op. cit., p. 389; Sutton op. cit., pp. 212-3; e.g. R. Davison, op. cit., p. 15.

which the brother was said to have opposed on political grounds, but there is nothing to suggest that he had any great influence or made any great impact, and he died unnoticed in 1808.[13]

It seems likely that neither the Jacobins nor the loyalists were as real as their enemies believed them to be. The *Journal*, whilst condemning disaffection generally, could never name any disaffected in Nottingham itself; in fact it welcomed the gathering of crowds to receive news of victories from the stage-coach, since such assemblies, it believed, proved unfounded the charges that Nottingham was disaffected towards its King and Constitution. Demonstrations of loyalty were the order of the day and Mayor Green had set a conspicuous example. Those who challenged the expediency of the war got what they deserved in June and July, and when political disturbances broke out again in various parts of the town in the November they were of so minor a nature as not to threaten order or cause any great concern Yet any assumption that a popular pro-war sentiment was at work must also take into account that political demonstrations were well-organised, that the town's only newspaper was encouraging people to demonstrate their loyalty actively, that any event that could be turned into an occasion was so turned, and that people had a vested interest in contributing their presence to the loyalist demonstrations since they provided much enjoyed opportunities to partake of food and drink at someone else's expense.[14]

It would, however, be true to say that after 1794 the war cause was never again to be so popular. When the loyalist mobs were beginning their work of destruction in 1793 the parliamentary reformers, essentially the same men who had declared against the war, were already petitioning parliament to extend the franchise, with the Rev. George Walker again drawing up the petition. There were over 2,500 signatures, a sizable group who could be expected to prevent the pro-war party assuming complete hegemony. It was also a fact that, in spite of Henry Green's mayoralty the Corporation was overwhelmingly opposed to the war, and when Green left office, in September, 1794, the worst excesses of the loyalists were at an end, though lively exchanges of opinion, and sometimes blows, still occurred. There had been

[13]Blackner, op. cit., pp. 357–8; W. H. Wylie, *Old and New Nottingham* (1853), p. 165.
[14]*Nottingham Journal*, 31st May, 29th November, 1794.

suppers to celebrate the acquittal of Hardy in November, 1795, and in the same month the Corporation met to consider government legislation against Seditious Meetings and Publications and the Bill to preserve the safety of the monarch and government. It viewed these with extreme distaste, an attitude reinforced by the Whig Club, but condemned, as expected, by the Secretary of the Constitutional Association. The *Journal* found the former Bill 'interesting and reasonable'. In December the alliance of Corporation, which evidently needed no Pitt legislation to maintain its authority, and manufacturing interests produced a further petition to the King for peace and criticised the government for its illiberal policy on the domestic front. To the petition was affixed the seal of the Corporation. Mayor Green's sway was at an end, and Charles Fox reigned supreme as hero of the Corporate body, his birthday being commemorated in certain Nottingham public houses in January, 1796. The Corporation did not, however, commit itself to the support of Dr. Peter Crompton, Radical candidate in the 1796 election. This contest, in keeping with tradition, was full of incident, but the violence of the campaign was hardly indicative of a revival of Jacobinism as has been recently suggested. The Whig mob put the Tory mob to flight not because the populace was now Jacobin but because they were better prepared and carried hidden truncheons, with which they beat the heads of opponents and broke the windows of their party headquarters. It was hardly a popular revival and triumph, for Crompton polled only half the votes of his two Tory opponents and was no more strongly supported by the framework-knitters than any other group. Still, there was a change of mood. There were recruiting riots in June, 1796, and when in October, 1797, Duncan's victory at Camperdown was announced it received a very poor welcome in contrast with the situation three years earlier. Petitions for the dismissal of the King's ministers and the restoration of peace were again organised and again by the same people as before, this time receiving over 5,000 signatures.[15]

[15]Parl. Debs., Vol. 30, 460-7, 21st February, 1793; Sutton, op. cit., pp. 226, 228, 230-1; *Nottingham Journal*, 7th November, 5th, 12th December, 1795, 23rd January, 20th, 27th February, 18th June, 2nd July, 1796, 1st, 15th April, 1797; Corporation Hall Books, 1795/6, pp. 12-18, 27th November, 1795, 1796/7, pp. 30-3, 20th April, 1797; E. P. Thompson, op. cit., p. 184; 1796 Poll Book; Bailey, op. cit., p. 171.

Bailey recorded a strong decline in popular enthusiasm for the war from 1797 and all accounts suggest that food riots were regaining their former, important role in Nottingham life. The important factor was not ideological conversion but the economic consequences of the war which were now being brought home to people. There is little reason to suppose that the gloomy forecasts of 1793 had been realised at this point, but 1797 was a bleak year, nationally as well as locally, and people were inclined to see it as a realisation of their worst fears. Robert Davison of Arnold wrote to Boulton and Watt of 'commerce, so nearly annihilated by war', and all through the correspondence between various Nottingham manufacturers and the Soho firm runs the theme of bad times resulting from the war. Business guile required that they should exaggerate their inability to pay high premiums for new steam-engines, but even the *Journal* was obsessed by the number of bankruptcies that had occurred in the country since the war started. The anti-war petitioners, lamenting the calamities that war had brought to the town, offered 1797 as a fulfilment of their earlier prophecies, but it was rather a national recession which temporarily marred a period of local expansion and fair prosperity.[16]

At the end of April, 1797, a meeting occurred at the home of a private individual, at which those in attendance pledged their support for the new town petition for the dismissal of the Ministry. This was the incipient Nottingham Corresponding Society, for there had been no branch in Nottingham before this time. On July 26th, a government messenger called on the Mayor to discuss a proposed meeting of the Society in support of an address to the nation on shorter parliaments. The Mayor was requested to use his influence and authority to prevent any disturbance, and the meeting did pass off peacefully. It took place on 31st July in the Market Place under the Chairmanship of Robert Brown, a framework-knitter, and was held, it was said, at the request of the London Corresponding Society. The vote was demanded for 'those who by their labour pay taxes to support placemen and pensioners' and annual parliaments were urged. After this the meeting gave its thanks to the Mayor and Aldermen present for their 'manly and impartial conduct', after

[16]Ibid.; Boulton and Watt Collection, Correspondence with Nottingham mill-owners, 1793-8; *Nottingham Journal*, 4th February, 1st April, 1797.

which the meeting dispersed in an orderly fashion. Both the Society and the town magistrates won the plaudits of the London Corresponding Society. The Home Secretary was not supplied with a copy of the Nottingham Society's regulations until March, 1798, when a newly-emerged informer, George Cartwright, forwarded one. This indicated that the Society was aiming at universal suffrage and annual parliaments; it was to have as many divisions as there were units of sixty; its meetings were to take place as far as possible at members' houses as this was best calculated to preserve order; and, apart from business matters, there was always to be an hour reserved for 'reading political books or discussing political questions'. Cartwright himself added the information that there were about 800 members; he regretted knowing nothing of their intentions, but the following month he related that the Society was believed to have 'plenty of arms'. In the November he got round to naming Robert Brown and Henry Shipley as Secretaries of the Society and asked that warrants should be sent for their arrest since they were suspected of having papers of great importance. But the government were apparently not very interested or impressed. In June, 1798, the *Journal* had reported that the Corresponding Society had met with such a poor response that it was considering becoming the 'Desponding Society', and that was the last mention it received in the local press, though the papers of the London Society suggest that the Nottingham branch was still in existence as late as March, 1799.[17]

Cartwright's interpretation of the Nottingham Society seems unlikely to have been a correct one. Apart from his own gossip, for which he was being paid and which will be examined further shortly, there is nothing to suggest that the Nottingham Society was anything other than a working class body advocating parliamentary reform. Its views were such as would find wide approval in Nottingham, and it alarmed the Tory *Journal* no more than it alarmed the Whig Corporation. Shipley, named by Cartwright, was a well-known figure, described fully by Blackner, and Robert Brown, so far from being a secret plotter, actually stood for election to the Junior Council as a Radical in February,

[17]*Nottingham Journal*, 22nd April, 29th July, 1797, 9th June, 1798; Report of Proceedings at a General Meeting of the Nottingham Corresponding Society, 31st July, 1797; H.O. 42/42, G. Cartwright to H.O. 7th March, 1798, H.O. 42/43, G. Cartwright to H.O. 15th June, 6th November, 1798; P.C. 1/43A, 153.

1798, polling 684 votes and winning Blackner's condemnation for his presumption in attempting to join his social superiors on the body Corporate. It would be folly to ascribe precise 'Jacobinical' ideas to the Nottingham Corresponding Society, and its almost total neglect by local commentators emphasises the unimportance of its role.[18]

The Corporation meanwhile settled down to a policy of steady opposition to the policies of the central government, missing few opportunities to register its discontent. For their pains the City Fathers received at their annual service at St. Mary's, in October, 1798, a lecture on the uses and abuses of liberty from the Reverend Dr. Wylde, a somewhat thinly-veiled injunction to support the legal government of the country. It was a well-deserved reminder if the reports of informer Cartwright through 1798 and 1799 were to be trusted, for his comments about armed Jacobins were spiced with allusions to 'our worthy magistrates', which were intended to implicate them in the conspiracies he described. On one occasion he even suggested a trap to prove the complicity of the magistracy, but mostly he passed on public-house gossip, of 1,500-1,800 well-armed Jacobins ready for a trial of strength with the local volunteers, of suspect chests from Birmingham, and shopkeepers ready to serve France if invasion came. Once it was necessary for Cartwright to ask for more prompt payment for what he called 'rendering a piece of acceptable service to my King and Country', and both his manner and the nature of his information render his testimony improbable, in particular his determination to implicate the magistracy, especially the Mayor, 'the very worst of all the Aldermen'. After January, 1799, he evidently found it no longer worth his while to bother writing.[19]

The government's trust in the magistrates was soon shown during the Corn Riots of April, September, and November of 1800, when Nottingham shared the national distress arising from corn shortage. Serious rioting was reported in both Nottingham and the country villages as crowds of men, reputedly a thousand strong, left the town and went in search of the millers and farmers, like the town bakers, the supposed authors of their troubles. The government praised the town authorities highly for their

[18]Sutton op. cit., p. 234; Blackner, op. cit., p. 306.

[19]*Nottingham Journal*, 6th October, 1798; H.O. 42/42, H.O. 42/43, H.O. 42/45, H.O. 42/46, Cartwright to H.O., March, 1798—January, 1799.

firm handling of the situation, though a doubt was expressed whether Corporation flour subsidies would not make the people unwilling to resume their normal purchases from the millers and bakers at market prices. On the suggestion that the situation might be exploited for political purposes, George Coldham, the town clerk, proposed that he should hire a spy to mingle with the crowds, but it is clear that the wrath of the mobs was directed entirely towards their failed sources of supply and not towards the authorities.[20]

Corporation members met in October to discuss the 'exorbitant price of all the necessities of life', and pretended, disingenuously, to have no opinion as to the causes of the evils and to have no wish to dictate to the King's 'wisdom and solicitude the ultimate means of removing them', but their role to date left no doubt about their real beliefs. And when peace was ratified in 1802 the *Journal*'s rejoicings cast doubts upon the validity of its own earlier arguments. It had usually denied that war was having bad effects on the nation's trade and industry; now it rejoiced to know that 'the stream of commerce will resume its genuine course'. The results of the peace for Nottingham would be extensive and manufactures would flourish in the general tranquility. It accepted the blessings of peace, having rejected previously the converse of this. And rejoicing and celebrations were general. In the prevailing atmosphere of goodwill and the temporary termination of party strife a man spoke out against enlistment and condemned as a crime the drinking of the King's health, but he escaped prosecution by an act of apology.[21]

During the brief period of peace there occurred in Nottingham two memorable elections which were to give rise to an informative debate on the nature of political dissent in the town, a debate carried on vocally, in the press, and in broadsheets and pamphlets, which was to give a comprehensive answer to those who sought to brand Nottingham as a centre of Jacobinism.[22]

[20]H.O. 42/49, H.O. 42/51, H.O. 42/52, H.O. 42/53 for Correspondence between Town Clerk of Nottingham and H.O.

[21]Corporation Hall Books, 1800/1, pp. 9-11, 10th October, 1800; *Nottingham Journal*, 28th March, 1801, 20th February, 10th April, 8th May, 1802.

[22]For a detailed account of the 1802 election see M. I. Thomis, *Old Nottingham* (1968), ch. 6, and for the 1803 election see M. I. Thomis, 'The Nottingham Election of 1803', *Transactions of the Thoroton Society*, 1961.

In the 1802 election the Tories, bearing the brunt of the war's unpopularity in its later stages, were at the receiving end of the violence of the mob, and the Whigs, justifying their failure to safeguard the rights and safety of their Tory opponents, referred repeatedly to their own demise eight years previously, and many saw the 1802 incidents as the days of the Whigs' revenge. Coke and his friends, according to one Whig view, had made themselves particularly odious by their part in the riots and duckings of 1794; now they were having their reward.[23]

Quite what these new manifestations, organised and spontaneous, revealed, people could not agree. 'Revolution's their aim, tho' they talk of reform', ran one election song, and Coke, the Tory candidate, himself asserted that the normal violence of the election crowd was mingled with a desire to overturn the legal government of the country. Precisely who wanted revolution and an overthrow of legal government was not explained. The Committee which tried the resulting election petition placed the blame for disorder squarely upon the shoulders of the local magistracy who had acted in a partisan manner, but there were no revolutionaries in their midst.[24]

From London John Bowles produced a highly coloured and erroneous account of the orgies and indecencies alleged to have been part of the Whig celebrations, from which he moved on to a general description of life in Nottingham since the French Revolution, a suggestive caricature but an unsubstantiated and uncorroborated account:—

'In that town', he wrote, 'a spirit of riot, outrage, disaffection, and impiety, has, for some years, and particularly since the French Revolution, displayed itself to the terror and annoyance of the peaceful and loyal part of the inhabitants; the constables have been, in general, disaffected characters, and, of course, unwilling to exert themselves in suppressing jacobinical tumults', and numerous loyal people of Nottingham 'have been long overborne by a tumultuous, ungoverned, and jacobinical mob'.[25]

[23]Vindex, *A letter to the Burgesses of Nottingham* (1803), p. 13.

[24]*Paper War*, 1803, op. cit., pp. 5, 261; *Report of Select Committee, 1803, to try the petitions on the Nottingham Election of 1802*, p. 281.

[25]J. Bowles, *A Postscript to Thoughts on the late General Election as demonstrative of the Progress of Jacobinism* (1803), pp. 119, 128.

N

It was a frightening picture, but no other account supports it and no records bear out its claims. A local press of basically the same viewpoint as the author failed completely to detect the forces and influence of which he complained. And his detailed account of the 1802 election celebrations at second hand produced detailed denials from numerous eye-witnesses. His purpose was clear—to denounce the Nottingham magistracy, whom he hated for their politics and their religion, and to brand them with sedition. Reaction to his taunt of 'Jacobinism' was illuminating. Did the word mean 'factitious turbulence', asked Vindex, for if so the destruction of life and property had prevailed back in 1794 without any complaints from those who now spoke up. But it was worsted manufacturer Robert Davison who answered the case most comprehensively. He saw no reason for precluding a free Briton from rejoicing at a Frenchman's participation in that freedom which he himself enjoyed. This did not mean the Briton wanted revolution; his constitution guaranteed his liberties, and revolution was to be dreaded and deprecated when the liberties were already won. Davison explained that revolution would be the ruin of him as a manufacturer and of his family. What he wanted was reform, which would perpetuate what was best in the British system and eliminate what was worst; and what, he asked, was meant by 'Jacobinism'?

'I consult my dictionaries, in vain, for an explanation of the word "Jacobinism"; it is a cant phrase, which men of sense and candour should refrain from using; at least they should affix a glossary; it is a mule in language, begotten by malevolent party spirit upon credulity; its construction is at diametrical variance with its etymology.'[26]

And an examination of the use of the term in Nottingham suggests that it was simply a smear word, calculated to excite an emotional response. Those on whom it was used were almost entirely men of substantial social and economic position, whose remotest thought was revolution in their own country. As reformers they might have had sympathy with some of the aims of the French Revolution though they spoke little on this subject. They almost certainly shared the Rev. Gilbert Wakefield's view that however much a man might wish for radical reformation by

[26]Vindex, *A letter to the Burgesses of Nottingham* (1803), p. 8; R. Davison, *Letter to J. Bowles on the subject of his 2 pamphlets lately published* (1803), p. 14, *Ten Letters*, op. cit., p. 23.

pacific means he could have little hope from violent revolutions. As revolutionaries themselves these men would not have known how to start. The leaders of the reform movement in Nottingham could hardly have been more inappropriately cast when labelled as 'Jacobins' or 'Revolutionaries'. The social and economic groups for whom revolution might have been a justifiable gamble barely stirred politically throughout this period and when they did it was only to support reform movements.[27]

In July, 1803, the country was again at war, but Nottingham reactions this time were far different from those of ten years earlier. The opponents who had spoken out in 1793 now went quietly; the enthusiasts who had gone noisily in 1793 were now sobered at the prospect of a long struggle ahead and the threat of French invasion. The Corporation of Nottingham, which had refused to make a donation to the war effort in 1798, now called a special meeting, voted 400 guineas to the government, and swallowed its previous discontent in a loyal address to the King, offering its firm and united support to defend the country by every means in its power. Disillusionment with Napoleon, locally as well as nationally, combined with a real threat to national integrity, had, for the time at any rate, stilled the voice of discord, and the *Journal* applauded the yielding of state broils and party rancour to the present crisis.[28]

Nottingham again called for volunteers and about 750 men were formed into two battalions. Previously, at the beginning of 1798, a voluntary corps of Infantrymen had been formed to serve in defence of Nottingham should the invasion materialise. Though it had its teething troubles and committee resignations it quickly elicited over £1,000 in subscriptions from the town's enthusiasts. Now the call again went out but only to men 'with property to defend'; the services of the remaining classes, they were told, were not at this stage required, though Bailey estimated that almost the entire adult male population were, in one way or another, being trained in the use of arms by the end of 1804. There was evidently no danger in entrusting the alleged Jacobins with such a role. There were Whig Officers too amongst the early appointments such as Francis Hart, a lieutenant, and

[27]G. Wakefield, *Memoirs of the Life of Gilbert Wakefield* (1804), Vol. II, p. 15.
[28]Corporation Hall Books, 1802/3, pp. 63-5, 27th July, 1803; *Nottingham Journal*, 30th July, 1803.

Richard Hopper, an ensign, both prominent reformers, though their Commander in Chief was Ichabod Wright, of a prominent loyalist county family from Mapperley. The volunteers undertook this time to march to any part of Britain in case of invasion and even to serve when required by the Civil Magistrates in the suppression of riot and tumult in their own districts. One correspondent thought that the efficiency of the volunteers was restricted by their tendency to chatter and whisper whilst being trained, but their enthusiasm was great and over 600 turned up for drilling even on a wet day.[29]

The fear of invasion and the changed attitude of the Corporation are clear. The magistrates assumed responsibility for organising all willing householders who were not in the volunteers to act as special constables should the invasion come, and one of the principal rooms at the Exchange Hall was converted into an Armoury Room. There was thus complete identification this time between the local government of Nottingham and the national purpose. When the Whig Club met in August, 1804, they looked forward to the prospect of Fox's joining the government, and in March, 1806, the Corporation forwarded another loyal address to the King, thanking him for the forming of the 'Talents' Ministry and expressing their willingness to make any sacrifice. This was a quite different feeling from that of the Revolutionary Wars, and it was the projected invasion that dominated all thoughts. In February, 1804, the French were reported to have landed in Scotland. When the real crisis came the Nottingham volunteers were declared to be at the ready, for the enemy attempt was about to be made. After Trafalgar, news of which was received thankfully, the Mayor himself sponsored the Nottingham contribution to a Patriotic Fund for the relief of widows of those killed in action, and all the Churches and Chapels of the town held charity sermons to help swell the funds. Not the least contribution made to the prevailing spirit in Nottingham was that of George Burbage, the proprietor of the *Nottingham Journal* for thirty years, who died in 1807. So enthusiastic was he as an advocate of the national cause and so anxious for success that it was said of him that in his accounts he killed more French

[29]*Nottingham Journal*, 3rd February, 28th April, 1798, 6th August, 5th November, 1803, 28th April, 1804; Bailey, op. cit., pp. 212-3; H.O. 50/82, Duke of Portland to H.O. 23rd August, 1803.

soldiers on paper than were contained in the whole of France.[30]

It was perhaps as well that the Nottingham volunteers were not required to face action. After Trafalgar their enthusiasm quickly waned; through 1806 Ichabod Wright, commanding both the Yeoman Cavalry and Infantry, had to report that he had lost many men from the Cavalry as a result of regulations he had been compelled to introduce to keep discipline. Of those remaining many were useless, never attending exercise or inspection, and failing to keep horses fit for service. By April, 1808, the Yeoman Cavalry had become so weak that it had to be disbanded and remaining officers transferred to the Infantry Corps.[31]

On their past record the Nottingham Whigs of the Corporation and outside it could not be expected to keep up this harmonious relationship with the central government for long. Though it was claimed that there was enthusiastic support for the Spanish patriots in August, 1808, and the Mayor actually supported the opening of subscriptions on their behalf at the end of the year, the essential basis for unity had gone when the invasion threat had been removed. The old arguments soon began to reassert themselves. The writing was already on the wall in August, 1806, when the Whig Club, toasting the Nottingham volunteers, referred enigmatically to 'the domestic as well as the foreign foe'. Through 1807 they were gradually resuming normal business with celebrations of Francis Burdett's return to the House of Commons, and by June, 1808, the 'Rights of Man', though fashionably abused according to its proposer, was again their toast.[32]

It was in 1808 too that the *Nottingham Review* first appeared, under the ownership and editorship of a printer, Charles Sutton, a New Connexion Methodist and political Radical. He quickly made it clear where his sympathies lay and was soon mobilising Nottingham opinion against both the way in which the war was being waged and its very continuation. For the first time the

[30]*Nottingham Journal*, 10th December, 1803; 4th, 11th February, 25th August, 1804, 17th August, 30th November, 1805; Corporation Hall Books, 1805/6, pp. 21-2, 3rd March, 1806; W. H. Wylie, op. cit., p. 160.

[31]H.O. 50/157, Ichabod Wright to H.O., 10th March, 1806; H.O. 50/200, Ichabod Wright to H.O., 8th April, 1808.

[32]*Nottingham Journal*, 16th August, 1806, 4th July, 1807, 6th August, 1808; *Nottingham Review*, 3rd June, 30th December, 1808.

people of Nottingham were given informed comment on the detailed conduct of the war; previously they had seen nothing but extracts from national papers. From exposures of particular alleged errors, such as the Convention of Cintra, Sutton quickly moved to the more general question of the terms on which the British government would be ready to make peace. This line of thought was at the same time developed by John Smith in the House of Commons. Elected in a 'pro-War Coalition' with Daniel Parker Coke in 1806 and again in 1807, he was beginning to move away from his backers and had asked on 29th February, 1808, how long the government envisaged continuing the war and whether they anticipated being able to negotiate more honourable and secure terms if the war continued two years longer than they could at that time. By 1810 Smith had become an extreme critic of the government, denouncing it for its profligate expenditure, especially in military departments.[33]

It was, however, the effect of the war on trade and industry which was the vital factor in determining growing opposition in Nottingham, and the *Review* echoed and inspired the arguments of the growing anti-war movement. It condemned the Orders in Council for their disastrous effect on manufacturing trades and warned, in June, 1809, of the dangers that the government's American policy would precipitate. When, in the September of that year, it discussed the approaching Golden Jubilee of the King's accession, it suggested that the occasion should not be celebrated in view of the irretrievable difficulties into which the reign had brought the country. Again it raised the question of peace terms and suggested that Britain should be ready to give up all her conquests as a start. Through the November came further urgings on the country's need for peace to avoid an increasing National Debt and national bankruptcy, and people were implored, in Nottingham and elsewhere, to overwhelm the government with peace-petitions, believed to be the only efficacious way of applying pressure. As 1810 opened there were further attacks on 'the folly of the government's policy' and the times were described as 'the most woeful epoch in English History'.[34]

[33]Parl. Debs., Vol. 46, 367, 29th February, 1808.

[34]*Nottingham Review*, 30th December, 1808, 2nd June, 22nd, 29th September, 13th October, 3rd, 10th, 24th November, 1809, 26th January, 1810.

The unaccustomed unity which had descended in 1803 with the renewal of the war and lasted as long as the invasion threat was now in ruins. There had been both Corporation and general town meetings in April, 1809, to demand an inquiry into the conduct of the Duke of York as Commander in Chief of the Armed Forces, and through 1809 the Whig Club had gone back to its old campaign for Parliamentary reform as a more important cause to support than prosecution of the war. Reformers all joined forces in May, 1810, under the leadership of the Corporation when that body drew up a petition to the King for the removal of the Ministers and to Parliament 'for a radical and temperate reform in the representation of the people'. 'Peace and Parliamentary Reform', the twin slogans of the following years, were now being heard together. A public meeting was held to follow up the Corporation's lead. It was attended by 5,000 men, according to the *Review*; the *Journal* estimated not more than 500, though it did concede that the meeting had been held in the Market Place as the Guildhall had not been large enough to accommodate it. It also conceded a great unanimity of feeling at the meeting and the almost immediate receipt of nearly 4,000 signatures of approval.[35]

The years 1811 and 1812 saw this mood increasing in intensity and the peace demands growing. Against a background of intense industrial unrest, of Luddite sabotage to supplement the more orthodox pressures and organisations of the framework-knitters, attention was inevitably directed towards the social and economic impact of the war. Letters and articles on the high cost of living occurred weekly. Attention was drawn to the number of paupers in Nottingham, which reached a new peak in April, 1813, when one third of the population was on poor relief. Men recalled the words of those who had opposed the war in 1793 and their original protests and petitions were reprinted to show how their supporters had been vindicated by events. The association of peace with prosperity was irresistible when war appeared to have such dire consequences, and as men lamented the increased cost of living and loss of work through 1811 they asked what would happen if war with America should also come. John Cartwright offered

[35]*Nottingham Review*, 7th April, 1809, 8th June, 1810; Corporation Hall Books, 1808/9, pp. 66-8, 4th April, 1809, 1809/10, pp. 52-4, 23rd May, 1810; *Nottingham Journal*, 20th May, 1809, 2nd June, 1810.

parliamentary reform as the only road to peace, but more people regarded it as a desirable consequence, and in the meantime kept up their traditional meetings and petitions against the government. In May, 1812, the death of Perceval was greeted with some show of joy by people who paraded in the streets, though this was less a political demonstration than the result of a bill stuck up in the town five days earlier which had held Perceval responsible for the Act making frame-breaking a capital offence. In June feeling was manifested in an incident at the theatre when men refused to remove their hats for the National Anthem as a gesture of protest against the King and his government. Disorder broke out, and the theatre had to be closed for a time. Although one correspondent complained of the 'supineness and apathy of Nottingham' on the matter of peace-petitions, this was intended to make the active more active. In August the Dissenters of the town organised their own peace-petition, and in December there were general demands that Nottingham should again make its voice heard to the rest of the country. Dissenting Ministers of every denomination were said to have supported the call for a general town meeting, at a time when St. Mary's parish alone was supporting over 8,000 paupers.[36]

The meeting was held at the end of 1812. The arguments put forward dealt almost entirely with economic grievances; the middle class could no longer bear the weight of oppressive taxes; the industrious poor were denied work; their maintenance from poor rates was totally inadequate, and the necessities of life were priced beyond their reach. Robert Denison, 'the universal exposer of public peculators', lamented the debts of the country arising from massive expenditure. Alderman Howitt came right down to earth with his description of overstocked warehouses, of customers who seldom came, and of the unavailing applications for work which were daily made. Another speaker declared that to enumerate all the sufferings and privations of the labouring poor would make the heart sicken. A petition to Parliament was presented by John Smith, who maintained that it had been adopted

[36]Parl. Debs., Vol. 61, 598, 6th April, 1813; *Nottingham Review*, 8th March, 27th December, 1811, 4th, 18th December, 1812. Sutton, op. cit., p. 300. The somewhat melodramatic account of the anti-Perceval demonstration in E. P. Thompson, op. cit., p. 570, is undermined by Coldham's letters to H.O. of 9th and 14th May, 1812, H.O. 42/123.

with a greater measure of unanimity than any political cause he could remember in the town. A counter-petition in favour of continuing the war was also organised but it received only some 700 signatures, in contrast to the 5,000 or 6,000 who signed the first one. In this new and more intense upsurge of anti-war feeling, the *Review* bitterly recalled that the initial purpose of the war had been 'to stifle the infant liberties of France' and for 'extinguishing the principles of political regeneration in Europe'.[37]

When the victories of Wellington towards the end of 1813 suggested that the end was in sight the *Review* was in no mood for rejoicing. It welcomed the expected deliverance from the 'thraldom of a war-faction domination' (the government) but it could not ignore that trading and manufacturing interests had suffered privations and losses for twenty years which were unequalled in any previous period. Its own contribution to peace displays was, significantly, a tableau of John Bull in the act of burning the Income Tax Bill. When the supposed end came and the statesmen assembled at Vienna the *Review* saw them as squabbling about who should have the greatest share of the plunder. Nottingham celebrated the peace but the celebrations were not without reminders of the times passed and present as hungry men jumped inside a roasted ox and impatiently began to tear the carcase apart with their hands, unwilling, or unable, to wait their turn.[38]

But this was the phoney peace. There was still Napoleon's Hundred Days to be endured. On the renewal of war John Blackner and fifty-three other men requested the Mayor of Nottingham to take the lead in organising yet another meeting of protest. This time the Mayor refused because of 'the present unsettled state of the public mind'. The Luddite outrages since 1811 had undoubtedly cooled the ardour of the Magistrates for popular demonstrations when the initiative came from outside their own body, though the Mayor did allow the use of the Guildhall for the collection of signatures, confirming the general sympathy of the Corporation with the venture. Almost 5,000 signatures were received. John Smith in the Commons seconded the amendment

[37]*Nottingham Review*, 1st, 8th January, 26th March, 1813; Parl. Debs., Vol. 61, 598, 6th April, 1813.

[38]*Nottingham Review*, 22nd October, 1813, 30th December, 1814, 3rd March, 1815; Sutton, op. cit., p. 312; *Nottingham Journal*, 11th June, 1814.

against the resumption of the war 'as a friend of humanity', winning great approval for his stand; the hated foe of 1806 was now the darling of the Nottingham Whigs. When peace really did come after Waterloo the Corporation reacted soberly; it decided to abandon the frivolous expenditure on public rejoicing normally accompanying such an event, instead opening a fund for the relief of soldiers, sailors, widows, and other warsufferers.[39]

And the *Review* shared this mood, being left to lament the temporary loss of its owner and editor, Charles Sutton, convicted at Nottingham Assizes in July, 1815, of showing contempt for the government, degrading the army, and encouraging the Luddites. The *Review* had long been under attack. The *Gazette*, an ultra-Tory paper owned by Richard Eaton, the hosier, and beginning its brief existence in January, 1813, confessed to feelings of disgust at the *Review*'s filth and accused it of 'instilling political wisdom into worshippers at the altar of jacobinic idolatry'. In May, 1812, Major General Hawker had informed his superiors that the editor, Charles Sutton, must be punished. 'He is a bad fellow', he wrote, 'and the sooner the writings of that man is stop'd the better' (sic). Sutton went too far in printing a satirical letter, allegedly from a British soldier in America, who claimed to be doing far worse things there as a war-hero than he had ever done when breaking frames back home as a criminal. He was sentenced to eighteen months' imprisonment in Northampton jail, a punishment, said his successor, not for libel but for opposition to the war. The prosecution, said to have been instigated by local Tories, made no difference to either the policy of the paper or the enthusiasm with which Sutton took up his causes on his release.[40]

*

[39]*Nottingham Review*, 5th May, 1815; H.O. 42/144, Coldham to H.O. 10th May, 1815; Parl. Debs., Vol. 67, 415-8, 25th May, 1815; *Nottingham Journal*, 15th, 22nd July, 1815.

[40]Sutton, op. cit., pp. 316-8; *Nottingham Gazette*, 25th February, 18th March, 1814; H.O. 42/121, Major General Hawker to H.O., 12th March, 1812; *Nottingham Review*, 1st September, 1815; Commentary on the legality of the trial of Charles Sutton, MS. fragment, Nottingham City Library, Archives Section, M.1001.

10

THE PENTRICH REBELLION

In the immediate post-war period Nottingham exhibited most of the characteristics which historians have noted about these years. In particular, it experienced the sometimes over-lapping reform and revolutionary movements, which have never been easy to disentangle or assess. In Nottingham the revolution-bogey acquired even more frightening proportions because of the town's still persistent Luddite troubles, and in June, 1817, the town was actually to contribute to the Regency's armed uprising, the Pentrich Rebellion. Yet even Pentrich cannot obscure the fact that the bogey was exaggerated; the revolutionaries in Nottingham were fighting not only the Tories but also the re-formers, who were organised and led by the Corporation Whigs. The latter proved their more dangerous enemies, and during these years the masses were influenced by the reformers rather than the revolutionaries; reforming initiative was seized from the latter and given official direction, losing its political menace and any social and economic overtones that it might have acquired.

Those in authority did not distinguish between the later Luddites and the early revolutionaries; Luddism seemed to merge imperceptibly into the extremist political agitation of the im-mediate post-war period. In fact, the belief that the Luddites had political designs arose from the unsubstantiated, unproven allegations of informers that this was so and the inability of the local magistrates to believe that men who had so successfully contravened the law in pursuit of industrial ends could not have deeper-laid schemes. The town clerk of Nottingham, George Coldham, appears to have accepted uncritically the revolution gossip fed to him by his informers and passed it all on to the central government. He lived in fear of attacks upon himself and the town magistrates through April and May, 1815, though there was not a single incident of violence during this period. The only slightly ominous development was a notice posted in the town and neighbourhood on 22nd April, urging people to resist all demands made by the government until it agreed to carry out certain reforming policies. This was almost identical to the suggestions made in 1831 by the Nottingham Whig leaders that people should pay no taxes until Parliamentary reform had been passed, but in the atmosphere of 1815 the words appeared full of menace. The county magistrates warned that these words implied rebellion against the state; the town magistrates even won praise from the *Journal*, a rare thing, for their peace-keeping role, and the working classes were warned not to attend illegal meetings. Public meetings were few; one was held, with Blackner himself a leading sponsor, in opposition to the renewal of the French War, a cause which the Corporation would have relished at any other time and which, even now, their M.P.s enthusiastically championed. But to Coldham this was a 'violent petition' which the anti-war party were fostering and might lead to further breaches of the peace. There was also an allegedly seditious meeting of unemployed held in Nottingham during May, at which one speaker, Peter Green, was arrested by the magistrates, but neither this nor the anti-war meeting constituted any real threat to the authorities.[1]

The second period of panic occurred in the Autumn of 1816. In the months following the last great Luddite coup at Lough-borough in June, 1816, when the culprits were being tracked down or awaiting trial, the air was again filled with talk of revolution. The word was common currency in Nottingham, reported one visitor, and the government ought to have been better informed. In fact, George Coldham and his successor, Henry Enfield, town clerks in this period, were constant correspondents of the Home Secretary, and they were never guilty of underestimating

---

[1] *Nottingham Review*, 28th April, 1815; *Nottingham Journal*, 29th April, 1815; H.O. 42/144, Coldham to H.O., 10th May, 1815; Darvall, op. cit., p. 150 from H.O. 42/144.

the problem. In October Enfield informed the Home Secretary of his intention to reimpose Watch and Ward in the town and notified him of the suspicious meetings that were taking place at public houses and the menacing appearance that the town presented. The county authorities were similarly plagued with notions of numerous malcontents possessed of arms. In November Enfield asked the government for the retention of cavalry forces in the neighbourhood because of their proven superiority in the control of unruly crowds, and on 9th December he reported that there was still 'talk of revolution' among the Luddites. The Lord-Lieutenant was also convinced that the 'lower orders were more disaffected than ever', but he did not define his terms.[2]

Again nothing happened beyond the appearance at the end of December of a poster headed 'Britons prepare yourselves', which offered no very precise message. Shortly before this the editor of the *Review* had commented that he had never known Nottingham more tranquil or peaceable. When trouble flared up in London in the form of the Spa Fields Riots everyone had to admit that Nottingham had in no way responded to the lead and that there had been no trace of commotion. There was, allegedly, 'much dispirit', amongst Nottingham's 'disaffected', whoever they were, at the government's quick action, but the allegation could be proven only by the absence of any trouble. And, in spite of all expressed fears to the contrary, not a single outburst occurred to disturb the political calm in the pre-Pentrich period. When the Home Secretary suggested in February, 1817, that the Spring Assizes should be transferred from Nottingham to the quieter centre of Newark to avoid possible trouble, both the town magistrates and the Lord-Lieutenant, the Duke of Newcastle, were sure that this was unnecessary and persuaded the Home Office not to go ahead with its proposals.[3]

[2]H.O. 42/153, Col. W. Shaw to H.O., 6th September, Enfield to H.O., 16th, 21st October, County Magistrates to H.O. 15th October, 1816; H.O. 42/155, Enfield to H.O. 20th November, Newcastle to H.O. 16th November, 1816; H.O. 42/156, Enfield to H.O. 9th December, 1816.

[3]Ne.C. 4954, E. S. Godfrey to Newcastle, 22nd December, 1816; *Nottingham Review*, 22nd November, 1816; H.O. 42/156, Enfield to H.O., 4th December, 1816; H.O. 40/3(1), Extracts of a letter received from Nottingham, 2nd December, 1816; Ne.C. 4936, 4929, 4937, correspondence between Newcastle and Sidmouth, 25-28th February, 1817; H.O. 42/160, Enfield to H.O., 28th February, 1817.

Already the Corporation Whigs were reasserting their traditional control of the popular movement, a control which Luddism had threatened to break. In a manner somewhat contradictory
to the town clerk's repeated requests for military assistance, they
sponsored petitions to Parliament in February, 1816, and again
in February, 1817, against the retention of a large standing army,
a danger to the 'liberties of the country'. John Smith, M.P.,
supporting his constituents, described them as 'consistent friends
of liberty'. Not all their conduct was consistent, but this was at
least a good Whig cause, which enabled the Corporation to move
back into the saddle. Also of a totally acceptable kind were the
demands for Parliamentary reform and a reduction in public
expenditure which were put forward in the following month.
The *Review*, whose ideas were usually a little in advance of the
orthodox Whig line, was happy to note the highly constitutional
form that the agitation was now assuming. Petitioning was the
means that it approved and this was the means that the Nottingham Whigs liked to employ. In September, 1816, a large public
meeting was held under Corporation sponsorship, which listed the
usual Whig grievances such as standing armies and excessive
taxation. This time a detailed account of the meeting reached the
Home Office from non-Corporation sources, but the town
clerk had failed to inform the central government only because
he had probably helped to organise the meeting himself and knew
that it constituted no threat. At a meeting in February, 1817, the
suspension of Habeas Corpus was added to the list of grievances,
a not surprising complaint but, like the attack on standing
armies, a little ironical in view of Enfield's alleged relief before
Pentrich at the end of May that the authorities had previously
removed potential trouble makers. Newcastle expressed his
conviction that the holding of public meetings was undesirable
since they agitated men's minds at a time when everything should
be done to avoid this. He failed to realise that by bringing
political discontent into the open and giving it public ventilation
the Corporation Whigs were doing more to render the discontent innocuous and keep down prospects of revolution than
his own purely repressive attitude would ever do.[4]

[4]Parl. Debs., Vol. 68, 949, 28th February, 1816; Corporation Hall Books, 1816/17,
pp. 34-8, 5th February, 1817; *Nottingham Review*, 29th March, 27th September, 1816,
14th, 28th February, 1817; H.O. 42/165, James Hooley to H.O., 29th May, 1817; Ne.C.
4982, Newcastle to Richard Sutton, 5th April, 1817.

The Hampden Club movement of the autumn and winter of 1816–17 falls somewhere between the official and unofficial reform movements of the time, or rather managed to incorporate people from both groups and be all things to all men. On 13th December, 1816, the *Review* published information of the growing number of Hampden Clubs in neighbouring towns, and the *Review* office itself printed copies of the constitution and regulations of the Nottingham Hampden Club. It was to have several divisions, though they were all to go under the one name; its aims were to be the securing of universal manhood suffrage and annual parliaments, and a new member could be introduced only by other members who could testify that 'he will not disgrace this Society'; subscriptions of $1\frac{1}{2}$d. per week were to be charged 'to cover pens, ink, paper, and printing'; and members were instructed to be 'perfectly legal and constitutional' in their conduct. The Home Secretary received accounts of an extensive network of Hampden Clubs throughout the county in January, 1817, and at the same time the *Review* reported flourishing groups at Beeston and Chilwell on the outskirts of the town and a Basford Club of over 100 members. The declared purpose of the Nottingham Club was purely constitutional and many people were ready to testify that they had attended meetings and heard nothing but Parliamentary reform discussed. But it is also beyond question that groups later met under the Hampden Club banner whose aspirations went beyond that point.[5]

The composition of the Nottinghamshire Clubs has been a matter of some disagreement. The 1817 House of Lords' Committee of Secrecy described them as consisting of the 'lower order of Artizans', with an avowed and expressed intent of conducting a revolution, an opinion recently supported by a description of them as being 'almost wholly proletarian in character'. This view could well be incorrect. The Leicester Hampden Club was made up of small tradesmen and superior artizans as well as stockingers, and Nottingham's would very likely have had a similar composition. A member from nearby Arnold wrote of the tradesmen and shopkeepers of considerable substance who were members in addition to the framework-knitters, and the Duke of Newcastle was very concerned in November, 1816, that 'the better as well

[5] H.O. 40/3(2); H.O. 40/4(1), W. Lockett to H.O., 12th January, 1817; *Nottingham Review*, 24th January, 1817, 24th April, 1818.

as the lower orders' were 'very disaffected'; when Newcastle talked of 'disaffected' he invariably meant 'reformers', and the Hampden Clubs were amongst his greatest worries at this time.[6]

On 13th March, 1817, Lord Sidmouth informed the County magistrates that the Blanketeers were expecting to be joined by a large number of individuals when they reached Nottingham, and he asked them to take effectual means to prevent them from progressing further. In fact the threat fizzled out. Newcastle was able to notify Sidmouth on the 19th that only one man had appeared in Nottingham from Manchester and he had been apprehended immediately. Nottingham itself had not stirred. At the same time the *Journal* was commenting that local Hampden Clubs were breaking up, following the suspension of Habeas Corpus, a view supported elsewhere; it interpreted the withdrawals as the departure of disappointed revolutionaries who had found that, whatever the situation in other countries, revolution in Britain was not possible. Whatever the revolutionary intent of those who withdrew, it is fairly clear that some who remained employed the machinery and personnel of surviving societies to plan the rebellion of June.[7]

The Pentrich Rebellion of June, 1817, is an event which has aroused the interest and passions of men of widely different views. At the time the *Review*, a supporter of reform by constitutional methods, found the rebels an embarrassment and was happy to shift the blame for the rising on to Oliver the Spy, who incited the trouble, 'turned discontent into treason', and 'forced the miserable people of Derbyshire and Nottinghamshire from their homes'. The *Journal*, similarly embarrassed by revelations about the use of government spies, shifted the blame from Oliver on to the shoulders of reform associations, such as the Hampden Clubs, and reform orators, such as Hunt, who were believed to be exciting public opinion. Whether Oliver played any major role

[6]Parl. Debs., Vol. 71, 444, 19th February, 1817; E. P. Thompson, op. cit., p. 641; A. T. Patterson, op. cit., p. 107; H.O. 40/4(1), William Burton's Confession, 22nd January, 1817; H.O. 40/4(3), Newcastle to Sidmouth, 6th November, 1816; H.O. 42/155, Newcastle to Sidmouth, 16th November, 1816.

[7]Ne.C. 49596, Sidmouth to Thomas Hildyard, 13th March, 1817, 4930, Newcastle to Sidmouth, 19th March, 1817; *Nottingham Journal*, 8th March, 1817.

in fomenting rebellion or simply acted as a paid informer remains an issue for disagreement.[8]

Even to allow Oliver the Spy a substantial role in the causation of the Pentrich Rebellion, it is still necessary to explain why the situation favoured his exploitation. The Nottingham Whigs believed that this could be explained in terms of the post-war depression and erroneous government policy, high taxation, the Corn Laws, and failure to move ahead with reforming policies, errors from which Nottingham was felt to be suffering particularly severely. The rebels themselves scarcely referred to economic discontent beyond 'going a revolutioning' 'to make times better', which was in line with the statements of William Stevens, a needle-maker, probably the leading Nottingham conspirator. The army had fought Napoleon, he said, to secure peace and comfort; these had not been forthcoming and, following the suspension of Habeas Corpus, soldiers, like civilians, shared the belief that nothing less than revolution would do.[9]

Economic motivation was not clearly defined, though an attempt has recently been made to explain the Pentrich rebellion in terms of a community 'at the heart of the conflict between unplanned economic individualism and an older way of life'; the stockingers, it is suggested, were some of the worst hit victims of *laissez-faire* and this is offered as an explanation of the rebellion's location. In fact, the rebels of Pentrich were 'stockingers, quarrymen, iron-workers, and labourers', as is admitted, a mixture of occupational groups. The Nottingham section might better be used to illustrate the behaviour of the stockingers, though the claim that 1817 was a crisis point in the application of *laissez-faire* principles is no more valid as an explanation of Pentrich than it is as an explanation of Luddism.[10]

Nor is it helpful to suggest that Nottingham was both chosen by Oliver for special treatment because of its industrial situation and destined by its history to play the role that it did. Nottingham

[8]*Nottingham Review*, 20th, 27th June, 1817; *Nottingham Journal*, 25th October, 1817. For the 'Oliver controversy' see R. J. White, *From Waterloo to Peterloo* (1957), Ch. XIII and E. P. Thompson, op. cit., pp. 649-669.

[9]Sutton, op. cit., p. 335; Ne.C. 4995a, Evidence of arrested men . . . taken on 10th June, 1817; H.O. 40/9, Oliver's Narrative.

[10]E. P. Thompson, op. cit., pp. 648-9, 667; Report of Proceedings concerning the trial of Jeremiah Brandreth (1817), pp. 6, 9-10.

appears not to have been given any special treatment by Oliver; he visited it very briefly on three occasions and performed very little business when he was there. And Nottingham's supposed 'revolutionary tradition', whatever that signifies, can be attributed to little more than Robin Hood and the Luddites; and the latter, far from providing an example to the revolutionaries of 1817, were responsible for a campaign from which the Pentrich Rebellion could hardly have been further removed.[11]

Whatever part economic grievances or revolutionary tradition played in promoting it, there seems little doubt that the Pentrich Rebellion was the anticipated culmination of political agitation and organization which had been growing locally for over a year. The Hampden Clubs, spreading throughout Nottingham-shire and Derbyshire in the autumn and winter of 1816-17, became the vehicle and in part the cause of growing political discontent. They feature prominently in the depositions of defendants and witnesses concerned in the subsequent trials, and it was from a Hampden Club meeting at the Golden Fleece, in Nottingham, that an informer gleaned information for the Town Clerk which proved to be a substantially accurate account of the plan which was launched on 9th June.[12]

Apart from the vague, unsubstantiated claims and beliefs about the subversive activities of the Hampden Clubs, no statement was made of official concern until February, 1817, when the House of Lords' Secret Committee reported that the neighbour-hood of Nottingham was one of the centres of the various country societies, such as the Hampden Clubs and Spencean Societies, which were plotting revolution. This brought a quick response from the reformers of Nottingham that they were 'grossly calumniated' by a report which 'represented them as seditious, disaffected, and treasonably disposed'. Evidence had not been offered and so the case could be neither proved nor disproved. One of the Duke of Newcastle's most reliable magistrates, Lancelot Rolleston, assured the Lord-Lieutenant on 5th April that there was not the slightest foundation for the idea that Nottingham was in any combination or contact with other parts of the Midlands and the North. The Duke quickly communicated the happy intelligence that Nottingham was neither directly nor

[11]E. P. Thompson, op. cit., p. 656.
[12]H.O. 42/165, Enfield to H.O. 23rd May, 1817.

indirectly engaged in any plot. But if the Secret Committee's report was an exaggerated view of the situation in February, 1817, it was a fair anticipation of what was going to develop by May and a more realistic appraisal of the situation than Newcastle's. William Stevens, the Nottingham needle-maker whose house was a meeting-place of the would-be insurgents and whose role was sufficient to cause him later to flee the country, described afterwards how support for revolution grew in Nottingham throughout March, April, and May.[13]

The scheme as it materialised was first mooted when Joseph Mitchell, a Liverpool 'reformer', passed through Nottingham in April and was drawn up during May. On the 5th of that month Thomas Bacon, the 'Derbyshire delegate', attended a meeting at Wakefield at which Oliver was present and brought back his report to the 'North Midland Committee' on which sat Brandreth, Turner, Ludlam, all later executed. From that time onwards preparations went ahead with Nottingham as the centre of the Midlands' organization. From Nottingham delegates went out to the Hampden Clubs on the Nottinghamshire-Derbyshire border, preparing their members to look to Nottingham for leadership when the time came. It was a Nottingham man who persuaded the Ripley Hampden Club to put their fears behind them as 'it was generally arranged all over the nation' and from Nottingham that Jeremiah Brandreth went out on 5th June to Pentrich to lead the rebellion. Though they were mostly Derbyshire men who were taken during the revolt, wrote Rolleston to Newcastle, they all claimed that they had been led on by Nottingham men. And there is little reason to suspect this version. When Oliver was taken to Nottingham on 26th May by Birkin of Derby it was here that he learned of the full, and limited, extent of the plans that had been made, of the fact that the villages for some twelve to fourteen miles around had been instructed to look to Nottingham for orders, and it was here that he met about twenty-six 'very determined characters', who said that 'nothing but a revolution would do for them' and later, on 7th June, that Nottingham would have to set the example. There was ample justification for the informers' reports and the somewhat naive

[13]Parl. Debs., Vol. 71, 416, 18th February, 698, 26th February, 1817; Ne.C. 4970, L. Rolleston to Newcastle, 6th April, 1817; 4931, Newcastle to Sidmouth, 8th April, 1817; Deposition of William Stevens, Cobbett's Political Register, 16th May, 1818.

suggestions raised in the press after the event that certain meetings had been held in Nottingham for purposes other than the discussion of Parliamentary reform. The conspirators, the *Journal* admitted, were mainly in Nottingham, though it was unable to support the Judge's view that Brandreth was a well-known figure, since it could discover virtually nothing about him.[14]

If the conspirators were mainly Nottingham-based so did their plan of action assume Nottingham's central role, for the town was to be the rallying point for the whole of the Midlands area. The marchers from Pentrich believed that when they reached Nottingham they would find the town in the hands of its people, the soldiers acting along with the civilians. An army would meet them there consisting of men from all over the area and they would even use Nottingham to establish their provisional government before rallying all their support, crossing the Trent, and proceeding to London.[15]

The most difficult to assess, and yet the most vital contribution to an understanding of Oliver's role in Nottingham, is his own account of it. This account illustrates clearly the difficulties which beset a man playing a double game. He had to give the appearance of knowledge and emotions which he did not possess yet to avoid precision and enthusiasm which he could not have carried off with conviction. He was intelligent enough to carry conviction and intelligent enough not to become fantastical. His technique appears to have been to allow others to do most of the talking and to answer them in generalities. His main deception was not that he made sweeping affirmations but that he failed to deny the sweeping affirmations of others. By Oliver's account his contribution was to allow others to think wishfully without contradicting them.[16]

Several factors suggest that this is a fair view. One is that Oliver's narrative is an unvarnished one, containing no flowery details, making no excessive attempt to incriminate people, describing the fearful and reluctant as well as those filled with bravado, and, above all, conveying the pathetic nature of the plot rather than

[14]Ibid.; Ne.C. 4996, Evidence of arrested men, 10th June, 1817, 4972, L. Rolleston to Newcastle, 10th June, 1817; H.O. 40/9, Oliver's Narrative; *Nottingham Review*, 14th November, 1817; *Nottingham Journal*, 25th October, 1817.

[15]Ne.C. 4994, 4995a, 4996, Evidence of arrested men, 10th June, 1817.

[16]H.O. 40/9, Oliver's Narrative.

its danger. Enfield, the town clerk of Nottingham, a good
Whig and a strong opponent of the government on all else,
was ready to vindicate Oliver and clear him of any deliberately
provocative role. And it is important to note that Brandreth left
Nottingham for Pentrich the day before Oliver paid his last visit
to Nottingham on 6th June. The decision was taken before
Oliver's arrival and was not later rescinded in spite of the strong
suspicions growing amongst the Nottingham Committee on the
7th that Oliver was in fact a spy. This must be taken in association
with Steven's statement on that day that he had made up his
mind 'to kill or be killed', which reinforces the idea that the die
was cast before Oliver returned to Nottingham.[17]

Sympathisers with the Pentrich rebellion, both contemporaries
and later commentators, have felt a great need to offer 'proof'
of an actual meeting between Oliver the Spy and Brandreth, the
leader of the rebels. Contemporary accounts of such a meeting,
invariably hearsay evidence, contain such a confusion of dates and
places that they are quite unreliable, and modern efforts to supply
documentary proof of such an alleged meeting have fared no
better. It is, of course, quite possible that Brandreth did attend
Oliver's meeting on 27th May at the Three Salmons, though the
Home Office denied that he had been present and were supported
in this view by Thomas Bacon, one of the leading conspirators.
When Oliver returned to Nottingham on the 6th, Brandreth had
already left for Pentrich, as the town clerk's informant told him.
And so there is no actual proof of a meeting, or even strong
evidence to support the idea of one, which was conceded by
defending counsel Thomas Denman when he attacked the man
'behind the curtain' and 'he who furnished the combustibles' but
admitted that there was no actual evidence on the point. Denman's belief in Oliver's responsibility was no more than the
belief of all good Whigs and Liberals that Brandreth and his
associates were victims of the 'odious system of espionage'. In
fact this obsession with proving a meeting between Oliver and
Brandreth has been particularly pointless, for the role of Brandreth in planning the rebellion from Nottingham, which is well
documented, indicated that he was repeatedly in the company of
men who did meet Oliver and must have been well aware of

[17]H.O. 42/168, W. J. Lockett to H.O., 20th July, 1817; H.O. 40/9, Oliver's Narrative.

Oliver's visits. This was not, however, sufficient to enable Brandreth's counsel, or that of his associates, to call Oliver as a defence witness. It seems likely that those who had actually met Oliver did in fact, as one historian has noted, stay at home on the night of the 9th, that of the rebellion.[18]

The role of the local magistracy and the government has also come under critical scrutiny for their failure to prevent the Pentrich Rebellion. Why, asked the *Review*, did the Magistrates of the town keep out of the way on the evening of the 9th, when Nottingham showed some signs of disturbance, instead of turning out to read the Riot Act and disperse the crowd? The paper would have been even more concerned had it known the full extent of the authorities' involvement. The Town Magistrates had secured full details of the plot by 23rd May, the County Magistrates were fully in the picture at the same time, and the Magistrates of Derby were fully informed by 25th May. Oliver, it is clear, supplied all the latest details to the authorities on his final visit of 6th-7th June, though the Lord-Lieutenant had been assured a week earlier that all the Magistrates were ready and that the people would not rise in great numbers. It is difficult to resist the conclusion of the government's parliamentary critics that the Ministry had allowed the plot to go on until it acquired a footing, that it had been allowed to come to fruition, and that the offenders had been treated to the publicity of a special commission rather than the normal processes of law so that the whole country might know of their offence and its punishment. Suggestions that the authorities could have stopped the rebellion but evidently wanted blood seem incontestable.[19]

[18]E. P. Thompson, op. cit., pp. 656-7 quotes from H.O. 40/6, Enfield to H.O., 1st June, 1817, and deposition of Stevens, Political Register, 16th May, 1818, to establish the latest 'proof'. The first statement establishes only that Stevens met Oliver, which has never been in question, whereas the second is so inaccurate in its dating as to suggest that its author either had a bad memory or that he lied; in either case his testimony on this point is of little value. For contemporary efforts at 'proof' see *Nottingham Review*, 23rd January, 1818, 22nd January, 1819; H.O. 40/3(8), Minute of Bennet's speech, 11th February, 1818; H.O. 40/10, Statement of Thomas Bacon; Report of Proceedings, op. cit., p. 78; R. J. White, op. cit., p. 165.

[19]*Nottingham Review*, 27th March, 1818; H.O. 42/165, Enfield to H.O., 23rd May, 1817, and Mayor of Derby to H.O. 25th May, 1817; Ne.C. 4971, L. Rolleston to Newcastle, 1st June, 1817; Parl. Debs., Vol. 73, 165; 5th February, 1818; E. P. Thompson, op. cit., p. 659.

Perhaps the most interesting question raised about Pentrich is its seriousness, whether this was a movement which the government was right to take seriously. In Nottingham itself, the centre of the rebel movement, activity was slight on the night of the 9th. There had been before that time, according to one account, a considerable amount of disaffection among the starving population, yet beyond a few attempts to fraternise with the military and a few wild, muttered intentions of attacking the barracks or sacking a gunsmith's shop 'little was thought of and still less attempted'. On the night of the 9th large numbers appeared on the streets, evidently expecting some disturbance, but the only development containing any menace occurred on the Forest. The House of Lords' Secret Committee later reported that about 100 men had assembled there two deep with pikes or poles, in the opinion of the Home Office a demonstration in Nottingham of intent to join the insurgents. These were the men described by Lancelot Rolleston, a County Magistrate, when he testified to the disturbed state of the town, and the Judge accepted them as proof that Nottingham was to play its part in the uprising. Another witness of the events, not called at the trial, found a further body of 100 men assembled in a shed by the Race Course Stand on the Forest, but these men like the rest dispersed peacefully at a late hour. The Under-Sheriff for the County reported these events to Newcastle and informed him also that two pikes had been found in the outskirts of the town. And these events, together with a few arrests of suspected trouble-makers, later released, were the total contribution of Nottingham to the rebellion itself. The earlier hopes and beliefs of a town in the hands of rebels before the Pentrich men arrived could not have been more falsely founded.[20]

In spite of the very poor showing of the rebels numerically, in the country areas and in Nottingham itself, it has been suggested that Pentrich should be given an important place in the annals of working class history. Its leaders were not country yokels but 'experienced revolutionaries', a title to be wondered at rather than explained, and they were attempting to promote one of the first wholly proletarian revolutions without any middle class support. In doing this they achieved heroic stature, and, but for the

[20]Sutton, op. cit., p. 339; Parl. Debs., Vol. 73, 571, 23rd February, 1818; H.O. 42/169, Locket to H.O., 10th August, 1817; Ne.C. 4972, R. Leeson and L. Rolleston to Newcastle, 10th June, 1817, 4994, 4995a, 4996. Evidence of arrested men, 10th June, 1817.

meddling of Oliver, might well have achieved greater success. There were at the time many tributes to the heroism of Brandreth; these arose partly because of the glamorous and romantic figure he cut, likened by Denman to Byron's 'Corsair', partly from his stoical behaviour during captivity, but largely out of sympathy for him as the supposed victim of Oliver's intrigues. There was no attempt to praise him as a man who might have succeeded and whose success would have been welcome. The anti-government *Review* persisted in the view, after the Rebellion, that the government was preserving artificially a crisis atmosphere and conspiring to keep troops in an area where they were totally unnecessary. This was, in fact, contradicted by the repeated begging letters from the town clerk of Nottingham, himself a liberal in politics, imploring the government not to withdraw troops from the area, but the fears of the local magistracy sprang more from the obsessive fear that was a relic of Luddism than from any actual evidence that they were seriously threatened; for any knowledge about the rebels and their plans suggests that they were not a force to be overestimated.[21]

From the accounts of Oliver, who could hardly have been concerned to play down the rebellion and underestimate its danger, can be seen the very ineffectual organisation that the men had built up. The illusory pictures of the travelling delegates had caused the men to have an entirely false impression of how strong they were and what could be attempted. Oliver reported that the villages around Nottingham were in no way organised or aware of any systematic plan; they looked to Nottingham for orders, but viewed the revolt with very mixed feelings, some dreading the prospect of rebellion through fear of what would befall their families. The confidence of the Nottingham men lay, said Oliver, in 'the direction of divine providence as they say; it does not appear to me that they have adopted any regular sistom (sic) to go by but depends entirely upon chance and the assistance of the great reformers who will not at present be seen among them until they make a great stand, which is all their dependance'. An

---

[21] E. P. Thompson, op. cit., p. 668. Thomas Bailey began his 'Monumental Inscription for Jeremiah Brandreth' (1817)—'This soul possessed a degree of personal courage, and an extent of self-command, which, under the smiles of fortune, might have enabled him to eclipse the fame of Marlborough and rival the glory of Napoleon'. *Nottingham Review*, 25th July, 1817.

interesting light on the organisation is also thrown by Enfield's informer in Nottingham. This man notified the town clerk on 23rd May that he had received a letter from Brandreth telling him that he had been appointed delegate for Bulwell, on the north-western fringes of the town, which meant that he was responsible for bringing out the men of Bulwell on the day. But the Bulwell rebels to be brought out were a purely hypothetical force, uncanvassed and unprepared; their leader was employed by the Corporation, which ensured that they remained so, and there was evidently no check made that the paper army was ready to march when the time came. This was not a plot to strike terror into the hearts of either the local or central government. They knew that they could safely allow it to mature and await the outcome with confidence.[22]

And if the Pentrich rebels were not exactly country yokels, there was nothing in their known plan of action and declared purpose to suggest anything other than a thoroughly naive and unsophisticated approach to the problem of waging a successful rebellion. There was no note of realism or reality to be detected, as their counsel comprehensively showed, and there is no reason to suspect that without Oliver the revolt would have gone better. There is no evidence of any widespread readiness to participate in rebellion in Nottingham or in the country districts; the latter won the highest praise from Sidmouth for their behaviour when the rebels passed through, and even those who did act did so, in many cases, with reluctance; Brandreth had great difficulty in persuading people to join him and even more in holding his band together. If the government determined to silence rebellion for all time, it was not because it ever reached dangerous proportions or was likely to do so but because it believed that rebellion should be silenced even if it arose in mild forms and because it was acting in part under the influence of local government officers, such as the town clerk of Nottingham, who had experienced a great fright from the Luddites.[23]

It is indeed instructive to view the Pentrich Rebellion against the background of Luddism, but not because the one was the

[22]H.O. 40/10, Oliver to Addington, 27th May, 1817; H.O. 42/165, Enfield to H.O. 24th May, 1817.

[23]Report of Proceedings, op. cit., pp. 120-1; Ne.C. 4945, Sidmouth to Newcastle, 14th June, 1817; Sutton, op. cit., p. 340.

continuation of the other, as has been alleged. The supposed common tradition which came down from Luddism to the Pentrich Rebellion seems to depend largely on the story, circulating in 1817 and totally unproven, that Brandreth had once been a Luddite. The really significant relationship between the two movements lies in their contrast, not their continuity. Mistaken or otherwise in their ventures, the Luddites knew precisely what they were doing and had a fair idea why they were doing it, their enterprises were brilliantly organised and they were technically successful, even if they failed to achieve their ultimate purpose. More important, they were limited in their aims and their objectives were purely industrial. Far from being a transitional movement beyond Luddism, Pentrich was a regressive movement, looking back, as one historian has said, to peasant revolts of earlier days, unlike Luddism, which was at least a successful exercise in working-class solidarity.[24]

The case of the Nottingham men who spent time in prison during the suspension of Habeas Corpus in 1817 is an illuminating example of the confusion that existed in the authorities' attempts to round up remaining Luddites at the same time as they were faced with the prospect of political revolution. In April, 1817, Gravener Henson, the well-known Nottingham trade-union leader, went to London to intercede on behalf of men convicted for the Luddite outrage at Loughborough the previous June. Henson had featured prominently in the reports of the town clerk's informers through 1815 and 1816 as an alleged Luddite leader and a would-be revolutionary, and when it was suggested to the Home Secretary that the real purpose of Henson's visit was 'to meet some deputies on treasonable practices', Sidmouth had him detained, questioned, and imprisoned 'on suspicion of being engaged in treasonable practices', notifying Newcastle of this on 11th April. There are no real grounds for believing that Henson was capable of anything perpetrated by Robespierre, as one confessing Luddite alleged; on the other hand it is wrong to believe that Henson, politically, could be identified with the Corporation leaders. The latter feared and mistrusted him and were glad to have him in prison at the time of Pentrich, however groundless their fears. What is beyond question is that Henson

[24]E. P. Thompson, op. cit., pp. 656, 669; *Nottingham Journal*, 25th October, 1817; R. J. White, op. cit., p. 166.

could not have been responsible for the offences with which he was associated in the May and June of 1817. Whilst he languished in Cold Bath Fields, colleagues of the men who had put him there were listing him as one of the main instigators of the Pentrich Rebellion. A national newspaper, the *Observer*, had Henson sitting on a Secret Committee which met Oliver at Nottingham on 27th May, and Henson himself, more amused than annoyed by the confusion, was later to note wryly that he had also been accused of drilling Nottingham revolutionary volunteers whilst he was in Cold Bath Fields.[25]

The confusion over Francis Ward was equally great. He, like Henson, was named by the Loughborough culprits as a leading Luddite organiser, perhaps the chief one. On the day after Pentrich the Nottingham magistrates were informed that Ward's house contained a store of arms; they searched it and found nothing. But before the end of the month Ward was taken by the magistrates, according to John Smith, the Nottingham M.P., because of strong evidence connecting him with the Loughborough job. This is curious since the warrants made out by the central authorities for Ward and three other men were for his apprehension on a charge of High Treason. There was confusion at every level. Ward himself later recalled how the Nottingham magistrates told him he was being arrested for the Loughborough business, but on his arrival in London Sidmouth informed him that he was suspected of high treason. In the Commons Castlereagh told Members that Ward had been arrested for Luddism and not for treason; yet Sidmouth accused him of wishing to change the government and being a leading agent behind the Pentrich Rebellion, which he fully denied. Part of this confusion was brought out by Lord Folkestone in Parliament. He asked, quite reasonably, why, if Ward was so great and notorious a political danger, he had not been arrested before Pentrich or immediately afterwards and not a fortnight later. He might also have asked why, if Ward was being detained for Luddism, he had not been

[25]H.O. 42/163, James Hooley to H.O., 8th April, 1817; Ne.C. 4942, Sidmouth to Newcastle, 11th April, 1817; H.O. 42/168, Confession of Thos. Savage, C. G. Mundy to H.O. 4th April, 1817; R. A. Church and S. D. Chapman, op. cit.; H.O. 42/165, James Hooley to H.O., 29th May, 1817; H.O. 40/9(4) Summary of the Proceedings relating to the Conspiracy formed in the West Riding, Notts., and Derbyshire for a general Insurrection; *Nottingham Review*, 23rd January, 1818, 22nd January, 1819.

arrested in March, when all the information had been laid against him and not in the middle of June. In fact Ward, like Henson, was tried for neither Luddism nor treason; both were released in the November; and Ward's story had a not unsatisfactory ending for him, for he was able to sue the *Observer* for wrongful allegations against him and win damages of £600. He described himself as being just a supporter of Parliamentary reform for over thirty years.[26]

The pattern of Nottingham politics after Pentrich was much the same as before, with the Corporation Whigs gradually winning their struggle to control the Nottingham reform movement. In retrospect, the failure of William Stevens and his friends on the night of 9th June to rouse those of similar inclinations can be seen to be decisive. Halévy found to his surprise that the hosiery districts were no longer the centre of political agitation in 1818; this was not really surprising, for the framework-knitters were normally preoccupied with industrial matters and the 1817 fiasco could hardly have given them a taste for politics. At the time the finality of this failure was not so evident. The local Tories still professed to believe that Nottingham was a 'hot-bed of sedition' and that reform was only another name for treason and sedition; large meetings during 1819 were still alleged to be demanding 'money, work, or revolution'. Newcastle could still receive panicky messages urging him to suppress the 'Ranting preachers' because of the danger that they might promote revolution, and in December, 1819, rumour of a revolution plot could still be received with infinite credulity. This year, a period of unparalleled suffering amongst the working classes, according to Bailey, was really the last year of panic. In February the editor of the *Review* denied that the 'lower orders' had any desire for revolution; in December the *Journal* asserted very dogmatically that secret drilling had been practised in Nottingham for some time and that the crisis was coming. The town clerk, still hearing reports of revolutionary talk at framework-knitters' meetings, demanded to know the

[26]H.O. 42/168, Mitchell's Confession, March, 1817; Parl. Debs., Vol. 73, 469, 475, 481, 17th February, 1818; H.O. 40/3(a); *Nottingham Review*, 2nd January, 1818; H.O. 40/5, Rough Minute Book, 1817, Ward examined, 21st June, 1817; Sutton, op. cit., p. 337; *Nottingham Review*, 22nd January, 1819.

evidence. No evidence could be presented, and the whole thing was proved to be a hoax, but not before the army had taken over Bromley House in the town centre, Nottingham become a garrison town, and its Members of Parliament been accused of concealing vital information of national importance from the House of Commons. The following week the *Journal* admitted that its stories were unfounded.[27]

The allegedly 'bloody purpose' of the Tories against the reformers had failed. But so too had the purpose of the revolutionaries. In spite of unemployment and poverty Nottingham remained peaceful and order good throughout 1819 as its Members of Parliament testified. When the stockingers went on strike in August they behaved with great restraint and caused no breaches of the peace, for which the town clerk was thankful. Their parades and demonstrations during the strike were not, as has been suggested, a show of strength to the community but a pathetic revelation of their great numbers but powerlessness. After the failures of Pentrich, the town clerk's informer had written in May, Nottingham would be the last place to rise in the future. By the end of 1819, according to the *Journal*, revolutionary radicalism was prostrate.[28]

The unofficial reform movement turned, through 1819, to public meetings, a sure sign that its menace was over. In July the Mayor had been invited by men of reforming inclination who were not favourable to the Corporation to call a public meeting to which Cartwright would be invited and at which grievances, especially the need for Parliamentary reform, would be discussed. The Mayor, evidently suspecting the intent of his petitioners, refused the request, but the meeting was organised privately. In spite of the absence of official blessing and the refusal of the *Journal* to publicise the meeting, it attracted 'between 5 and 10 thousand people'. No national figures appeared, and the people

[27]E. Halévy, *The Liberal Awakening* (1926) p. 56; See *Nottingham Journal* throughout 1817, 1818, and 1819; H.O. 42/187, Enfield to H.O., 1st May, 1819; Ne.C. 4960 Thomas Hildyard to Newcastle, 17th June, 1819; Bailey, op. cit., p. 308; *Nottingham Review*, 12th February, 1819; *Nottingham Journal*, 11th, 18th, December, 1819; *Nottingham Review*, 17th December, 1819; Parl. Debs., Vol. 77, 1529, 23rd December, 1819.

[28]*Nottingham Review*, 17th December, 1819; Parl. Debs., Vol. 77, 1125-6, 14th December, 1819; H.O. 42/194, Enfield to H.O., 2nd September, 1819; E. P. Thompson, op. cit., p. 681; H.O. 42/187, I. H. Barker to H.O., 12th May, 1819; *Nottingham Journal*, 6th January, 1821.

had been warned not to let an 'Oliver' come amongst them. Visiting speakers, in advocating universal suffrage, annual parliaments, and the ballot, attacked 'pretending reformists' as more dangerous than Tory Ministers and condemned the Nottingham Whigs 'in terms of unqualified abuse'. Clearly the meeting was as concerned to attack its pretended friends as its avowed enemies. In November and December two proposed meetings that were to have taken a similar line failed to material-ise. In the latter month the town magistrates met the county officials under the chairmanship of the Duke of Newcastle to discuss the enforcement of the Act against Seditious Meetings and to combat 'the visionary schemes of Radicals', but the danger was now passed. The *Journal* would inveigh against the 'Radical rabble' and 'disaffected reformers' intermittently for some time, but even it had eventually to admit that 'Radical reform' was no longer a bogey. It declined in the early 20s in part because of working class preoccupation with industrial activity, of which they had always felt a greater need, and because of the almost complete success of the Corporation Whigs in controlling the popular reform movements, selecting the causes to be supported, and channelling discontent in acceptable directions.[29]

In so far as a Radical wing remained in these years it was a small, almost intellectually élite, movement which collected money to assist those in prison for their political conduct, or those imprisoned for offences of 'printing and publishing blasphemous publications'. No account of its work has remained beyond a few scanty press notices. The movement was represented by the Nottingham Permanent Subscription Fund, which assisted 'the persecuted friends of Reform', or the 'Friends of Freedom' who relieved Richard Carlile and his family. They doubtless assisted too in the case of Mrs. Wright, the local lace-mender who was imprisoned for selling copies of Carlile's Addresses in 1822. These were Nottingham's 'radical enclaves' of the 20s rather than any bodies of men which planned revolution or even seriously challenged the ability of the Corporation Whigs to lead the Nottingham reform movement.[30]

[29]*Nottingham Review*, 16th, 23rd July, 29th October, 10th December, 1819; *Nottingham Journal*, 17th July, 1819; 1st January, 1820; 1st January, 1825.

[30]*Nottingham Review*, 23rd February, 14th September, 1821, 6th December, 1822, 31st January, 1823; E. P. Thompson, op. cit., p. 729-30.

Perhaps the best illustration of Corporation control is the Peterloo meeting of September, 1819. The Manchester massacre was bound to evoke a great response in Nottingham, and the Corporation anticipated and guided this by themselves organising a great meeting and demonstration against the Manchester magistrates and the Tory government which had upheld their conduct. It was 'one of the most numerous public meetings ever held in Nottingham', but it was held under the authority of the magistrates, who were themselves amongst the main speakers. The reappearance of the aged Robert Denison, a veteran of Tory-Jacobin feuds earlier, whose ideas were more advanced than those of the Corporation, on a common platform with the Whigs, and a conveniently derisive comment from the *Journal* on Peterloo as 'a lesson to those deluding the people', did much to restore the Whigs to their former position. The meeting was quickly followed by a dinner to celebrate Lord Rancliffe's famous election victory of 1812; toasts were drunk to 'the Sovereignty of the People' and 'the Swinish Multitude', and the common touch was again near to being found.[31]

At the same time as the Corporation was re-establishing its position, the Duke of Newcastle and a number of country gentry issued a post-Peterloo declaration, attacking such meetings and the work of the Radical reformers. This has been described as a typical reaction to Peterloo. But it also needs to be contrasted with the reaction of the town leaders. The aristocracy and gentry in adopting a purely negative and repressive attitude did nothing to help preserve civil harmony. The town authorities championed the causes of Peterloo and Parliamentary reform, put on a massive display, and proved that public meetings need not be dangerous, and by their own leadership they avoided the dangers feared by their county colleagues.[32]

Throughout 1820 the Corporation was loud in its support for Queen Caroline. It was a classic non-issue, as Newcastle realised. People were encouraged to become excited about the case, and, when the Whigs triumphed, they were encouraged to celebrate as if their final emancipation had been achieved. Illuminations and firework displays were organised and more than thirty sheep roasted for public consumption. The poor would certainly have

[31]*Nottingham Review*, 1st, 22nd October, 1819, *Nottingham Journal*, 21st August, 1819.
[32]Sutton, op. cit., p. 352; R. A. Church, op. cit., p. 105.

been glad enough to partake of the free food, and the whole episode gave them something more for which to thank their governors.[33]

This is not to say that Whig politics in Nottingham were directed towards purely selfish ends. Great campaigns were waged throughout the 20s for Catholic Emancipation as well as for the repeal of the Test and Corporation Acts and the Corn Laws. These often involved serious divisions of opinion inside Nottingham society and provoked much bitterness. The *Journal*, representing in this the local Tories and Anglican Clergymen, pursued a fanatical line in defence of the Anglican monopoly. Its hatred of Catholics exceeded even its scorn for Protestant Dissenters, and it bitterly denounced Wellington and his fellow apostates for their failure to stand firm and resist the demands of the religious minorities. Though it no longer feared 'Radicalism' it condemned 'the new school of Liberalism, keeping out of sight the good old principle of loyalty to the King and Constitution', and its invective reached new heights. What the Whigs did in this period was to concentrate reforming zeal on certain limited and precise reform proposals on which all Nottingham reformers could agree. Others temporarily were suspended. When Wellington became Prime Minister in January, 1828, they again knew that they could speak for all but the Tories when they opposed his appointment. He was an aristocrat and a soldier and a man whose views on parliamentary reform were not to their liking. And Parliamentary reform was increasingly becoming the issue to which all others were believed subordinate.[34]

After a decade dominated by strikes, the lace-boom and its subsequent collapse, a decade in which politics were of secondary importance, interest in politics began to revive and new and deeper divisions to appear. The control of the Nottingham movement for Parliamentary reform was to be the supreme test of the Old Whig Corporation.

[33]Portland MSS., PwH, 489, Newcastle to Portland, 17th September, 1820, wrote 'It does not seem to me that the people are in earnest when they declare for the Queen, they do so many for seditious and mischievous purpose, many for amusement and many for the sake of making a row'; *Nottingham Review*, 24th November, 1820.

[34]*Nottingham Journal*, 20th August, 1825; *Nottingham Review*, 25th January, 1828.

II

THE REFORM OF PARLIAMENT

In the years before the French Revolution the Parliamentary reform movement had widespread support throughout the county as well as in the borough of Nottingham. Even the *Journal* was in these days pro-reform as long as the movement had the distinguished patronage of Pitt and sought a redress of grievances without widespread departure from the principles of the constitution.[1]

George Walker of High Pavement was an active propagator of reform ideas through the county from 1780 and was ably seconded in his speeches and writings by his friend Gilbert Wakefield. Their arguments and demands were very much in harmony with the respectable reform movements of the day, being concerned with the two main questions of reducing the amount of 'influence' at the disposal of the government and abolishing rotten boroughs so that a re-distribution of seats would take place to secure fairer representation of the country's important interests. These concerns can be clearly related to a Nottingham background. Nottingham, as an industrial centre of growing importance, felt that it was rightly represented in Parliament and maintained the right of other such economic interests to be so represented. And these interests could not be properly represented and Parliament could not function properly when Members looked to faction leaders or the government instead of to their constituents and constituency

[1]For the background of the 18th Century Parliamentary Reform Movement see G. S. Veitch, *The Genesis of Parliamentary Reform* (1913); *Nottingham Journal*, 29th January, 5th, 26th February, 1785.

P

matters. The presence of independent Members, that is constituency rather than party Members, was something that mattered a great deal in Nottingham. Important too was the fact that Nottingham was a populous borough with a large electorate; this made it resentful of the small boroughs which had equal representation. It prided itself on its independence of the local aristocracy and resented the perpetuated influence of the aristocracy through pocket boroughs. And, being a business and industrial community, it resented the continued existence of placemen and sinecure-holders, parasites on the national economy, unlike the manufacturers of Nottingham who worked for their income and contributed, if insufficiently, to the wealth of the country.

These are some of the considerations which influenced the Nottingham Parliamentary reform movement; under the influence of the French Revolution it temporarily exhibited more democratic tendencies, with a petition in 1793 proposing manhood suffrage, but it was usually more concerned to rid the constitution of evils that had crept in and restore it to some original, idealised form than to carry forward its development and write in some new principles. When Thomas Denman was later, as Whig Member for Nottingham, to describe himself as a 'conservative reformer', he was representing the views of his supporters much more accurately than they ever realised. With Parliamentary reform, as with opposition to the French Wars, enlightened self-interest rather than pure enlightenment lay at the base of local attitudes.[2]

The last gesture of the Parliamentary reformers before the War threw their activities into disarray occurred in February, 1793. After being in correspondence with Grey, and clearly acting under his guidance, George Walker drew up a reform petition, signed by 2,500 people in Nottingham, which complained that 'the constitution of these Kingdoms has passed into the grossest abuses, so as to insult the common sense of the nation with a name when the reality is gone' and demanded the introduction of manhood suffrage. It was presented in the House of Commons by a town Member, Robert Smith, and aroused the anger of Pitt, who condemned it for showing insufficient respect for the House and reverence for the constitution. Burke went further, noted its 'seditious tendency', and demanded punishment

[2]Sir J. Arnould, op. cit., p. 394.

for those responsible, for he saw it as 'only a small part of the fruit of the doctrines which had lately been propagated by certain societies, that England had no constitution'. Whether this meant anything to the author of the petition can only be guessed at, but the excitement of Pitt and Burke was certainly out of proportion to the intentions of Walker and the signatories. Charles James Fox, who enjoyed high prestige in Nottingham, confessed that on the suffrage question he did not go along with the petitioners, but he strongly upheld their right to hold such views.[3]

The subject of Parliamentary reform was evidently still under discussion a year later, in May, 1794, when the *Journal* urged the cessation of all meetings on the matter because of the dangers of assembling large crowds together at the time of such ferment. The public meetings did stop. The cause of reform passed temporarily into the hands of the various groups which met at a few public houses, owed their origin to the French Revolution, and never enlisted more than marginal support in the town. In 1797-8 the Nottingham branch of the Corresponding Society again made the debate public, but this organisation had only a brief and uninfluential existence.[4]

During the period of peace, 1801-3, Parliamentary reform again featured in the Whig programme, but not centrally. In 1806 and 1807 the Whigs could barely disturb the sitting coalition of pro-War Members, and it was not until 1809 that the cause again began to feature prominently in official political circles. Soon after his re-election in 1807, John Smith, M.P., though still as yet unsympathetic towards reform, had evidently received a number of letters from his constituents urging him to speak against the possession of pensions and sinecures by M.P.s. He voiced his constituents' feelings but did not share them. Two years later he was still in the same position, for the Whig Club sent him a request for his attendance in the House when a debate on Parliamentary reform was about to take place. By 1810 the Nottingham Whigs were back in normal service, petitioning Parliament for reform and using the Corporation to convey their demands. The *Review* had now appeared to press the cause upon its readers and during June, 1810, it collected and printed most comprehensive

[3]*Nottingham Journal*, 2nd March, 1793; Parl. Debs., Vol. 30, 460-5, 21st February, 1793.
[4]*Nottingham Journal*, 3rd May, 1794.

lists of all the places, sinecures and offices held by peers, Members of the Commons, and their relatives, friends and dependants. In the same month John Smith presented a petition and remonstrance from the people of Nottingham, attacking the unrepresentative nature of Parliament and the return of half of the House of Commons by 150 peers. The previous month Smith had presented a petition from the Magistrates, Aldermen, Council, and Livery of Nottingham, asking for a 'temperate and radical reform' of Parliament. This enigmatic request covered conventional proposals to economise on the spending of public money and to eliminate the smaller boroughs.[5]

The 'friends of reform' in Nottingham were now organised as a group and dining together, but this presaged no new radical trends in their thoughts. The grievances and solutions remained the same. A purifying of the system, the elimination of pensions and title-holders, the restoration of the 'legislative rights of the People according to the Constitution', whatever that meant, 'no taxation without representation' even, all these demands stemmed from a belief that the system had gone wrong and needed to be restored to its former excellence. The reformers were still backward-looking. The only new life grafted on to the old stock was the association of the peace movement with Parliamentary reform. 'Peace and Parliamentary Reform' was the slogan given by the *Review*; it was broadcast by Major Cartwright, who maintained that reform was the only road to peace, and it was taken up by Robert Denison, the 'Major Cartwright of Nottingham' and indefatigable organiser and speaker on behalf of both causes. There can already be seen the magical qualities that Parliamentary reform was beginning to have ascribed to it. Before 1814 it was the means to peace with France; in 1817 it was said to be necessary for the solution of the country's economic problems; and in 1826 the *Review* committed itself to the opinion that 'a reform in Parliament is the grand panacea for the country'. This view the Nottingham Whigs were very ready to disseminate, which helps to explain the tremendous build-up and excitement that preceded the 1832 Reform Act and the bitter disappointment and frustration that followed it, producing a

[5]Parl. Debs., Vol. 54, 750, 7th July, 1807; *Nottingham Journal*, 20th May, 1809; Corporation Hall Books, 1809/10, pp. 52-4, 23rd May, 1810; Parl. Debs., Vol. 53, 303-4, 8th June, 201-2, 30th May, 1810.

break-up of the town's political patterns and a basis for realign-
ment.[6]

The period immediately preceding the 1832 Act revealed a
new tension in Nottingham political life and growing signs that
the Whigs of the Corporation were having difficulty in restraining
the passions of reformers. Indeed, the reform campaign was
organised on two levels, by the Corporation through its customary
institution, the town meeting, under the supervision and control
of the magistracy, and by the Nottingham Political Union, a not
altogether welcome stranger which threatened, but failed, to
wrest the initiative from Corporation hands.

The approach of the Corporation Whigs was according to
practice. By sponsoring a popular cause they could, on past
performances, have reasonable expectation of keeping it within
reasonable limits. They could also turn any event into a public
occasion and substitute festivities for further agitation when the
limited end had been achieved. In August, 1830, a public meeting
was held in Nottingham to express support for the 'French
Revolution' of that year, and subscriptions were opened on
behalf of those who had suffered during the troubles. It was
typical of the Corporate body that it then nominated three of
its members to go to Paris to make an official presentation to the
French Government on behalf of the people of Nottingham. In
the October the Mayor organised a reform meeting which,
amongst other things, denounced the corruption still believed to
be rife, advocated the Ballot (this cause was becoming increasingly
popular in Nottingham because of the prevalent stories of the way
in which the Duke of Newcastle treated his tenants), and deprecated the high rates of taxation, a recurrence of the theme of
economic grievances behind the reform movement. More than
8,000 signatures were quickly gathered for a petition, and when
Thomas Denman presented it he was able to claim that it had been
signed by over half the adult males in the town. Such petitions
were to be a regular feature of the year 1831, when the Corporation did its part by organising them and keeping the government
under bombardment. That of March, 1831, acquired a record
number of 9,030 signatures in a record time of three and a half

[6]*Nottingham Review*, 6th July, 1810, 10th January, 1817, 27th October, 1826.

days, after Richard Hopper had supported the reform schemes on the grounds that 'the proposal to enfranchise the middle classes, who are the strength and stamina of the country—can be for no other interest than that of the community'. This was the authentic Corporation voice, echoed later by a letter from a 'working-man' who rejoiced because the Bill was enfranchising his master, whose interests were identical with his own. Russell defined his Bill's purpose in April, 1831, as the raising of a bar to the accomplishment of the wishes of those who looked forward to more extensive and violent change, a sentiment in harmony with those of Nottingham's leaders.[7]

When the Bill became law the magistrates set the Parish bells a-ringing, organised collections to pay for celebrations throughout the town, and, under Corporation auspices, a Reform Celebration Committee was instituted for the 'organisation of rejoicings'.[8] This disproportionate enthusiasm for so modest a measure indicated clearly the limited outlook of the Corporation, as did their immediate dropping of the cause of Parliamentary reform once the 1832 Act was passed. The rejoicings of the Corporation were only in part for the triumph of the Bill; they were probably in part to celebrate their own success in keeping the Political Union under control. Parliamentary reform had given them some bad moments, especially on the night of October 10th, 1831, when the Castle was fired, but this had been the work of hooligans. More alarming, because of its radical social as well as political implications had been the work of the Nottingham Political Union.

There had always been some undercurrent of dissatisfaction from more ardent reformers with the way that the Corporation oligarchy dominated and directed town politics. In 1830 this was given a very definite working class tinge and assumed more formidable proportions. In January, 1830, William Shoults, later Secretary of the Nottingham Political Union, attacked the widely-held belief that moderate Parliamentary reform plus free trade would solve the nation's problems as 'the delusive doctrines of some of our political economists'. A month later, a 'Radical reformer' suggested that no permanent relief would come to the

---

[7]*Nottingham Review*, 20th August, 22nd October, 1830; 11th March, 1831, 18th May, 1832; Parl. Debs., Vol. 103, 627, 22nd November, 1830, Vol. 105, 1688, 19th April, 1831.
[8]*Nottingham Review*, 10th August, 1832.

working man as long as the middle classes were willing to come forward and keep the poor quiet by dispensing soup and cheap blankets. This sounded very much like ingratitude and it virtually labelled the Nottingham soup-dispensers as the tools of the aristocracy. Dissatisfaction was increased by the arrival of Cobbett in Nottingham, under official Corporation patronage, to lecture on the subject of Parliamentary reform. From these lectures he received £69 and when some of his audience expected that part of this would be given away to charity they were disillusioned to hear Cobbett's lament that a round figure of £70 had not been reached—for six hours' work. This sum of money could hardly have been raised just by the poor stockingers of the town. The visit of a figure of such national prominence attracted the curious from all social and political groups. William Parsons, for instance, a lawyer and a Tory, went along with his friends to witness the spectacle. He, like critics on the Whig side, such as Thomas Bailey, found Cobbett's visits a disillusioning experience; it seemed to him that Cobbett was for anything which suited his own purpose, and that his prime concern was to put money into his own pocket. The stage was now set for some supplementary organisation for the opinion no longer adequately represented by the Corporation Whigs.[9]

It was the *Journal* which was the first to spot the possible menace in the new phenomenon of the Political Unions when it reported on the Birmingham Union on February 6th, 1830, doubting its wisdom and wondering if such bodies might not contain an implied threat to the independence of Parliament. The *Review's* reply was to chastise the reformers of Nottingham for their delay in following the Birmingham example. Delay was short. On March 1st, a 'private meeting' was held to discuss the formation of a Nottingham Political Union to work for 'effectual reform'. It was to be a union between 'the middle and lower classes of the people of this town'. But things worked out badly at first. When its first general meeting was held on July 5th, its committee had to report only slow progress. On their own confession they were men of 'no decisive character in Nottingham—influential only

[9]*Nottingham Review*, 22nd January, 19th, 5th February, 1830; T. Bailey, *Strictures on Mr. Cobbett's Second Lecture* (1830); Diaries of William Parsons, 1830-1871, 3rd February, 1830.

in their zealous adherence to the cause of reform'. This was probably an over-modest assessment. Of the four people who filled the
offices of Secretary and Treasurer in the Union, three were men
of some social standing, and two of them in positions of un-
rivalled influence. Richard Sutton had taken over the *Review* on
his father's death in 1829, Robert Goodacre was the founder of the
Standard Hill Academy, the most important private school in
Nottingham, strongly patronised by the business community,
whilst Benjamin Boothby was an iron merchant and iron-
founder, running the largest firm of its kind in Nottingham, the
premises of which occupied almost the whole of Granby Street.
But their members in July were still few in number, and the
Committee offered the following explanation: some people
were afraid to join; others hung back because they saw that
'those they had been in the habit of regarding as their political
pastors' were not taking an interest in the Union; some kept out
because they felt that the Union cut across party boundaries, not
realising that party names were operating to the exclusion of
genuine political principle; many 'operative mechanics' were
excluded because of their inability to pay the subscription, and
because of this it was decided to abolish the subscription.[10]

For whatever reasons, and all these alleged ones were most
suggestive, it was agreed that the majority of reformers in Nottingham were standing aloof. And this remained so. When the
'Radical Reformers' dined together on November 9th, George
Whitehead, in a call for unity amongst all reformers, regretted
that more of them were not members of the Political Union as he
himself was. The main speaker on this occasion was Richard
Sutton of the *Review*, one of the few middle class people to be
associated with the Union, who defended the right of all men to
vote and argued the need for Annual Parliaments. Sutton, it will
be remembered, was never one of the Corporation clique and
since his assumption of control of the paper he had committed it
to supporting a thorough-going reform programme of manhood
suffrage, Annual Parliaments, and the secret ballot. In the early
months of 1831 numbers rose and by March the Union could
attract about 700 to its meetings, though this was nothing compared with the thousands who flocked to town meetings under

[10]*Nottingham Journal*, 6th February, 1830; *Nottingham Review*, 26th February, 5th March,
9th July, 1830; Mrs. A. Gilbert, *Recollections of Old Nottingham* (1904), pp. 44-5.

official patronage. Numbers were now being swelled by employers as well as operatives, it was claimed, though later in the year the middle classes were still being harangued for their failure to join.[11]

The reform proposals were revealed at the end of February and must have been, like Elizabeth's first Bill of Supremacy, 'a cold douche for ardent zealots'. Radicals were advised of the need to see the measure through, even though it did not go as far as many of them wished. Richard Sutton continued to call for the ballot and manhood suffrage and made disturbing references to 'the poverty of millions'. But the progress of the Political Union remained desultory. It organised its own modestly supported petition in September, 1831, but never in these preliminary stages did it become the force that the Birmingham Union was or threaten to replace the town meeting as the popular mode of political expression in Nottingham. It was such a town meeting, on October 10th, that was for once to get out of control and to present the authorities with a problem never previously encountered in such magnitude, if anticipated in the lesser outbreaks of violence and disorder earlier in the century.[12]

On Saturday, October 8th, news arrived that the Lords had rejected the Reform Bill. The Mayor was immediately regaled by no fewer than nineteen different requisitions from separate groups to hold a public meeting on the subject, which he undertook to do at the earliest possible time, Monday morning. The next day, Sunday, brought no further news but some inflammatory gossip from the mail-coach that in London the reformers were taking up arms. This excited people further and acts of violence were perpetrated throughout the day against the property of persons known, or thought, to have signed an anti-reform petition recently organised in the town. The Riot Act was read, but the magistrates had great difficulty in keeping the outbreaks of violence under control. On the Monday the crowds assembled for the well-publicised meeting long before the appointed hour of eleven o'clock. They were eventually addressed by a number of prominent local leaders, such as Lord Rancliffe, an ex-M.P. for the town,

[11]*Nottingham Review*, 12th November, 1830, 4th March, 7th January, 28th October, 1831.

[12]J. E. Neale, *Elizabeth I and her Parliaments* (1953), Vol. 1, p. 59; *Nottingham Review*, 4th March, 1831; C. Gill, *History of Birmingham* (1952), Vol. 1, p. 209.

and Corporation figures Alderman Oldknow and Thomas Wakefield. Thomas Bailey, the historian, was himself one of the speakers. One of their themes was the need for orderly behaviour, but with the ending of the meeting matters went completely out of control. Apart from many small acts of depredation against property, three major outrages were committed. One was an attack on Colwick Hall, the home of John Musters, Squire of Sneinton and a prominent Tory magistrate, known for his strict enforcement of the Game Laws; the second was the notorious onslaught on Nottingham Castle, the property of the Duke of Newcastle, which was fired and reduced to a shell in a matter of a few hours; the third occurred on the following day when crowds proceeded to the silk mill at Beeston belonging to William Lowe, another well-known Tory, and destroyed it by fire. These incidents, forming one of the most dramatic parts of the story of the passing of the Great Reform Bill, have been very widely reported, and the burning of the Castle, in particular, has become a Reform Bill legend. The connection between these incidents and Parliamentary reform and Parliamentary reformers is not absolutely clear.[13]

On the question of immediate responsibility for the outrages, contemporary local accounts and later ones written by eye-witnesses were unanimous in laying the blame on people other than the reformers themselves. When Sir Charles Wetherell spoke in the House of Commons on October 13th in denunciation of the 'Radicals' who had burned down the Castle for no other reason than that the Duke of Newcastle was an opponent of the Reform Bill, he was taking a line that the Tory *Nottingham Journal* could not countenance. No doubt the Duke's politics and his local notoriety as a borough-owner and evicter of tenants helped to single him out as an object of popular rage, but not even the local Tories held the reformers directly responsible for the outrage. A correspondent of Lord Middleton's, Samuel Parsons, though bitterly critical of the Corporation Whigs and the failure of the magistrates to prevent trouble, identified the

[13]This account is largely based on Bailey, op. cit., pp. 371-80 and Sutton, op. cit., pp. 423-9. The suggestion that the crowds 'also burnt several factories, as the symbols of capitalist tyranny' (G. M. Trevelyan, *Lord Grey of the Reform Bill*, 1920, p. 315) is wildly inaccurate factually and almost pure romance in interpretation.

rioters not as Parliamentary reformers but as a mob made up of 'the very dregs of society'.[14]

It is to be expected that the reformers of Nottingham would find the riots of 1831, like the revolutionary movement of 1817, an embarrassment and a danger to their own cause, and that they would identify the rioters as depraved criminals, not reformers. And on this occasion, as on so many others, there was a readiness to blame country people and strangers to the town rather than locals when trouble was caused. But these views were not simply rationalisations and supporting evidence for them is not lacking: the coincidence of the crisis with Goose Fair, which always attracted crowds from outside the town and furnished opportunities for petty crime; the cancellation of Nottingham Races which denied the pickpockets their customary sphere of operations; the contemporary reports that the number of country people attending the 1831 Fair was the largest ever. The crowds who flocked into town after the Castle fire to partake of the entertainment were so unfamiliar with the townsmen that they almost attacked Alfred Lowe of Highfield House instead of William Lowe, the Tory proprietor of Beeston silk mill, and had nowhere to sleep that night and so spent the night in the meadows and could be seen returning to the villages the following morning. These factors, together with the unanimous voice of local commentators and historians in blaming thieves, vagrants, and the disorderly, suggest that the outrages can hardly be attributed to Parliamentary reformers. Much of their behaviour, argued the *Review*, seemed more the work of regular thieves than the friends of reform, and the visiting judge at the County Assizes then being held was willing enough to pronounce the reformers guiltless of the offences that were being perpetrated. Reports of the subsequent trials indicate a series of disorganised, riotous episodes without leadership into which people were drawn by a mixture of motives, none of which concerned the reform of Parliament.[15]

[14]Parl. Debs., Vol. 110, 711, 13th October, 1831; Middleton MSS. MiF. 12, Samuel Parsons to L. Middleton, 1st December, 1831.

[15]*Nottingham Review*, 7th, 21st October, 1831, 27th January, 1832; Sutton, op. cit., p. 423; Bailey, op. cit., pp. 373, 380; Orange, op. cit., Vol. 2, pp. 885-6; Wylie, op. cit., p. 355; J. T. Godfrey, *History of the Parish and Priory of Lenton* (1884), p. 470. The much debated issue of whether the Nottingham magistrates could actually have prevented the destruction of the Castle is considered in M. I. Thomis, *Old Nottingham* (1968), Ch. 2.

To say that the outrages were not the work of the Parliamentary reformers but of lawless, ill-disposed people is not, however, to deny the importance of the reform controversy as a setting for troubles which, without the crisis concerning the Lords' rejection of the Reform Bill, would not have reached such magnitude. The Nottingham crowd, at all times combustible, was particularly so at this time of great political excitement and frustration. And the Duke of Newcastle was believed to be in part responsible for the frustration they felt. He was unpopular in Nottingham on many grounds. In November, 1828, he had issued leases for building in the Park, part of his own town property, subject to the condition that no house should be used for a prayer-meeting, or 'conventicle for the diffusion of sentiments contrary to the doctrines of the Church of England', which was believed by the nonconformists, the majority of the town, to be a piece of religious intolerance. In April, 1829, the *Mercury* commented on Newcastle's notoriety as an enemy of the constitution, depriving people of their elective franchise and 'doing what he would with his own'. The case of the deprived Newark electors received strong condemnation from Thomas Denman, whose language was so fierce that Newcastle complained of being brought into contempt in his own county, though it could well have been argued that his own action had already brought him into contempt. When Newcastle, appropriately, presented the small Nottingham petition against Russell's proposals his popularity was at its nadir. After his Castle had been fired he was warned by both the Home Secretary and one of his own magistrates not to attempt to visit Nottingham personally. The warning was scarcely necessary, for on his own admission he was afraid to go to Nottingham as he would either be murdered or raise a riot.[16]

Nor must the economic and social background to the troubles be ignored. Views have recently been expressed that the depressed social and economic condition of the working population was a greater incentive to riot than hostility to the Duke of Newcastle, and that the episode was indicative of a deep disturbance at the

[16]*Nottingham Review*, 14th November, 1828; *Nottingham Mercury*, 11th April, 1829; Parl. Debs., Vol. 103, 750-5, 3rd December, 1830; H.O. 41/10, Melbourne to Newcastle, 31st October, 1831; Ne.C. 5003, J. D. Gell to Newcastle, 18th October, 1831; Quoted by G. M. Trevelyan, op. cit., from H.O. 52/15.

foundations of society. Local commentators such as Mary Howitt stressed the economic background to the troubles, as did Mrs. Gilbert in her *Recollections of Old Nottingham*, though the latter produced some unreliable figures of wages and interpreted the cause of the riots somewhat wildly as a reaction to depression after years of unexampled prosperity. It is a not unfamiliar situation of local trade depression and attendant unemployment which, besides Goose Fair, helps to explain why there were so many people about from amongst whom a mob could be raised, and when, in the words of a *Review* correspondent, 'political sentiment lit the torch, a real or fancied consciousness of social wrongs applied it to its destination'. The episodes in Nottingham itself must be seen too against a whole background of incendiarism in the surrounding districts in the closing months of 1831 and the opening ones of 1832. The *Review* saw behind the outbursts 'the wants and necessities of the working classes' and voiced the fear that unless the government and men in authority showed the utmost vigilance a war of labour against property could develop, this 'above all things to be dreaded'. At the same time the editor received an illiterate production from a nearby village, listing the grievances of the poor; that the rich had taken their cottages away, employed Irishmen in harvest work, robbed them of their winter's work by using threshing machines, and kept their bread dear by means of the Corn Laws. This was the 'real or fancied consciousness of social wrongs' which was believed to be responsible for the outbreaks of lawlessness around Nottingham, for the 'spirit of insubordination' existing among a portion of the populace. Incendiarism was still spreading with the most fearful ravages in the neighbourhood, reported the *Journal* in November, 1831, but it doubted if this had anything to do with politics.[17]

It is perhaps instructive to ask again at this point how concerned the working class were with politics and, in particular, with the cause of Parliamentary reform. The entry of working class leaders and trade unions into the political arena had usually been for the pursuit of some measure concerned with industrial regula-

[17]J. M. Golby, 'The Duke of Newcastle and the Nottingham Reform Riots', Robert Mellors Prize Essay, Nottingham University, 1959; E. P. Thompson, op. cit., p. 815; M. Howitt, Autobiography (1809), p. 226, Mrs. A. Gilbert, *Recollections of Old Nottingham* (1904), pp. 38-9; *Nottingham Review*, 7th October, 11th November, 1831, 20th January, 1832; *Nottingham Journal*, 12th November, 1831.

tions. Politics as such had been largely eschewed. When the Reform Bill agitations took place the stockingers obediently attended the officially-organised meetings and signed petitions, but they were well schooled in this. Bailey's lyricism about reform as the hope of the people by day and their dream by night seems somewhat extravagant. After all, the Nottingham franchise was already a popular one, the vote had not brought the working man any improvement in his physical conditions, and a Reform Bill to impose national uniformity on the borough franchise could well end up with the Nottingham working man losing his right to vote. Extravagant too is a more recent assertion that the ordinary man of Nottingham wept when reform was defeated and rejoiced when it succeeded. This is an inference from the alleged fact that the ordinary man had no say in Parliament and needed Parliamentary reform to give him one. In the case of Nottingham this is quite untrue. The stockingers cast between half and two-thirds of the votes in any Parliamentary election as a result of the Burgess franchise, and it would have needed a very radical measure indeed to have increased the popular element in the Nottingham electorate. As it was, Russell's first Bill threatened to eliminate the Burgess vote for all future generations, retaining it only for the life-time of existing voters, with Russell rejecting as 'quite impossible' a Tory amendment to prolong Burgess voting rights in perpetuity. It is not likely then that the working classes would feel very strongly involved in a Bill which was progressively to eliminate them from the electorate; nor is it likely that they would later have found the eventual Act a subject for great celebrations, for by it they simply retained what they already had. Neither the violence of October, 1831, nor the festivities of August, 1832, can be explained in terms of Bailey's dream, shattered and then restored. It is, of course, very likely, in spite of the failure of the popular local franchise to bring benefits to the working classes, that Whig propaganda had some success in suggesting that the Reform Act would mean an alleviation of the lot of the working man. It is also likely that the terms of the various Reform Bills were never fully understood by the working classes in spite of the publicity and detailed accounts in the local press. The Whigs could count on general support from the working classes over reform, but the disappointment and frustration that followed 1832 were this time to lead to a specifically working class political movement, Chartism.[18]

The nearness of England to revolution in 1831 has been a much debated theme, and the proposition continues to receive support. In Nottingham there was hardly any middle class leadership to direct the working classes along any revolutionary course. The Corporation's political mission was as much to avoid revolution as to achieve reform, the middle classes were chided for their failure to patronise the Political Union, and they were said, at the time of the troubles, to be thoroughly on the side of the authorities and ill-disposed towards the rioters. That left the Political Union. Soon after the October riots the Union received a letter from Joseph Hume, informing members that the purpose of the Political Union was not simply to carry through reform; it was also to strengthen the hands of the magistrates in preserving public peace and property. But the Nottingham Union, with its few middle class and many working class members, had little in common with the Corporation's political approach, and its Radical members had been too long snubbed by the magistracy to care overmuch about its problems. There was no resort to violence, but the Union did enjoy a great rise in membership after the riots, and by January 6th, 1832, more than 2,500 men had joined. It remained rather quiescent as an organisation, but its very existence produced a crop of alarming, though totally unsubstantiated, rumours in the period immediately after the riots.[19]

At the end of October the Lord-Lieutenant, the Duke of New-castle, began to pass on local gossip to the Home Office in much the same way as he had done in the Luddite period. Melbourne, more than some of his predecessors in the office, was sceptical about the stories he received from Nottingham and precise evidence was demanded about men alleged to be arming. This was not forthcoming, but the stories continued. On November 13th, a county magistrate, Lancelot Rolleston, wrote that the Political Unions were progressing fast in Nottingham and district and that money was being collected to buy arms. A musket and bayonet could, he said, be obtained for 16/8 and the daily

[18]Bailey, op. cit., p. 373; D. Gray, 'Nottingham in the 19th Century', *Transactions of he Thoroton Society*, 1951; Parl. Debs., Vol. 6, 886, 30th August, 1831.

[19]E. P. Thompson, op.cit., p. 817; *Nottingham Mercury*, 15th October, 1831; *Nottingham Review*, 11th November, 1831, 6th January, 1832.

coach from Birmingham was bringing supplies into the town. On the 28th the story was repeated by someone who had just passed through Nottingham and heard that the Political Union was levying weekly contributions of 6d. from members, buying muskets, and giving them out amongst the people. Smiths, the bankers, in fear of some sort of attack, asked the Home Secretary for help and Melbourne agreed to their receiving a supply of hand grenades in case of need, but this did not indicate Melbourne's acceptance of the stories circulating. On November 30th, he warned the county authorities of the dangers of exaggeration and asked again for details of the arming and training of the Political Union and reminded them that an extract previously sent about drilling on the Forest had turned out to be about a mere five men; he suspected that other stories could be the same. A very sarcastic letter followed on December 3rd, expressing confidence that appropriate steps had been taken over the 'nocturnal training and exercise in the vicinity of Nottingham'. He was still vainly seeking details on the 12th, and the county magistrates, still having nothing but rumours, were still not able to supply any. It seems certain that Melbourne, 100 miles away, judged the situation better than the men on the spot. Though the town clerk prepared his womenfolk an escape route through a neighbour's back-garden should his home be attacked, his fears were unfounded. Nottingham was peaceable and quiet after the riots of October 8-11th and remained so at the time of the prisoners' trials in January, 1832. The authorities feared the Political Union as a source of rebellion. Its limited mass support and the known character of its leaders, such as Richard Sutton, the New Methodist owner of the *Review*, suggest that the fear was groundless.[20]

But political tension remained high. The Duke of Newcastle, as Lord-Lieutenant of the county and therefore responsible for law and order, was in an anomalous position with his own property involved. He showed a tactless, almost vengeful, desire to seek out the criminals and bitterly resented, with local Tory backing, the prudent decision of the government to relieve him of the

[20]H.O. 41/10, Melbourne to Newcastle, 6th, 30th November, 3rd December, 1831; H.O. to Samuel Smith and Co., 29th November, 1831; H.O. 44/25, L. Rolleston to H.O., 13th November, 1831; H.O. 44/24, Mr. Banks to H.O., 28th November, 1831; High Pavement Biographical Catalogue of Portraits (1932), p. 23; *Nottingham Mercury*, 15th October, 1831, 6th January, 1832.

embarrassment of being judge where his own interests were involved. A Special Commission was appointed, excluding New-castle, a piece of spite by Lord Melbourne, he believed, and in January, 1832, it met to try the offenders. Newcastle's persistence left him almost devoid of sympathy in Nottingham, and popular feeling rallied to the cause of the prisoners who awaited trial. Unfortunately, the local magistrates, in their desire to keep excitement down, avoided publicity in their police activities and managed to give the impression of a conspiratorial group secretly rounding up suspects for the purpose of a sacrificial gesture. The *Review* asked for an explanation of the silence surrounding their activities and their failure to notify the public of the men taken, the precise crimes for which they were to be charged, and why the men had not been given adequate opportunity to provide for their defence. On January 4th, the Special Assize opened. The authorities were unable to find anyone against whom they could prove responsibility for the firing of the Castle; but nine men were found guilty of the Beeston and Colwick outrages, of whom five were condemned to death and four to be transported. Again official proceedings appeared unsatisfactory to many. There were bitter complaints of the treatment of the prisoners, the nature of the witnesses used by the crown, and the general means used to obtain convictions.[21]

At the end of December, 1831, a committee had been formed at the Fox and Hounds to collect funds for the defence of the prisoners; this had no official backing from Corporation dignitar-ies or others of social standing and consisted of men of the 'same station in life as the prisoners'. One of them was Gravener Henson, who, with his vast experience of committee work and organisa-tion of petitions, was given charge of the funds collected. With customary feeling Henson launched himself into the work. On January 31st, a petition signed by 17,000 people from Nottingham was presented by Sir Francis Burdett for securing a respite of the executions. The petition contained the charges that the prisoners had been given insufficient time to prepare their defence and that threats and privations had been resorted to by magistrates to get their confessions. These were denied by two local Members,

[21]Ne.C. 4903, J. S. Gell to Newcastle (undated), 5058, Melbourne to Newcastle, 31st December, 1831; *Nottingham Journal*, 21st January, 1832; *Nottingham Review*, 23rd December, 1831, 20th January, 17th February, 1832.

Q

Ferguson for the borough and Denison for the county. The plea was refused, and on the next day the condemned men were executed to accompanying cries of 'Murder' and 'Blood'. Henson now led the agitation for a Parliamentary inquiry into the whole question of the conduct of the Commission and the behaviour of the magistrates. In this work he was obstructed by the local press; the *Journal* and the *Mercury* refused outright to publish the charges, whilst the *Review*, for once, sided with authority, refusing to become an 'accuser of men whose public situation places them in a station of vast responsibility'. This was an uncharacteristic line for the *Review* to adopt. In spite of it, the Committee collected 3-4,000 signatures for their petition, which was eventually presented by Hunt on June 22nd after Cobbett and O'Connell, two expected sources of help, had refused their assistance. The conduct of the Commission was not allowed to be questioned further, but the charges concerning the treatment of prisoners were passed on to the magistrates concerned, who found them to be 'false and slanderous'. Hunt complained of the mockery involved in allowing an interested party to inquire into its own conduct, but there the matter ended. The reputation of the Nottingham magistracy and the *Review* and *Mercury* for being 'supporters of the cause of Freedom' seemed sufficient to convince M.P.s that the magistrates had not offended on this occasion and that the petition was, in the words of one Nottingham M.P., 'the work of very few hands'.[22]

Reforming opinion was now clearly divided and the impending triumph of reform was soured before it occurred; nor could the jollying-round of Corporation organisers prevent this. On the other hand the Tories could do little to resist the tide of opinion, and Thomas Denman even noticed Tory banners waving amongst the anticipated Whig ones when he visited Nottingham in April, 1832. But the fears remained. Events of the previous October, when the Lords had rejected the First Reform Bill, had set a frightening example; if the Lords should repeat their step trouble would recur; in April, for instance, manufacturers were said to be refusing to give out raw materials in case reform should again be rejected by the Upper House and workmen should vent their

[22]*Nottingham Review*, 23rd December, 1831, 2nd March, 1832; S. Maccoby, *English Radicalism, 1780-1832* (1955), Vol. 3, p. 41; Parl. Debs., Vol. 111, 1049-51, 31st January, 1832, Vol. 115, 953-9, 22nd June, 1832, Vol. 116, 990, 1243, 1st August, 1832.

wrath on their employers' goods. That a second crisis did not occur must have given the Corporation's celebrations in the August more meaning than many participants realised.[23]

The situation was not then all loss to the Tories, who could afford to sit back and see the split develop. Their worst moment had occurred when Wellington had brought in Catholic Emancipation; this had been the great betrayal and what followed was endured with an almost masochistic delight. Wellington had let them down over the Catholics; he could also be conveniently blamed for the reform trouble. Had he been willing to tackle the question of reform himself, he might have accomplished a moderate solution which would have saved the country from what the *Journal* considered to be the radical proposals of the Whigs. As it was, the Tories must bow to the storm and accept the consequences of their own folly. Some attempt was made at nominal protest when an anti-reform petition bearing 400 signatures was organised at the end of September, 1831, but this did no more than supply the rioters with names. In one moment of wild romance, the *Review* offered the ingenious explanation that the riots were Tory-instigated for the purpose of discrediting reform, but this was no more believed than an earlier assertion that a demand for adult manhood suffrage by an association of Nottingham operatives was also a Tory plot to bring reformers into disrepute. The Tories needed no such ingenuity whilst the reformers showed themselves so ready to attack each other.[24]

When the shouting was over and attempts were made to assess the changes brought about by the Reform Act in Nottingham itself, both sides agreed that its effect was slight, though the Tories believed that they had rather more cause for rejoicing than the Whigs. The *Review* earlier calculated that the electorate would probably remain about the same since 1,000-1,500 non-residential burgesses would be disfranchised but these would be replaced by 1,200-1,500 new voters, the £10 householders. The *Journal* rejoiced that the Act had swept away the great majority of the honorary burgesses, the spurious creations of the Whig Corporation and probable Whig voters, and dogmatically calculated that 5,213 people were entitled to vote under the new

[23]Sir J. Arnould, op. cit., p. 348; *Nottingham Review*, 20th April, 1832.

[24]*Nottingham Journal*, 7th May, 24th September, 1831; *Nottingham Review*, 3rd February, 1832, 20th May, 1831.

system. This was a slight increase on the pre-1832 situation, though neither before nor after the Act could anyone state with conviction the exact number of voters. Before 1832 the number was never fixed nor known with certainty since large numbers were usually temporarily disfranchised through receiving parish aid, and the eligibility of dozens of others was invariably challenged on the grounds that they were not legally elected burgesses. After 1832 the party struggle acquired greater force over the registration of electors and the right to be registered, and the old warfare about the eligibility of burgess voters did not cease. The retention of the burgess vote, now supplemented by that of the £10 householder, meant that Nottingham continued to have a very broadly-based franchise, which was to help make possible the election of Feargus O'Connor in 1847.[25]

[25]*Nottingham Review*, 4th March, 1831; *Nottingham Journal*, 1st September, 17th November, 1832.

12

THE RE-SHAPING OF
NOTTINGHAM POLITICS 1832-5

The menace of the Political Unions, which in Nottingham failed to attract the support of many of those normally leading reforming causes, was as clearly seen by the Whigs as by the Tories. On the one hand the Tories saw that a union of middle and working classes might destroy the influence of 'the upper classes of society' and put an end to what they rather perversely called 'freedom of election' and unhesitatingly branded such extra-Parliamentary organisations as 'unconstitutional'. On the other hand it was a Whig government proclamation of November, 1831, which suggested that the Political Unions were 'illegal and subversive of the King's authority'. And it was Nottingham M.P. Thomas Denman who saw the choice of 1831-2 as being between reform peaceably carried through by the Government or reform proposed by the clubs and unions and carried through by convulsion. The latter was not the wish of the Corporation Whigs, however willing they might on occasion be to utilise the mass-meeting.[1]

The Bill became an Act, but the Nottingham Political Union remained. The *Journal* asked what would now happen; the government, it believed, vainly thought that the unions would dissolve themselves; ministers had connived at a power which would now be difficult to control and 'incalculable mischief' would arise from

[1]*Nottingham Journal*, 5th, 26th November, 1831; J. Arnould, *Memoir of Thomas, First Lord Denman* (1873), Vol. 1, p. 391.

'the waves of popular disaffection' which had been conjured up. The Nottingham Union had certainly no intention of disbanding, and its post-reform Act work was in many ways more interesting than its earlier efforts. It declared its intention to work for other reforms, such as the abolition of the Corn Laws and the Septennial Act, and the repeal of certain taxes; and it eventually settled down to holding regular weekly meetings on Monday evenings to discuss political subjects, such as the further extension of the franchise. In July, 1832, William Shoults, shortly to become secretary of the Union, denounced the new Act as having done nothing for the working classes, though the latter had been used to secure it, a theme which historians were later to take up. Political radicalism and working class grievances, long kept apart by the Corporation Whigs, were now coming together. The following month the editor of the *Review* connected Parliamentary reform and continuing economic distress. The working class were asking, he reported, what good reform had done them. The answer he suggested was that the Act was not yet fully operative, but that answer would not suffice for long and the question continued to be asked, especially of those who had offered reform as a panacea for all ills.[2]

A new enemy was now appearing. In place of the Tory, borough-owning aristocracy, who had kept their opponents together for so long, were appearing the treacherous Whigs, who had changed, but hardly reformed, the political system and were now commencing their disillusioning programme. They had hanged the agitators of Nottingham and Bristol and in Nottingham it was felt that Thomas Denman, as Attorney-General, might well have intervened to save the condemned men. In February, 1833, the Nottinghamshire Union, having failed to secure the co-operation of the Mayor, summoned its own public meeting to condemn the treachery of the government in pursuing an illiberal, coercive Irish policy, no different from that of previous Tory administrations. This policy was consistently defended by the *Mercury*, the organ of the orthodox Corporation Whigs, and O'Connell became one of its main targets of attack. The Union itself was divided into those who followed the *Review*'s advice that they should accept the limitations of the government and

[2]*Nottingham Journal*, 11th August, 1832; *Nottingham Review*, 6th July, 16th November, 1832, 11th January, 1833, 27th July, 31st August, 1832.

recognise that all in all a good job was being done and those who thought that the good fight should continue to be fought mightily. The latter convened a meeting in June to demand the dismissal of ministers, but a mere 600-700 turned up. At the beginning of November William Shoults, the secretary, expanded his earlier theme of July, 1832, and proclaimed that unions among the working classes should go beyond their present limited political objectives and predicted the occurrence of 'a war of the artizans against the capitalists'. At the same time the Nottinghamshire Union issued a manifesto containing four of the points of the People's Charter, lacking only equal electoral districts and the payment of M.P.s. Whig treachery, supporters were told, must not be allowed to rival Tory despotism. Some action was required.[3]

Strangely enough the action came not from the Political Union but from another, less formalised, *ad hoc* association which was hardly an organisation but which was taking political action by the middle of 1833; this was the system of newsroom delegate meetings. In May, 1833, there occurred a meeting of delegates from 'different newshouses, factories, and other places where bodies of men assemble together', when the conduct of Nottingham's two M.P.s was considered and unfavourably judged and a resolution adopted that other candidates must be sought for the future. This implication of political organisation at the factory level is most intriguing, almost evoking thoughts of 'workers' Soviets'. Unfortunately, this tantalising incident was followed by no continuous, traceable developments of any length. The meeting of May 2nd, which occurred at the Newton's Head, a popular resort of trade unionists on earlier occasions, proposed that the various newsrooms, friendly societies, and factories should appoint two delegates for a further meeting on the 13th; at this second meeting a committee of thirteen was appointed to find a candidate to run against the official Whigs. A week later a third meeting occurred, when one delegate had

[3]The Nottingham Political Union had by this time become the Nottinghamshire Political Union, *Nottingham Journal*, 1st March, 1833; *Nottingham Mercury*, 16th March, 1833; *Nottingham Review*, 21st, 7th, 14th June, 8th November, 1833; R. F. Wearmouth, *Some Working Class Movements of the 19th Century* (1948), p. 55, states that most of the provincial Unions had been dissolved by the Spring of 1833. The survival of the Nottinghamshire Union to this point was evidently exceptional.

the temerity to defend the government, 'which called forth a strong burst of radical indignation'; there was talk at this meeting of a National Convention, an anticipation of the Chartist pattern. After this the meetings either lapsed or ceased to be reported, but the committee found their candidate for July, 1834, a Norfolk barrister, William Eagle. His nomination was proof that the malcontents were no longer satisfied to accept the leadership of the Corporation Whigs. There was, admitted the *Review*, a complete division between the Whigs and the Radicals, who had previously acted together to support 'liberal' candidates. The radical *Review* took an equivocal view but inclined slightly towards the official Whigs as some Tories were rallying round Eagle in the hope of dishing the Whigs.[4]

After the election there is evidence that the unofficial organisation, based on the newsrooms and public houses, was again active. On November 16th the Radicals delegated by 'their various clubs' addressed the monarch on the subject of 'the treacherous and imbecile Whigs', formulated their demands for political reform, again virtually a 'Charter', and demanded the 'annihilation of the Poor Law Amendment Act'. Equally interesting is their condemnation of the free-trade system, for this offered further scope for realignments inside Nottingham's traditional political structure. Delegates met again at the Newton's Head the following week and resolved to support no Parliamentary candidate who refused to adopt their political programme. Shortly after this the Corporation Whigs appear to have made a great effort to patch up the differences. On January 2nd the *Review* rejoiced at the restored unity, but the leader of the Radicals at the Newton's Head, Benjamin Boothby, again disturbed the calm by crossing swords with Hobhouse, the Corporation's Whig M.P., who refused to be pledged to household franchise, shorter Parliaments, and the ballot. For this Boothby was thanked by his supporters for his stand against 'the apostates'. The latter were again reviled at the end of March, when the Radicals petitioned Parliament on behalf of the Dorchester labourers and against the new Poor Law. Their views on the work of the new Whig enlightenment could hardly have facilitated the attempts of Thomas Wakefield to bring the Radicals back into the fold by means of the new Re-

[4]*Nottingham Review*, 17th May, 1833, 25th July, 1834; *Nottingham Journal*, 18th, 25th May, 1833.

form Associations formed at the end of June to register voters and 'to promote the free and independent exercise of the franchise'. It was not now simply that the Radicals were determined to press for the extension of political rights but that the social and economic policies of Whiggery had created bitter opposition amongst people whose co-operation had previously been relied upon. The *Review* reflected this change. Immediately after the Reform Bill became law it had stressed the need to vote for 'the right people'; by January, 1833, it was calling for 'some representation of the common order, of the poor and industrious classes', though it did not say how this was to be effected; by July, 1835, the editor was condemning the retention of property qualifications for M.P.s and demanding 'a sprinkling of working men in Parliament'. When the Whigs failed to accommodate the working classes, with whose support Parliamentary reform had been achieved, and positively antagonised them with their measures, the doctrine of virtual or indirect representation of the working classes was no longer valid. The next step was direct representation and the next campaign that of the Chartists.[5]

If the post Reform Act years of Whig government brought disillusionment with the national leaders, so too did these years produce a crescendo of opposition to the principles and methods of those who controlled local government in Nottingham. It was one more weakness of reformist politics in Nottingham that they were led by people who were failing first to remove the beam from their own eye. For years the Tories had hammered away at this theme, that the oligarchical rule of the town Whigs was just as fitting an object for reformers' attention as the weaknesses in the national legislature; for years the thick-skinned had ignored the challenge whilst the more sensitive offered the half-hearted justification that Nottingham had the good fortune to have a 'liberal Corporation' and so there was no real problem. The government's proposal to reform the old Corporation inevitably met with a mixed reception inside Nottingham. Pretending reformers could hardly oppose such a clearly-needed reform; members of the Corporation protested their willingness to be reformed as long as reform was to be general throughout the country, but when a member proposed in Common Hall a

[5] *Nottingham Journal*, 21st, 28th November, 1834, 3rd April, 26th June, 1835; *Nottingham Review*, 2nd, 9th January, 1835, 15th June, 1832, 4th January, 1833, 3rd July, 1835.

Corporation address in favour of the Bill he could find no seconder. There were, however, 10,000 people in Nottingham to sign a privately organised petition in its favour. And when the Commissioners came to Nottingham they met a host of people of similar political inclination to the Corporation who condemned What George Gill called 'the oligarchical usurpation of the Corporation' and deprecated the exclusive system that operated. The pretensions of the Whig oligarchy to represent the reformers of Nottingham were destroyed, not to mention their claims to speak for the whole town. Nor did the national government help to restore their credit when its proposals became clear. Nottingham's existing burgesses were to be the last ones, and their legal claims to privileges and property rights within the town were to disappear. Also, the institution of a rate-paying qualification for the municipal franchise in place of the traditional 'rights of the poor burgesses' meant that the electorate would in fact be reduced in size and become a socially more exclusive body, though this point should not be over emphasised when the extent of previous 'popular control' is remembered. It did, however, give one more argument to those who wished to show that the Whigs were abandoning the poor. When the candidates submitted themselves for election to the council under the new Act they seemed anxious to avoid the appearance of being tied to party-labels and traditional groups inside the town. The *Review* managed to distinguish between the 'Reform' and 'anti-Reform' candidates, but the lines of demarcation were not always clear. In the new body the Whigs only just managed to win a majority, of two, over the Tories, and almost three-quarters of the personnel were new members. Some of the old Corporation had been defeated; many had not taken the chance. Thomas Wakefield, one of the few surviving members from the former body, became the first Mayor of the new Corporation, but Nottingham politics had been given a major shake-up and the established rule of the Whigs was now in jeopardy.[6]

[6]*Nottingham Review*, 28th June, 1828, 1st November, 1833, 25th September, 1835; Evidence of Senior Councillor J. R. Allen, reported in *Nottingham Journal*, 8th November, 1833; *Nottingham Review*, 21st, 14th August, 27th November, 1835; reports of Evidence in *Nottingham Journal*, 1st, 8th, 15th November, 1833; D. Gray, *Nottingham through 500 years* (1960), p. 177; D. Fraser, 'The Nottingham Press, 1800-50', *Transactions of the Thoroton Society*, 1963.

It might be said that the success of the Whigs of the old Corporation, like that of any eighteenth- or nineteenth-century government, lay in the extent to which they could prevent the emergence
of issues, or at least permit the emergence of only those which
they wished to encourage. The political campaigns of the old
Corporation were for fixed and limited political objectives, and
when each was achieved the people of Nottingham were given
oxen to roast and fireworks' displays to applaud. They were not
encouraged to make political issues out of the problems nearest
to them, low wages, poverty, unemployment, and bad working
and living conditions, and it is one of the characteristics of the
post-Reform Bill years that social and economic issues of this
sort for the first time came to receive public ventilation and to
become questions of politics. That the trade unionists assembled to
discuss the Dorchester labourers should also condemn the Poor
Law Amendment Act and that the Radical political groups meeting to demand further Parliamentary reform should also protest
about the Dorchester labourers indicated a new approach for both
trade unions and politicians.[7]

The first of the new economic/political issues was factory reform. In February, 1832, a petition was organised, in support of
Sadler, to prevent the employment in factories of children under
the age of nine. This collected over 2,000 signatures. That the
number was so small probably arose from the fact the organisers
of the campaign were, at first, purely private individuals and that
Corporation support and resources were not thrown behind
them. The *Review* urged that all who had the welfare of the
working classes at heart should sign but then advanced a
purely economic rather than a moral motive for so doing, that the
competition of child labour kept down the wages of working
men. It soon became evident that the Nottingham reformers who
could be relied upon to support political reforms could not all be
relied upon to support this one. The *Review* believed it to be only
marginally relevant to the problem of the poverty which caused
parents to send their children out to work, some thought that
only further Parliamentary reform could help the working man,
whilst one correspondent of the *Review* condemned Sadler as an
enemy of liberty and offered opposition to him as the new liberal

[7]*Nottingham Review*, 4th April, 1834; *Nottingham Journal*, 28th November, 1834, 3rd
April, 1835.

cause. The Nottingham Tories responded readily to the challenge of the Whig-Radical defection and made themselves the apostles of factory reform. They were loud in their praise for Sadler, and it was suggested that he was under heavy attack for his politics as well as for his social reform, that he was hated because he was a Tory. Richard Oastler, too, was loudly acclaimed by the Nottingham Tories, who made him an honorary member of their Constitutional Club and feted him both for his ideas on factory reform and for his Tory principles. The inference intended to be drawn was clear. Only the Tories were befriending the working men on a matter that really affected their interests, in comparison with something like Parliamentary reform with which they had been deluded. The Whigs and Radicals were denounced for their indifference or even for their outright opposition, as shown by the outlook of the *Mercury*. They had failed to turn up at meetings organised in support of Sadler in Nottingham, and at Westminster their government was trying its hardest to get rid of Sadler's Bill and shelve the question of factory reform. The idea of a Parliamentary Commission was a stunt and a time-waster; the Tories were in favour of Sadler and his Bill and against the government and its policies. Meetings were held in Nottingham in the closing months of 1832 in support of factory reform, but the 'Friends of Sadler', even with the backing of the Constitutional Club, could not mobilise opinion in face of Corporation indifference or hostility. A meeting at the beginning of March, 1833, was only half full, and a mere 3,000 signatures were appended to a further petition to Parliament.[8]

Mrs. Mary Tatham could write to her daughter, Mrs. Richard Oastler, that factory legislation aroused no great interest in Nottingham because the factories thereabouts were so well-regulated, but not everyone shared her complacency. A 'numerous meeting' was held at Radford, on the fringes of the town, in August, 1833, which condemned the motion of John Heathcoat by which lace factories were excluded from the operation of Althorpe's Act and drew attention to the evils of child-employment in local lace factories. Heathcoat, though now in business in the West Country, had still substantial contacts and interests in

[8]*Nottingham Journal*, 18th, 25th February, 3rd March, 10th November, 6th October, 1832, 8th March, 12th July, 1833; *Nottingham Review*, 24th February, 14th September, 2nd March, 1832, 8th March, 1833; *Nottingham Mercury*, 17th August, 1833.

Nottingham. His contacts included William Felkin, a man of rising influence in Nottingham affairs, a Liberal and an Evengelical, who himself opposed the inclusion of lace in the 1833 Act on the grounds that this would retard the transition to steam-power in the industry. The *Review* reported further that it had organised conferences with many lace operatives in the town which had driven it to the opinion that lace factories were mistakenly excluded from the operation of the Factory Act. The Tories were loud in their denunciation of these 'blood-chilling' factories, and later government commissioners enumerated the evils to be tackled even if their imagery was less vivid.[9]

A more important issue locally than factory reform was the working of the new Poor Law, which, more than anything else, was responsible for alienating the Whig leadership from the affections of the working classes. The full effects of the 1834 Act were largely felt after 1835 but already by that date its implications were evident. From 1819, when he became Parish overseer in St. Mary's, Absolem Barnett had begun to apply the principles later to be associated with the 1834 Act. His writings on the administration of the Poor Law and his evidence to the commissioners clearly reveal Barnett's sense of his mission to encourage thrift and self-reliance and eliminate idleness, vagrancy, and public expense by refusing outdoor relief and forcing men to endure the deliberately harsh conditions of the workhouse as the alternative to making their own provision for themselves and their families outside. He told the commissioners how 'he baffled the complaints of the paupers', 'their opposition grew gradually weaker and weaker', and he won repeated victories over those who sought public assistance. After the Act 'Absolute' Barnett, as he became known, was in charge of the new Nottingham Union and became the number one enemy of the working classes by his harsh and apparently unfeeling administration. The Nottingham Whigs, great champions of the principles of self-reliance, industry, and prudence, which the new Act was supposed to foster, largely approved the principles and working of it even if Barnett seemed something of a tyrant. A few, such as Alderman William Roworth, changed their opinions as a result of seeing the Act in practice. Rowarth realised that in Notting-

[9]Rev. J. Beaumont, *Memoirs of Mrs. Mary Tatham*, op. cit., p. 324; *Nottingham Review*, 23rd August, 1833; *Nottingham Journal*, 29th March, 1833.

ham's economic pattern of permanent depression in hosiery, with fluctuations that brought bouts of even more intense depression, the workhouse system could never be fully applied. In time of extreme distress there would always be need for charity and outdoor relief, and the refusal of such outdoor relief on a temporary basis produced 'many and great evils'. He cited many cases of neglect and inhuman conduct from the poor law officials in their attempt to live by the law of 1834. Others, such as the Anglican parson, W. J. Butler, saw that Nottingham's situation must mean intolerable overcrowding in the workhouses, where there was an allegedly high death-rate among children in consequence, and that it would still prove impossible to dispense with traditional outdoor relief. The 1834 Act was no answer for Nottingham and attempts to enforce it produced both misery for the poor inside and outside the Union workhouse and bitter relations between the supporters and opponents of the Act in Nottingham public life.[10]

And this was one of the first fruits of the reformed Parliament and Whig government. An unholy alliance of Radicals and Tories began to take shape in spite of the *Mercury*'s attempt at self-consolation that to suppose that the Tories and Radicals could form a union would be to suppose that which could never come to pass. In March, 1835, the Radical delegates from the public houses and newsrooms examined the Act 'in its principle, its actions, its origin, its agents, its instruments, and its victims' and saw 'one mass of crime and misery, one withering antithesis of all that is manly, to all that is English, to all that we revere as wise or politic, as equitable or humane'. In April, over 5,000 signatures were collected for a petition demanding its immediate repeal. A year earlier the *Journal* had declared an immediate opposition to the Poor Law Amendment Act, shared by the Nottingham Tory association, the Constitutional Club, and on November 21st, 1834, the latter issued a significant declaration, addressing the Radical reformers as spokesmen for the poor and urging them, in view of their demand for the 'annihilation' of the Act, to consider carefully their relations with the main party

[10]A. Barnett, *The Administration of the Poor Laws* (1833); *Report of Commission of Inquiry into the state of the Poor Law*, 1834, p. 257; *Nottingham Mercury*, 12th December, 1835; W. Rowarth, *Observations on the Administration of the New Poor Law in Nottingham*, 1840; Rev. W. J. Butler, *A Friendly Letter addressed to Richard Oastler, Esq.*, 1838.

groups. With the town's Anglican clergymen in the van of a protest movement, as happened over the Poor Law, politics were clearly undergoing an important change.[11]

But if Whig government brought the working classes of Nottingham a new problem in the shape of the new Poor Law, their biggest problem was still the depression of local industry and the poverty resulting from this. The Whig reforms, it was soon observed, had brought no prosperity to Nottingham's poor. Lord Grey had given people 'a beautiful gilded plaything to amuse them, in the shape of the Reform Bill, but the gilding had now worn off', by March, 1834, and their position had not materially improved. Nor was there any confidence in free-trade and *laissez-faire* as solutions to local economic problems, however good they might be for the country as a whole. Gravener Henson had condemned the morality and efficacy of *laissez-faire* as an answer to workmen's problems in 1823; the Radicals, with Tory help, now took up the same cry and stressed the selfishness of the industrialists and manufacturers. The anti-Corn Law campaign of the local Whigs, according to the *Journal*, was designed to bring down wages, and the *Journal* quoted with relish the views of a local Whig who had admitted his belief that high wages were the greatest evil under which the country laboured.[12] On the question of trade unions too the working classes found in the years 1832-5 that the local Whig establishment, for so long tolerant and permissive, was hardening its attitude and viewing with great hostility the experiments in general union which were a feature of these years. And if the continued depressed condition of the hosiery trade and the consequent sufferings of the framework-knitters were not the fault of the business men and manufacturers who controlled Nottingham, the same could not be said of the insanitary homes in which they lived and the insanitary streets in which they walked.

The working classes of Nottingham had little for which to thank the Whigs, locally or nationally, and, not surprisingly, they

[11]*Nottingham Mercury*, 6th December, 1834, 11th April, 1835; *Nottingham Journal*, 3rd April, 1835, 16th May, 21st November, 1834; Rev. W. J. Butler, op. cit., p. 13, wrote 'No group has taken such a decided part against the law as the Anglican clergy'.

[12]*Nottingham Journal*, 12th December, 1834, 28th June, 1833; *Report of Proceedings of Public Meeting on Nottingham Forest, 31st March, 1834, on the 6 members of the Trades Union at Dorchester* (1834).

were courted very assiduously by the Tories in the years immediately following the Reform Act. Even before the Act the Tories had ostentatiously toasted Lord Wharncliffe and wished success to his Bill to outlaw the truck system. Now they drew attention to the cold reception that Sadler was getting from the Whigs for his proposals for factory reform; when he addressed a meeting in Nottingham in March, 1833, the local Whigs were conspicuous by their absence, whereas the Tories were sponsoring his campaign and giving him every assistance. When the Constitutional Club met at the end of the same month, the theme was again the need for social reform and better conditions for workmen. A speaker remarked how a starving population had asked for bread and had its cry answered with 'Schedules A and B', and he went on to make the familiar comparison between the West Indian slaves and those of the factories. At the same time the Radicals were condemning those who were 'all for the blacks' but unwilling to 'emancipate the whites'. The aim of the Tories, said the *Journal*, was to secure the poor their rights as well as the rich their privileges; one such right was fair wages, which the free-traders were trying to bring down. By May, 1834, the Tories had found another piece of common ground with the Radicals and working-classes when they began their attack on the Poor Law Amendment Act. In November, 1834, the Tories addressed Radicals directly:—

'I admit', said the writer, 'the Tory stands opposed to you as Radicals, but the Whig stands opposed to you as poor men. The Tory pities and would fain remove in his own time and way that poverty and distress which, in their own times and ways, the Whigs endeavour at once to increase, to perpetuate, and to punish.' The Tories, as the much lesser of two evils, should, he concluded, be supported.[13]

And this theme was continued. Whilst the government was causing the country to be visited by a 'locust plague of Commissions' prosperity locally was not rising. No longer could the French wars or Tory government be blamed; now it was the new free-trading policies which were held responsible, and in March, 1835, the Tories took the lead in organising a petition to the Board of Trade which claimed to show the evils befalling the

[13]*Nottingham Journal*, 16th July, 1831, 8th, 29th March, 17th May, 1833, 1st September, 1832, 21st November, 1834.

manufacturing interests from the adoption of free trade theories. Now it was the Tories who could write of poverty prevailing in Nottingham in the midst of plenty, of whole streets where people ate meat but once a week, had only half the bread they needed, and rarely saw tea, sugar, or butter. The standard of living issue operated against the government of the day and now it was a Whig government which had to answer the accusations. More potent, however, was to be the issue of the Poor Law, the real grievance that the Tories could exploit. They could derive a certain advantage from posing as the champions of the poor burgesses who were being threatened by the spoliation clauses of the Municipal Corporations Act, but it was over the new Poor Law that the Whig-working class gulf really developed, which permitted the Tories to drive home their claim to be the better friends of the poor.[14]

With the shake-up that Nottingham politics were at last receiving after decades of anaesthetising Whig rule and with the introduction of social and economic questions into the political debate, it is not surprising that the next twelve years of Nottingham's history were to witness first the election of a Conservative M.P., in 1841, with the assistance of Radical and Chartist votes, and then the election of a Chartist M.P., in 1847, with the assistance of Conservative votes.[15]

---

[14]*Nottingham Journal*, 21st November, 12th December, 1834; 6th March, 26th June, 1835.

[15]A. C. Wood, 'Nottingham, 1835-1865', *Transactions of the Thoroton Society*, 1955.

SELECT BIBLIOGRAPHY

1 Primary Sources

I. UNPUBLISHED

Public Record Office. The most useful series were:

(a) Home Office Papers

    Correspondence and Papers, Disturbances:
        H.O. 40. Correspondence, etc., 1812-1855
        H.O. 41. Entry Books, 1816-1898
    Correspondence and Papers, Domestic and General:
        H.O. 42. George III. Correspondence, 1782-1820
        H.O. 44. George IV, and later. Correspondence, 1820-1861
    Expired Commissions:
        H.O. 47. Judges' Reports, 1784-1829
    Correspondence and Papers, Military:
        H.O. 50. Correspondence, etc., 1782-1840

(b) Privy Council Papers

    P.C. 1/41. Papers relating to Corresponding Societies

University of Nottingham:
    Middleton MSS. (Mi)
    Newcastle MSS. (Ne.C.)
    Portland MSS. (PwH)
    Diaries of William Parsons, 1830-1871
    Minute Books of High Pavement Vestry Meetings, 1777-1812 and 1813-1876
    High Pavement School Attendance Registers
    Boulton and Watts MSS.: photostat copies of Nottingham items, which are part of the full collection at Birmingham Reference Library.
    Felkin MSS., typescript copy

Borough Records (Nottingham Central Library):
    Corporation Hall Books and Accounts, 1785-1835
    Framework-knitters' Papers, 1812-14
    Letters from London Magistrates on Luddites, M. 429
County Record Office, Nottingham:
    Clerk of the Peace Papers, E. S. Godfrey. 1806-43
British Museum:
    Place Collection, Add. MSS. 27, 798—27, 817

2. OFFICIAL PUBLICATIONS

Parliamentary Debates, 1785–1835

Report of Select Committee on Nottingham Election Petitions, 1803

Reports of Select Committee on Framework-knitters' Petitions, 1812

Report of Select Committee on State of Children Employed in Manufactories, 1816

Report of Select Committee on Framework-knitters' Petitions, 1819

Report of Select Committee on Artizans and Machinery, 1824

Report of Children's Employment Commission, 1833 and 1843

Report of Commission to Inquire into the State of the Municipal Corporations, 1835

Report of Commission for Inquiry into the Administration and Practical Operation of the Poor Laws

Report of Select Committee on Postage, 1837–8

Reports of Select Committee on Laws affecting the Export of Machinery, 1841

Reports of Royal Commission on State of Large Towns and Populous Districts, 1844–5

Report of Royal Commission on the Condition of the Framework-knitters, 1845

3. PUBLISHED CONTEMPORARY OR NEAR-CONTEMPORARY WORKS

Allen's *Illustrated Hand-book and Guide to Nottingham and its Environs*, Nottingham, 1866

Anon.   *Address to the Citizens of Nottingham*, Norwich, 1825.

Address to the Honest Burgesses of Nottingham, Nottingham, undated.

Address to the Inhabitants of Nottingham, 1793.

An impartial Account of the Proceedings of the Nottingham Committee of the Methodist Society, Nottingham, 1797.

Observations, on the late Contested Election at Nottingham, 1803.

Remarks upon the Controversy between the Rev. George Wilkins and the Rev. J. B. Stuart, London, 1823.

Report on Proceedings of Public Meeting held on Nottingham Forest, March 31, 1834, regarding the sentence on the 6 Members of the Trade Union at Dorchester, Nottingham, 1834.

Seeds of Sedition, Important Discovery, Nottingham, 1793.

Statement of some of the late proceedings in relation to the General Baptist Church at Nottingham, Nottingham, 1817.

To the Inhabitants of Nottingham, 1793.

Articles of Union for a General Lunatic Asylum in Nottingham, Newark, 1810.

Bailey, T.   *Address to the Teachers of the Nottingham and Basford General Baptist Sunday Schools*, Nottingham, 1814.

Eulogium on the Character of Mr. Robert Raikes, Nottingham, 1815.

Monumental Inscription for Jeremiah Brandreth, Nottingham, 1817.

The Entertaining Performances of the Election Jugglers, Nottingham, 1819.

Sermon on the Death of Byron, London, 1824.

Ireton, London, 1827.

Bailey for Ever (Election Verse), Nottingham, 1830.

Strictures on Mr. Cobbett's Second Lecture, Nottingham, 1830.

Eulogium on the Character of William Wilberforce, Nottingham, 1833.

Speech on the Corn Laws delivered at a Meeting of the Nottingham Town Council, February 19, 1838.

The Rights of Labour with Proposals for a New Basis for National Suffrage, London, 1844.

Wesleyan Methodism and its alleged Reform Movement, Nottingham, 1850.

The Annals of Nottinghamshire, London, 1853.

Village Reform—The Great Social Necessity of Britain, Nottingham, 1854.

Handbook to Nottingham Castle, London, 1854.

Discourse on the Causes of Political Revolution, London, undated.

Baines, E.   *History of the Cotton Manufacture in Great Britain,* London, 1835.

Barnett, A.   *The Poor Laws and their Administration,* London, 1833.

Beaumont, J.   *Life of Rev. Joseph Beaumont,* London, 1856.

Memoirs of Mrs. Mary Tatham, London, 1838.

Becher, J. T.   *Table for the Regulation of Friendly Societies,* Newark, 1825.

The Anti-Pauper System, Newark, 1824.

Blackner, J.   *History of Nottingham,* Nottingham, 1815.

Bowles, J.   *Letter to Charles James Fox,* London, 1802.

Thoughts on the Late Election as demonstrative of the Progress of Jacobinism, London, 1803.

The Salutary Effects of Vigour, London, 1804.

Brown, J.   *Memoir of Robert Blincoe,* London, 1832.

Brown, W.   *The Spirit of the Times,* Nottingham, 1822.

Butler, W. J.   *Friendly Letter to Richard Oastler,* London, 1838.

Burbage (printer)   *Account of Proceedings at Meeting of Freeholders of Nottinghamshire, Newark, March 8, 1785,* Nottingham, 1785.

Carpenter, B.   *Early Presbyterianism in Nottingham,* London, 1862.

Cartwright, F. D.   *Life and Correspondence of Major Cartwright,* London, 1826.

Cartwright, J.   *A letter to the Electors of Nottingham,* London, 1803.

Hampden Clubs, London, 1816.

Celebration of the Triumph of Reform at Nottingham, Nottingham, 1832.

Cobbett, W.   *Political Register* (Annual Register), 1802-35.

Rural Rides, London, 1885.

Cokayne, T. — *Report of the Evidence given before the Commissioners appointed to enquire into Municipal Corporations*, Nottingham, 1833.

Davison, R. — *Letter to John Bowles*, Nottingham, 1803.
Ten Letters, Principally on the subject of the Late Election, 1803.

Dunn, J. — *History, Antiquities and Present State of the Town of Nottingham*, Nottingham, 1807.

Felkin, W. — *History of the Machine-Wrought Hosiery and Lace Manufacturers*, London, 1867.

Foxcroft, A. — *Letter to Mr. Robert Davison*, Nottingham, 1803.

Gelsthorp, T. — *A Gift to the Poor*, Nottingham, 1812.

Gilbert, Mrs. — *Biographic Sketch of Rev. Joseph Gilbert*, London, 1853.

Gilbert, A. — *Recollections of Old Nottingham*, Nottingham, 1904.

Godfrey, J. J. (ed.) — *MSS. relating to the County of Nottingham in the possession of James Ward*, London, 1890.

Hall, R. — *A Reply to the Principal Objections advanced by Cobbett and others against the Framework Knitters' Friendly Relief Society*, Leicester, 1821.

Harwood, G. H. — *A History of Wesleyan Methodism*, London, 1854.

Henson, G. — *The Civil, Political and Mechanical History of the Framework-knitters*, Nottingham, 1831.

Howitt, M. — *My Own Story*, London, 1845.
Autobiography, London, 1889.

Howitt, W. — *Historical Sketch of the Progress of Parliamentary Reform*, London, 1840.
The Three Death Cries of a Perishing Church, Nottingham, 1835.

Hutton, G. — *An Appeal to the Nation*, Nottingham, 1798.

Kilham, A. — *Account of the Trial of Alexander Kilham before the General Conference in London*, Nottingham, 1796.

Laird, F. C. — *A Topographical and Historical Description of Nottinghamshire*, London, 1810.

Life of Alexander Kilham (compiled), Nottingham, 1799.

Local Directories for the period.

Lowe, R. — *General View of the Agriculture of the County of Nottinghamshire*, London, 1794.

Nott, J. — *Advice to sundry sorts of People*, 1793.

Nottingham Corresponding Society Proceedings, 1797, Nottingham, 1797.

Nottingham Journal, 1785-1835

Nottingham Review, 1808-35

Nottingham Gazette Prospectus, 1813

Nottingham Gazette, 1813-15

Nottingham Mercury, 1825-35

Orange, J. — *Nottingham Annual Register, 1840*, Nottingham, 1840.
History and Antiquities of Nottingham, London, 1840.

Poll Books for 1796, 1802, 1803, 1806, 1812, 1818, 1820, 1826, 1830

Roworth, W. — *Observations on the Administration of the New Poor Law in Nottingham*, London, 1840.

Salt, W.   *Memorials of the Methodist New Connexion*, Notting-
                         ham, 1827.
Society for Constitutional Information (J. Cartwright, 1792).
Statutes and Directions for the government of the General Hospital, Nottingham,
    1821.
Stretton MSS. on the History of Nottingham. Notes by William Stretton
    (died 1928) privately printed, Nottingham, 1910.
Sutton, C. (pub.)   *Paper War at the Nottingham Election of 1803*, Notting-
                         ham, 1803.
                         Paper War at the Nottingham Election of 1806, Notting-
                         ham, 1806.
                         *Collection of Addresses, etc. on the Nottingham Election
                         of 1812.*
                         *Proceedings of the Trial of Jeremiah Brandreth and others
                         for High Treason*, Nottingham, 1817.
                         Strangers' Guide through the town of Nottingham,
                         Nottingham, 1827.
Sutton, J. F.   *The Date-Book of Nottingham, 1750-1850*, London,
                         1852.
Sutton, R.   *The Gallow's Hill Remembrancer*, Nottingham, 1845.
                         *Correct List of all the Executions at Nottingham since
                         1201*, Nottingham, 1860.
Taylor, J.   *Sermon on the Character of the late Rev. George Walker*,
                         Nottingham, 1807.
Throsby, J.   *History and Antiquities of Nottingham*, London, 1795.
'Vindex'   *Letter to the Burgesses of Nottingham*, 1803.
Wakefield, G.   *Address to the Inhabitants of Nottingham on the subject
                         of the Test Laws*, London, 1789.
                         Cursory Reflections . . . (on) *the Repeal of the Corporation
                         and Test Acts*, Birmingham, 1790.
                         *Correspondence of G. Wakefield with Charles James Fox,
                         1796-1801*, London, 1813.
                         *Reply to some parts of the Bishop of Llandaff's Address
                         to the People of Great Britain*, London, 1798.
                         Memoir of the Life of Gilbert Wakefield, London, 1804.
Walker, G.   *Substance of Speech at General Meeting of the County of
                         Nottingham at Mansfield, February 28, 1780.*
                         Sermons, Vols. I and II, London, 1770.
                         The Dissenters' Plea, Birmingham, 1790.
                         Essays on Various Subjects, London, 1809.
Walker, G., Jun.   *Memoir of the Rev. George Walker*, London, 1809.
Walton, R.   *Random Recollections of the Midland Circuit*, London,
                         1873.
Wilkins, G.   *Letter to Earl Grey on the subject of Ecclesiastical Reform*,
                         Nottingham, 1832.
                         *Letter to Lord John Russell on the subject of The Church
                         Rates*, Nottingham, 1837.
                         *Letter to Rev. J. B. Stuart on the subject of the Nottingham
                         National Schools*, London, 1822.

Wylie, W. H.   *Old and New Nottingham*, London, 1853.
Wylie, W. H. and   *A Popular History of Nottingham*, Nottingham, 1893.
Briscoe, J. P.

II Secondary Sources

1. UNIVERSITY THESES

Chapman, S. D.   *Life of William Felkin, 1795-1874.* Nottingham
         University, M.A. Thesis, 1960.
         The Midlands Cotton and Worsted Spinning Industry,
         1769-1800. London University Ph.D. Thesis, 1966.

Golby, J. M.   *The Political and Electoral Influence of the 4th Duke of*
         Newcastle. Nottingham University M.A. Thesis,
         1961.

Thomas, A. W.   *The History of Nottingham High School.* Nottingham
         University Ph.D. Thesis, 1956.

Weller, J. C.   *The Revival of Religion in Nottingham, 1780-1850.*
         Nottingham University B.D. Thesis, 1957.

2. ARTICLES IN PERIODICALS

Bramley, J.   'Robert White Almond', *Transactions of the Thoroton*
         Society, 1956.

Butler, R. M.   'The Common Lands of the Borough of Notting-
         ham', *Transactions of the Thoroton Society*, 1950.

Chambers, J. D.   'Nottingham in the early 19th Century', *Transactions*
         of the Thoroton Society, 1941, 1942, 1943.
         'Victorian Nottingham', *Transactions of the Thoroton*
         Society, 1959.
         'The Vale of Trent, 1670-1800', *Economic History*
         Review, Supplement 3, 1957.
         'The Worshipful Company of Framework-knitters,
         1657-1778', *Economica*, 1929.

Chapman, S. D.   'The Evangelical Revival and Education in Notting-
         ham', *Transactions of the Thoroton Society*, 1962.
         'Working Class Housing in Nottingham during the
         Industrial Revolution', *Transactions of the Thoroton*
         Society, 1963.

Church, R. A.   'James Orange and the Allotment System in Notting-
         ham', *Transactions of the Thoroton Society*, 1960.

Fraser, D.   'The Nottingham Press, 1800-1850', *Transactions of*
         the Thoroton Society, 1963.

George, M. D.   'The Combination Laws reconsidered', *Economic*
         History, 1927.

Gray, D.   'Nottingham in the 19th Century', *Transactions of the*
         Thoroton Society, 1951.

Hunter, J. M.   'Sources of Capital in the Industrial Development of
         Nottingham', *East Midland Geographer*, December,
         1961.

Marshall, J. D.   'Nottinghamshire Labourers in the Early 19th Century', *Transactions of the Thoroton Society*, 1960.
'The Nottinghamshire Reformers and their Contribution to the New Poor Law', *Economic History Review*, April, 1961.

Russell, J.   'The Luddites', *Transactions of the Thoroton Society*, 1906.

Thomis, M. I.   'The Nottingham Election of 1803', *Transactions of the Thoroton Society*, 1961.
'The Politics of Nottingham Enclosure', *Transactions of the Thoroton Society*, 1967.

Wadsworth, F. A.   'Two Nottingham Schools', *Transactions of the Thoroton Society*, 1941.

Warren, J. C.   'The Life of John Blackner', *Transactions of the Thoroton Society*, 1926.

Wood, A. C.   'The History of Trade and Transport on the River Trent', *Transactions of the Thoroton Society*, 1950.
'George, Lord Rancliffe', *Transactions of the Thoroton Society*, 1954.
'Nottingham, 1835-1865', *Transactions of the Thoroton Society*, 1955.
'Nottingham Parliamentary Elections', *Transactions of the Thoroton Society*, 1956.

3. BOOKS

Allen, W. G.   *John Heathcoat and his Heritage*, London, 1958.
Armytage, W. H. G.   *A. J. Mundella, 1825-1897*, London, 1951.
Arnould, J.   *Memoir of Thomas, First Lord Denman*, London, 1873.
Ashton, T. S.   *The Industrial Revolution, 1760-1830*, London, 1949.
An Economic History of England in the 18th Century, London, 1955.
Aspinall, A.   *Politics and the Press, 1780-1850*, London, 1949.
Early British Trade Unions, London, 1949.
Austin, G. C. A.   *Nottingham Market Place*, Nottingham, 1941.
Birley, R.   *The English Jacobins, 1789-1802*, London, 1924.
Bland, W. P.   *The Abel Collins Charity*, Nottingham, 1944.
'Bon-bon'   *A Popular History of Nottingham Goose Fair*, Nottingham, 1904.
Bowden, W.   *Industrial Society in England towards the end of the 18th Century*, New York, 1925.
Bramley, J.   *Guide to Nottingham Castle*, Nottingham, 1878.
Briggs, A.   *The Age of Improvement*, London, 1959.
(ed.)   *Chartist Studies*, London, 1959.
(ed.)   *Essays in Labour History*, London, 1960.
Briscoe, J. P.   *Old Nottinghamshire*, London, 1881.
Brown, C.   *Lives of Nottinghamshire Worthies*, London, 1882.
History of Nottinghamshire, London, 1891.
Brown, F. K.   *Fathers of the Victorians*, London, 1961.

Brown, L.   *The Board of Trade and the Free Trade Movement, 1830-42*, London, 1958.

Buer, M. C.   *Health, Wealth and Population, 1760-1815*, London, 1926.

Butler, J. R. M.   *The Passing of the Great Reform Bill*, London, 1964 edn.

Chambers, J. D.   *Nottinghamshire in the 18th Century*, London, 1932.

Modern Nottingham in the Making, Nottingham, 1945.

Population Change in a Provincial Town, Nottingham, 1700-1800.

Studies in the Industrial Revolution, ed. L. S. Presswell, London, 1960.

Chapman, S. D.   *The Early Factory Masters*, Newton Abbott, 1967.

Church, R. A.   *Economic and Social Change in a Midland Town, Victorian Nottingham, 1815-1914*, London, 1966.

Church, R. A. and
Chapman, S. D.   *Gravener Henson and the Making of the English Working Class, Essays in honour of J. D. Chambers*, ed. G. Mingay and E. Jones, 1967.

Clapham, J. H.   *Economic History of Modern Britain*, London, 1926.

Clark, S. F.   *The History of the Derby Road Baptist Church, Nottingham*, Nottingham, undated.

Cole, G. D. H.   *Attempts at General Union, 1818-34*, London, 1953.

Cropper, H. S.   *The Freemen of Nottingham and their Estates*, Nottingham, 1880.

Cuthbert, N. H.   *The Lace Makers' Society*, Nottingham, 1960.

Darvall, F.   *Popular Disturbances and Public Order in Regency England*, London, 1934.

Driver, C.   *Tory Radical, The Life of Richard Oastler*, New York, 1946.

Easton, H. T.   *The History of a Banking House (Smith, Payne and Smith)*, London, 1903.

Erickson, C.   *British Industrialists, 1850-1950. Steel and Hosiery.* London, 1959.

Fay, C. R.   *Life and Labour in the 19th Century*, London, 1947.

Gill, C.   *History of Birmingham*, Vol. I, London, 1952.

Gill, H.   *Nottingham Castle*, Nottingham, 1904.

Godfrey, J. T.   *History of the Parish and Priory of Lenton*, London, 1884.

History of Friar Lane Baptist Church, Nottingham, London, 1903.

Granger, J.   *Old Nottingham*, Nottingham, 1902.

Gray, D.   *Nottingham through 500 Years*, Nottingham, 1960.

Guilford, E. L.   *A History of Abel Collins' Charity*, Nottingham, 1915.

Nottinghamshire, London, 1910.

Halévy, E.   *The Liberal Awakening*, London, 1926.

Hall, A. W. G.   *The Post Office in Nottingham*, Nottingham, 1947.

Hammond, J. L. & B.   *The Skilled Labourer, 1760-1832*, London, 1919.

Hayek, F. A. (ed.)   *Capitalism and the Historians*, London, 1954.

Henderson, A. R.	*History of Castle Gate Congregationalist Church*, London, 1905.
Hobsbawm, E. J.	*The Machine Breakers, Past and Present*, I, 1952.
	The Age of Revolution, London, 1962.
Hodder, E.	*Life of Samuel Morley*, London, 1887.
Jaeger, M.	*Before Victoria*, London, 1956.
King, R. W. and Russell, J.	*A History of Arnold*, Nottingham, 1913.
Lincoln, A.	*Some Political and Social Ideas of English Dissent, 1763-1800*, London, 1938.
Lomax, J.	*A History of Quakers in Nottingham, 1648-1948*, Nottingham, 1948.
Maccoby, S.	*English Radicalism*, Vols. 2 & 3, London, 1955.
Machin, G. I. T.	*The Catholic Question in English Politics, 1820-30*, London, 1964.
Mantoux, P.	*The Industrial Revolution in the 18th Century*, London, 1961.
Mather, F. C.	*Public Order in the Age of the Chartists*, Manchester, 1959.
Mellors, R.	*Old Nottingham Suburbs*, Nottingham, 1914.
	Men of Nottingham and Nottinghamshire, Nottingham, 1926.
Milton, W.	*Religion and Business, Memorials of Thomas Adams of Nottingham*, London, 1874.
Namier, L. B.	*The Structure of Politics at the Accession of George III*, London, 1957 edn.
Patterson, A. T.	*Radical Leicester*, London, 1954.
Prest, J.	*The Industrial Revolution in Coventry*, London, 1960.
Raven, H.	*Nottingham*, Nottingham, 1932.
Redford, A.	*Labour Migration in England, 1800-50*, Manchester, 1964 revised edn.
	Economic History of England, 1760-1860, London, 1931.
Rudé, G.	*The Crowd in History, 1730-1848*, New York, 1964.
Russell, J.	*A History of Bromley House Library*, Nottingham, 1916.
Smith, D. M.	*The Industrial Archaeology of the East Midlands*, Dawlish and London, 1965.
Swinnerton, H. H.	*Nottinghamshire*, Cambridge, 1910.
Taylor, F. W. V.	*History of the Bluecoat School, Nottingham*, Nottingham, 1956.
Thomis, M. I.	*Old Nottingham*, Newton Abbott, 1968.
Thompson, E. P.	*The Making of the English Working Class*, London, 1963.
Trevelyan, G. M.	*Lord Grey of the Reform Bill*, London, 1920.
Unwin, G.	*Samuel Oldknow and the Arkwrights*, London, 1924.
Varley, D. E.	*History of the Midland Counties Lace Manufacturers' Association*, Long Eaton, 1959.
Walker, V. M.	*Mr. Treasurer, Nottingham—before 1835*, London, 1957.
Wallas, G.	*Life of Francis Place*, London, 1898.

Wearmouth, R. F.   *Some Working Class Movements of the 19th Century*, London, 1948.

Webb, S. & B.   *History of Trade Unionism*, London, 1920 edn.

Wells, F. A.   *The British Hosiery Trade*, London, 1935.

Williams, F. S.   *Nottingham Past and Present*, Nottingham, 1879.

Whitehead, W.   *Old and New Nottingham*, Nottingham, 1874.

White, R. J.   *Waterloo to Peterloo*, London, 1957.

Wood, A. C.   *History of Nottinghamshire*, Nottingham, 1947.

INDEX